DEMOCRACY & PHILANTHROPY

THE ROCKEFELLER FOUNDATION AND THE AMERICAN EXPERIMENT

By Eric John Abrahamson
Sam Hurst
Barbara Shubinski

Innovation for the Next 100 Years
Rockefeller Foundation Centennial Series

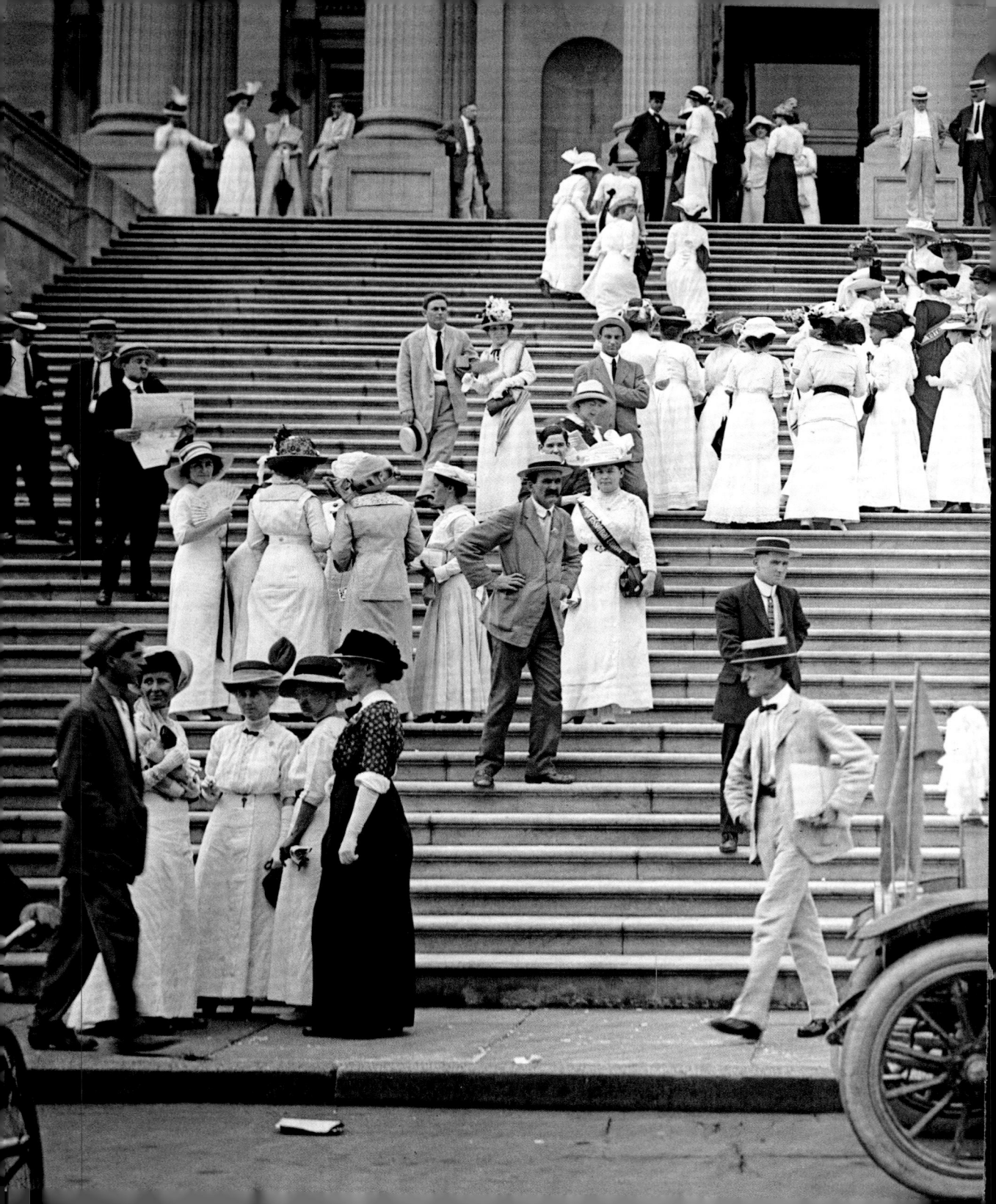

© 2013 by
The Rockefeller Foundation
Foreword copyright Justice Sandra
Day O'Connor
All rights reserved.

Top: Rockefeller Archive Center
Bottom: John Foxx. Getty Images.

Book design by Pentagram.

Democracy & Philanthropy:
The Rockefeller Foundation and
the American Experiment

Printed in Canada.

Published by
The Rockefeller Foundation
New York
United States of America

In association with Vantage Point
Historical Services, Inc.
South Dakota
United States of America

ISBN-13: 978-0-9796389-6-1
ISBN-10: 0-9796389-6-8

Rockefeller Foundation
Centennial Series
Books published in the Rockefeller Foundation Centennial Series provide case studies for people around the world who are working "to promote the well-being of humankind." Three books highlight lessons learned in the fields of agriculture, health, and philanthropy. Three others explore the Foundation's work in Africa, Thailand, and the United States. For more information about the Rockefeller Foundation Centennial initiatives, visit http://centennial.rockefellerfoundation.org/

Notes & Permissions
The Foundation has taken all reasonable steps to ensure the accuracy of the information provided in the book; any errors or omissions are inadvertent. This book is published without footnotes or endnotes. A manuscript version with citations and references for all sources used is available at http://centennial.rockefellerfoundation.org/

Captions in this book provide information on the creator and the repository from which the images in this book were obtained. The Foundation has made its best efforts to determine the creator and copyright holder of all images used in this publication. Images held by the Rockefeller Archive Center have been deemed to be owned by the Rockefeller Foundation unless we were able to determine otherwise. Specific permission has been granted by the copyright holder to use the following works:

Ruthie Abel: 8-9, 110-111
Art Resource: 26
The Johns Hopkins Bloomberg School of Public Health: 57
Department of Special Collections and University Archives, Marquette University Libraries: 84, 86
Regents of the University of California, Lawrence Berkeley National Laboratory: 101, 102
Estate of Bob Serating: 126-127
Sony Music Entertainment: 139, 141
Newark Public Library: 150
New York State Archives. New York (State). Governor. Public information photographs, 1910-1992. Series 13703-83, Number 1381_2047_2: 157
Boyd Lewis, Courtesy of Kenan Research Center at the Atlanta History Center: 166, 167, 168
Jonas Bendiksen: 88-89, 170-171, 233, 241
Spelman College Archives: 172-173, 175
Dartmouth College Library: 187
Suzie Fitzhugh: 200
New Haven Register: 202

	Preface from Dr. Judith Rodin	14
	Foreword – Justice Sandra Day O'Connor	18
I	The Charter Fight	24
II	Government by Experts	52
III	Philanthropy at War	90
IV	The Arts, the Humanities, and National Identity	112
V	Foundations Under Fire	144
VI	Equal Opportunity for All	174
VII	Democracy and Design in America's Cities	210
	Conclusion: Resilience and the American Spirit	239
	Acknowledgments	246
	List of Illustrations	248
	Index	256

"It has been frequently remarked that it seems to have been reserved to the people of this country, by their conduct and example, to decide the important question, whether societies of men are really capable or not of establishing good government from reflection and choice, or whether they are forever destined to depend for their political constitutions on accident and force."

Alexander Hamilton
Federalist No. 1

"Those coasts, so admirably adapted for commerce and industry; those wide and deep rivers; that inexhaustible valley of the Mississippi; the whole continent, in short, seemed prepared to be the abode of a great nation, yet unborn. In that land the great experiment was to be made, by civilized man, of the attempt to construct society upon a new basis; and it was there, for the first time, that theories hitherto unknown, or deemed impracticable, were to exhibit a spectacle for which the world had not been prepared by the history of the past."

Alexis de Tocqueville
Democracy in America

PREFACE

By Dr. Judith Rodin
President of the Rockefeller Foundation

Ten years after the end of the American Revolution, Alexander Hamilton wondered whether human beings were capable of establishing good government based on "reflection and choice." If not, he suggested, they would be ruled forever by those who would seize power by force. Alexis de Tocqueville, the French writer who came to the United States in the 1830s to study American democracy, would echo Hamilton's concerns. He called the United States a "great experiment" in politics and culture. His two-volume work entitled *Democracy in America* seemed to ask the fundamental question: could a pluralistic society with regional, economic, ethnic, and religious differences sustain a democratic government that would accommodate and draw strength from the underlying diversity of its culture?

Soon after the publication of *Democracy in America*, the American Civil War seemed to suggest that the answer was no. At Gettysburg in 1863, President Abraham Lincoln reminded Americans that the great civil war that had engulfed the nation would test whether the United States or any nation "dedicated to the proposition that all men are created equal" could endure. The tens of thousands of soldiers who died at Gettysburg, according to Lincoln, had given their lives so that "government of the people, by the people and for the people shall not perish from this earth." One hundred and fifty years later, American democracy is still a work in progress and Tocqueville's great experiment is relevant to people around the world who aspire to democratic government.

In his travels throughout the United States, Tocqueville was particularly impressed with what we would today call the nonprofit or civic sectors of society. He noted Americans' tendency to form associations to address common problems, rather than to always turn first to government for solutions. He wrote about the absence of a powerful aristocratic class in the United States and the egalitarian character of the culture. Tocqueville believed that these things went hand-in-hand, and that mutual aid strengthened the bonds of citizenship and democracy at the same time.

The Industrial Revolution, however, transformed the United States. In the last half of the nineteenth century entrepreneurs including John D. Rockefeller, Andrew Carnegie, and J.P. Morgan built personal fortunes that were far beyond Tocqueville's imagination and, even by today's standards, of unprecedented size. When these men decided at the beginning of the twentieth century to use a great portion of their wealth to create the first broadly purposed, private foundations, modern philanthropy was born—and with it, a deep anxiety over the role of great concentrated private wealth engaged in social projects in a democracy.

John D. Rockefeller's plan to create and endow the Rockefeller Foundation in 1910 engendered opposition in Congress and among some groups in the general public. People feared that Rockefeller's money, directed toward solving problems of broad public concern but without public oversight or administration, might undermine the great experiment in democracy that Hamilton, Tocqueville, and others had envisioned. The opposition was so strong that the Rockefeller Foundation was eventually incorporated by the state of New York, rather than the United States Congress.

But abandoning the idea of a federal charter did not mean forsaking the American people or the American experiment. As *Democracy & Philanthropy* shows, the Rockefeller Foundation has worked assiduously over the course of the last century to earn and keep the public trust. From its earliest days

PREFACE

the Foundation has published an extensive annual report that detailed every grant and investment and provided the names of all trustees and principal officers involved with the Foundation's operations. In the 1950s and 1960s, when Congress expressed grave concern about abuses perpetrated by some institutions within the philanthropic community, the Rockefeller Foundation's relationship with the people's elected representatives and the American experiment was tested again. On those occasions, the Foundation provided detailed reports on its work to satisfy Congressional investigators.

Perhaps more importantly, the Rockefeller Foundation has played an active role over the course of a century in promoting many of the ideals that are critical to the American experiment. Through the work of our earlier sister organization, the General Education Board, and then the Foundation itself, we sought to promote equal opportunity for individuals and families of color marginalized by institutionalized racism. Various initiatives in the social sciences worked to strengthen the institutions of democratic government. Programs in the arts and humanities helped nurture a complicated sense of American identity that embraced diversity and the idea of a pluralistic society. During two world wars, the Foundation did its part to protect the ideals of democracy and freedom of expression. To be sure, all of these programs were bounded by the pervading attitudes of their time, but the Rockefeller Foundation has been remarkably persistent and consistent over the years in its efforts to promote the values embedded in the basic framework of American democracy.

In many ways, this journey is tied directly to our charter. When John D. Rockefeller established the Foundation, he intended that we would work to promote the well-being of humanity "throughout the world." Throughout our history, we have embraced his global vision by working to foster international collaboration and to address the needs of poor and vulnerable people on nearly every continent. This made the Rockefeller Foundation America's first global foundation. In the 1950s particularly, but all through our history, this basic commitment has fostered tension with some in the United States who have asserted that working internationally is somehow un-American.

In creating the Foundation, however, Rockefeller did not see a conflict between his effort to help the world and his passion for his home country. Neither do we. In fact, some of our most well-known international programs—in public health, for example—began here in the United States. Just as Alexis de Tocqueville recognized that mutual aid strengthens the bonds of civil society, we realize that our work to promote the well-being of humanity throughout the world makes for a stronger global community.

Headquartered in New York City, chartered by the state of New York, and bound by laws passed by elected representatives of the state as well as the nation, the Rockefeller Foundation is unavoidably and proudly an American institution. The essays in this book explore moments when the Foundation has been tested in its relationship with the American people and their representatives. It also highlights the many ways in which the Foundation and private philanthropy have contributed to the ongoing evolution of the American experiment.

Opponents of John D. Rockefeller's foundation in 1910 expressed grave concerns regarding the role of great concentrated private wealth in a democracy. These fears have not been resolved. Indeed, the tension between the public and private nature of philanthropy fuels an ongoing discussion within the philanthropic sector. And in Washington, at various times, our nation's leaders have continued to debate the importance of philanthropy to the health of our nation. At the Rockefeller Foundation, we believe that these tensions are fundamentally creative. They push us to keep innovating, to find new ways to cooperate with the private and public sectors to promote the well-being of all Americans. This is the essence of American pluralism and the force that lies at the heart of the American experiment.

FOREWORD

By Honorable Sandra Day O'Connor
Retired Justice, U.S. Supreme Court

The National Cathedral in Washington, D.C. was packed with dignitaries on June 11, 2004. They had come from around the world for the funeral of President Ronald Reagan. They included the former communist leader of the Soviet Union, Mikhail Gorbachev. Presidents and prime ministers spoke, along with Jewish, Greek Orthodox, Muslim, Roman Catholic, and Episcopal clerics. As the Armed Forces Chorus sang the "Battle Hymn of the Republic," the mournful sound of this great Civil War-era song reverberated in the vaulted ceiling of the cathedral, reminding us that the contested nature of American democracy can never be taken for granted.

Before he died, Nancy Reagan asked me to participate in the ceremony. I had known the Reagans for many years. In 1981, during the first year of his presidency, President Reagan nominated me as a Justice on the U.S. Supreme Court. The nomination fulfilled his campaign promise to appoint the first woman to the nation's highest court.

I was asked to read from a sermon by John Winthrop, a founder and governor of the Massachusetts Bay Colony. Winthrop wrote and delivered his address, "A Model of Christian Charity," aboard the *Arabella* traveling in 1630 from England to the American harbor that we know today as Boston. The speech famously called upon the Pilgrims to establish a community in New England that would be "as a city upon a hill," and to live with one another as if "the eyes of all people are upon us."

That sermon was deeply religious, but Winthrop also articulated a secular vision of what would become the democratic society of the United States. In Winthrop's mind, and as our Founders intended, we are responsible as citizens for the fate of our community and for the strength of our democracy. "We must not look only on our own things," Winthrop said, "but also on the things of our brethren."

John D. Rockefeller knew this responsibility. Heir to New England's Puritan traditions and deeply immersed in his Baptist faith, he saw himself as a steward of his wealth. He created the Rockefeller Foundation in 1913 to "promote the well-being of mankind throughout the world." In doing so, he demonstrated a rare sense of citizenship and personal responsibility.

But members of Congress were deeply suspicious of Rockefeller's philanthropy. They echoed the fears of Thomas Jefferson, James Madison, and other Founders who were concerned that great wealth might eventually corrupt our democracy. Even today in the United States, as the reaction to the Supreme Court's decision in the *Citizens United v. Federal Elections Commission* case makes clear, we are uneasy with the role of private wealth in the public sector.

The Founders believed that virtuous citizens represented the greatest counterweight to the corruption of wealth. Jefferson and Madison associated virtue and good citizenship with the same selfless and community-minded ideal that John Winthrop articulated onboard the *Arabella*. Citizenship meant more than casting a vote, it demanded that we participate in civic life, that we speak out *and* compromise to build consensus and move our communities and our nation forward on the important issues of the day.

I share these sentiments. Since retiring from the Supreme Court in 2006, I have dedicated a great deal of my time to the promotion of civics education, especially among our young people. With philanthropic support from individuals and organizations, I founded iCivics in 2009 to help reverse America's

FOREWORD

declining civic knowledge and encourage citizen engagement. We develop curricula and tools that make learning fun and, above all, engage young people in the democratic process.

In 2006, I also became a trustee of the Rockefeller Foundation. Working with my fellow trustees and in collaboration with President Judith Rodin, I came to realize that the Foundation has been deeply committed to the development of democracy for a long time. As *Democracy & Philanthropy* illustrates, this work includes pioneering programs to professionalize the civil service, develop the social sciences as a tool for better policymaking, cultivate the arts and humanities to explore the complex character of American society, promote equal opportunity for all our citizens, invigorate the creativity of our cities, and strengthen our communities so that they reflect the resilience of the American character.

Over a hundred years, the work of the Rockefeller Foundation in the United States demonstrates that philanthropy does not threaten our democracy. It is in fact a safeguard of our freedom. In the diversity of philanthropic institutions in the United States, we find countless community leaders and social entrepreneurs testing new ideas to address the most challenging issues facing our society today.

John D. Rockefeller once said that "we have come to the period when we can well afford to ask the ablest men to devote more of their time, thought, and money to the public well-being." Many women and men embraced this challenge in Rockefeller's day. Our own generation and the generations that follow must rise to this challenge.

Thanks to our success as a nation, we do not need Rockefeller's great wealth to practice philanthropy or to lend a hand to strengthen our democracy. We need only cultivate our individual sense of responsibility. This was the challenge that John Winthrop offered to the Pilgrims. It is the challenge that the Rockefeller Foundation has embraced along with generations of American leaders, to shape our democracy as a city upon a hill, a model of freedom for the eyes that are upon us.

We the People

...insure domestic Tranquility, provide for the common de[fence]... and our Posterity, do ordain and establish this Constitu[tion]...

Article

Section. 1. All legislative Powers herein granted shall [be vested in a Congress of the United States, which shall consist of a Senate and House] of Representatives.

Section. 2. The House of Representatives shall be compo[sed]... in each State shall have the Qualifications requisite for Electors of the [most numerous Branch of the State Legislature.]

No Person shall be a Representative who shall not ha[ve]... and who shall not, when elected, be an Inhabitant of that State [in which he shall be chosen.]

Representatives and direct Taxes shall be apportioned am[ong the several States]... Numbers, which shall be determined by adding to the whole Num[ber of free Persons]... not taxed, three fifths of all other Persons. The actual Enumer[ation]... and within every subsequent Term of ten Years, in such Mann[er]... [thi]rty thousand, but each State shall have at least one Repres[entative]... [shall be] entitled to chuse three, Massachusetts eight, Rhode-Island an[d]... [ei]ght, Delaware one, Maryland six, Virginia ten, North Caro[lina]...

When vacancies happen in the Representation from an[y State]...

The House of Representatives shall chuse their Speaker [and other Officers]...

Section. 3. The Senate of the United States shall be compose[d]... Senator shall have one Vote.

Immediately after they shall be assembled in Conseque[nce]...

DEMOCRACY & PHILANTHROPY

Chapter I

THE CHARTER FIGHT

In 1910, John D. Rockefeller wanted to create the largest, richest private foundation in the world. The work of the foundation would not be confined to one state; it would be national and international in scope—America's first global foundation—so his representatives asked the U.S. Congress for a federal charter. Some members of Congress were adamantly opposed to the idea. They feared that this great concentration of private money, directed toward public policy issues and not subject to the will of the people, would undermine the foundations of American democracy.

Rockefeller may not have been the richest man in the United States in 1910, but he was close. He had founded the Standard Oil Company in 1870, and the company had become the world's first and largest multinational. It dominated the petroleum industry.

In a country without aristocracy, Rockefeller stood among the titans of the Gilded Age. His contemporaries included Andrew Carnegie, J.P. Morgan, Cornelius Vanderbilt, Jay Gould, and others once known as "robber barons," but in reality he had no peer. In an era without corporate or individual income taxes and a bare minimum of government regulation, these men amassed huge fortunes. Rockefeller's wealth was said to be equivalent to one sixty-fifth of the entire gross domestic product of the United States. There were rumors that he intended

Political cartoonists at *Puck*, the nation's leading magazine of political satire, frequently depicted John D. Rockefeller Sr. as a greedy manipulator of the American political system. In this 1906 image, he appears in Uncle Sam's clothes, preening while Senator Nelson W. Aldrich perches, as a vulture, on an oil can. (Frank A. Nankivell, Library of Congress.)

to endow his foundation with $1 billion—a sum greater than the entire federal budget in 1910.

The United States had never seen personal fortunes like Rockefeller's before, and many people in 1910 worried about the influence of America's great industrialists on public policy. The government that Lincoln had proclaimed to be of the people, by the people, and for the people "is no longer," President Rutherford B. Hayes wrote in his diary in 1888. "It is a government of corporations, by corporations and for corporations – How is this?" By the time Theodore Roosevelt became president, there was widespread anger at and fear of the power of "the trusts" —especially Standard Oil. Many people cheered in 1909 when the government announced it had filed a civil antitrust lawsuit against the company.

French writer Alexis de Tocqueville came to the United States in 1831 to study American culture. In *Democracy in America*, he explored the tensions between liberty and equality. The charitable associations Americans formed to address common problems, he said, played a key role in "the great experiment" of American democracy. (Théodore Chassériau. RMN-Grand Palais / Art Source, NY.)

At the same time, charity and philanthropy were deeply embedded in the civic culture of the United States. Puritans bound for North America in 1630 had been deeply moved by John Winthrop's shipboard sermon envisioning the new English society in North America as "A Model of Christian Charity." Benjamin Franklin imagined a country where industrious citizens, working together through various mutual aid organizations and charitable institutions, would create a more egalitarian society than the world had ever seen. And fifty-five years after the start of the American Revolution, a young French noble, Alexis de Tocqueville, would marvel at the ways in which Americans organized themselves for the common good. He viewed these civic associations as essential elements of the American experiment with democratic government. Philanthropy represented an extension of this democratic spirit.

But Rockefeller, along with steel magnate Andrew Carnegie and several others, envisioned philanthropy on an unprecedented scale. By 1910, Rockefeller had already established the Rockefeller Institute for Medical Research (1901), the General Education Board (1902), and the Rockefeller Sanitary Commission for the Eradication of Hookworm Disease (1909) to fight hookworm infestations in the American South. Carnegie had created the Carnegie Foundation for the Advancement of Teaching, and in 1911 the Carnegie Corporation of New York. In 1907, Margaret Olivia Slocum Sage had endowed a foundation named for her late husband, the Russell Sage Foundation, with $10 million. These new institutions were rich beyond the imagination of previous charities, and many were founded with broad mission statements that seemed to empower their private boards of trustees to do almost anything. John D. Rockefeller's closest advisors thought that was a good thing; his adversaries did not.

Development of the Idea

Rockefeller's philanthropy was rooted in his Baptist Christian upbringing. He gave to charity from his wages as soon as he started working as a teenager. By the late 1880s he had already given millions of dollars to church missions and other charities. But as his wealth continued to grow, he found it harder work to give away his money responsibly than to make it. As an entrepreneur and an executive, Rockefeller was constantly looking for people with talent who could take over realms of his business activities. As he began to look toward retirement, he met Frederick T. Gates.

Outwardly, Gates was distinctly unlike Rockefeller. In demeanor, he was outspoken and dramatic where Rockefeller was taciturn and demure. "He combined

The Rockefeller Sanitary Commission, formed in 1909, established county dispensaries to battle hookworm disease in the American South. Between 1901 and 1913, John D. Rockefeller Sr. endowed a number of new philanthropic entities to promote medical research, education, and public health. This work culminated with the creation of the Rockefeller Foundation in 1913. (Rockefeller Archive Center.)

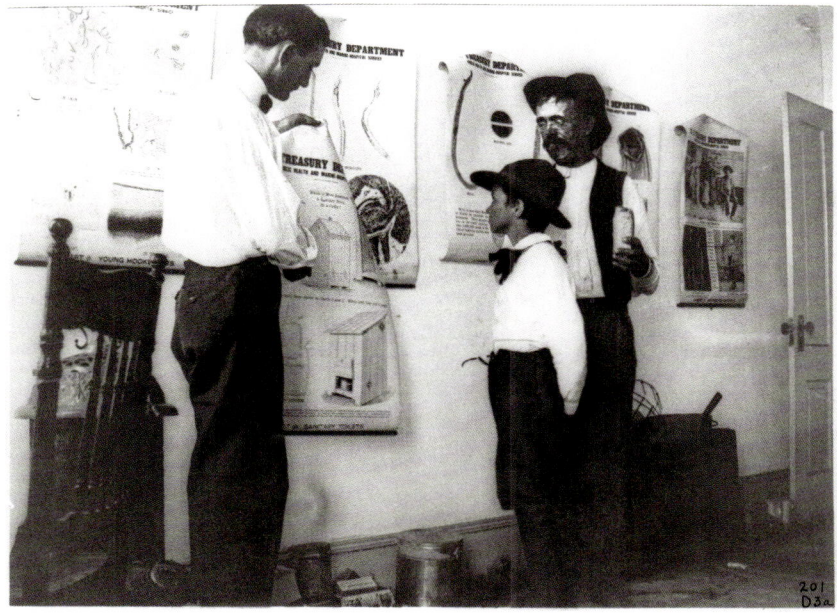

Democracy & Philanthropy

Frederick Gates (seated) and Simon Flexner (standing) were long-time advisors to the Rockefellers. Gates developed the strategic vision for Senior's philanthropy, and served as a mentor to Junior as he made philanthropy his life's work. Meanwhile, Flexner became the director of the Rockefeller Institute for Medical Research. Both men were trustees of the Rockefeller Foundation. (Rockefeller Archive Center.)

bold imagination and large horizons with shrewd business capacity and driving energy," wrote Raymond Fosdick, who would later become president of the Rockefeller Foundation. Born in 1853, Gates was the son of a New York Baptist preacher, who had become a schoolteacher at age fifteen to help his family pay its bills. Graduating from the Rochester Theological Seminary, a Baptist institution, Gates moved to Minneapolis to become a pastor at the Fifth Avenue Baptist Church. Through his involvement in mission activity of the state's Baptist organization, Gates met George Pillsbury, the flour magnate, and got his first taste of advising the wealthy on their philanthropy when Pillsbury came to him regarding a bequest he intended to make to support a Baptist academy in Minnesota. Gates ended up leading the effort to raise money to match Pillsbury's gift, and his success as a fundraiser drew the attention of national leaders in the Baptist community.

In 1888, Gates was picked to lead the American Baptist Education Society, with a primary goal of developing a great university in Chicago, which brought him into contact with John D. Rockefeller. Leaders of the society hoped that John D. Rockefeller, who had already given hundreds of thousands of dollars to Baptist initiatives, would make a lead gift to launch the project. Rockefeller was ambivalent about the project. He thought the vision was grandiose. When Gates wrote to him seeking support for a more modest beginning, Rockefeller invited him to lunch. Clearly impressed with Gates, Rockefeller suggested that they travel together the next day on the train to Cleveland (with Gates heading on to Minnesota).

Gates was impressed by Rockefeller's demeanor. "Mr. Rockefeller is broad, clear-headed, self-poised, devoted to what he regards as duty, little influenced by considerations of position, or the authority of advocates of special causes. A child with a clear case would have as much weight with him as an eminent man," Gates wrote to his parents after the encounter.

Rockefeller's support for equal opportunity was evident long before the Rockefeller Foundation was established. In 1884, Spelman Seminary (later College) in Atlanta, which served African-American women, was named after Rockefeller's wife and her parents. The family had been active in the antislavery movement. On index cards, Rockefeller staff recorded his contributions to the institution. (Rockefeller Archive Center.)

Chapter One: The Charter Fight

Gates' intellect and methods helped boost Rockefeller's confidence in the University of Chicago concept and led him to endow the university. The relationship between Gates and Rockefeller, however, soon shifted dramatically. During a meeting in March 1891, Rockefeller confessed to Gates that the appeals to his philanthropy and charity had become overwhelming. He was incapable of giving without the due diligence to reassure himself that the money would be well spent, but he didn't have the time or energy to investigate the organizations to which he was inclined to give – to say nothing of the work of turning down the hundreds of appeals to which he was not interested in contributing. He needed either to shift the burden of giving to someone else or "cease giving entirely," according to Gates. In 1892, Rockefeller asked Gates if he would be willing to move to New York to help. In Rockefeller's mind, Gates was the perfect choice since most of Rockefeller's giving went to Baptist organizations and Gates knew this terrain. Gates accepted the job. Soon thereafter, Rockefeller directed all appeals to Gates.

"I did my best to soothe ruffled feelings, to listen fully to every plea, and to weigh fairly the merits of every cause," Gates wrote, but as he began to direct the enormous flow of Rockefeller's benevolence, he confirmed that Rockefeller's frustration at not being able to exercise sufficient due diligence with all of his beneficiaries had been well founded. Gates

29

discovered "not a few of Mr. Rockefeller's habitual charities to be worthless and practically fraudulent."

Working with Gates, Rockefeller transitioned to a practice of "wholesale" philanthropy. For example, rather than give directly to local appeals from Baptist congregations or pastors, he increased his giving to state and national organizations and let them do the due diligence on local projects. Internationally, Rockefeller had been giving to a host of foreign missionary projects, each one seeking his assistance individually. Working with Gates, Rockefeller "cut off every one of these private missionary appeals" and referred them back to the Baptist Foreign Mission Society, which Rockefeller strengthened with larger contributions.

Gates was astonished to discover how many individuals wrote to Rockefeller seeking money for themselves. "These appeals came in multitudes from every part of the United States and, after Mr. Rockefeller became widely known, from nearly all foreign lands and the islands of the sea." They came "in a flood" each time the newspapers reported on a Rockefeller donation or gift. At one time, Gates counted 50,000 such requests within the space of a month. "Few were answered, but every one was opened for a glance as to its character. Our office force was swamped with them."

John D. Rockefeller Senior and Junior in 1918. Deeply religious, each in his own way, their philanthropy was motivated by their understanding of Christian teachings. At the same time, each believed in the rule of reason, especially as it applied to civic culture and government in the United States. (H.T. Koshiba. Rockefeller Archive Center.)

Rockefeller increasingly recognized that even with Gates managing his philanthropy full-time, he could not keep pace with the need to give money away and to do it wisely. As Rockefeller biographer Ron Chernow points out, he was often vilified in public for hoarding his money. Everywhere he went people asked him for help. Newspapers noted that his giving did not keep pace with Andrew Carnegie's. Moreover, as Gates warned him, his fortune was building and was becoming so large that it would be a burden to him and his family.

Rockefeller was focused on the problem. In 1899, speaking on the ten-year anniversary of the founding of the University of Chicago, he called on the other great entrepreneurs of his generation to be generous: "Let us erect a foundation, a trust, and engage directors who will make it a life work to manage, with our personal cooperation, the business of benevolence properly and effectively."

Rockefeller's son, John D. Rockefeller Jr., played a key role in the decision to create the Rockefeller Foundation. In 1897, after graduating from Brown University, Junior – or "Mr. Junior," as he was known to Rockefeller's staff – began working in his father's office. Under Gates's mentorship, Junior embraced philanthropy as his life's work. Together, he and Gates advised, cajoled, encouraged, and responded to John D. Rockefeller's philanthropic impulses.

By 1907, the idea to create an institution with a very broad mission had begun to build momentum among this small group. A panic on Wall Street that year was reversed by the actions of several New York capitalists, including Rockefeller, who earned some measure of goodwill in Washington. The following year, a chance encounter between John D. Rockefeller and Senator "Pitchfork Ben" Tillman of South Carolina gave Rockefeller an opportunity to charm a potential critic in Congress.

On the strength of these events, John D. Rockefeller Jr. spoke to his father-in-law, Senator Nelson Aldrich of Rhode Island, about the creation of a foundation. Aldrich was known as the "General Manager of the Senate." He was the most powerful member of the "old guard" Republicans who dominated the institution at the end of the nineteenth century. With Aldrich's help, Junior hoped the Rockefeller Foundation bill would sail through the Senate.

But Aldrich's influence was waning. With the election of Robert M. "Fighting Bob" La Follette to the Senate from Wisconsin in 1905, a new "Progressive" wing of the Republican Party gained power and challenged the old guard's control of the Senate. In combination with Populist Democrats, these Progressives attacked the trusts and financial interests associated with Rockefeller, J.P. Morgan, and Wall Street. Given the changing political climate in Washington, obtaining a state charter in New York might be easier.

Frederick Gates favored a federal charter, especially after reading a report written by attorney Starr J. Murphy. Variously described as quiet and efficient, as well as witty, gracious, and warm, Murphy lived in Montclair, New Jersey, where he had gotten to know Frederick Gates. Impressed with

Attorney Starr J. Murphy managed the initial effort to secure a federal charter for the Rockefeller Foundation. He worked with New Hampshire Senator Jacob H. Gallinger to introduce the bill. In testimony before the Senate, he reassured Congress that it would have the power to intervene if trustees used the assets for improper purposes. (Rockefeller Archive Center.)

Murphy's demeanor and intelligence, Gates had recruited Murphy to help with various Rockefeller projects. In 1904, Murphy left private practice to join Rockefeller's staff.

Murphy noted that there was very little consequential difference between a New York and a federal charter. He thought a New York charter could be easily won. But if he went first to Congress and was rejected, he might have a harder time of it in New York. Still, Gates favored a federal fight. "I would not hesitate to throw this charter right into the arena and let the wild beasts fight over it if they like."

Gates thought the issues were on Rockefeller's side. As he tried to anticipate the debate in Congress, he formulated the questions. "Will Mr. Rockefeller's enemies make a bitter fight against his right to give away his own money as he deems fit? If they do, will they win or will Mr. Rockefeller win?" He thought if Rockefeller's enemies sought "to prevent his doing good to his fellow men" the opposition would backfire. "Mr. Rockefeller has given away vast sums of money; he is using the great fortune which he has acquired for the promotion of human welfare. That is a feature of his character and life which is never mentioned by his enemies." Gates hoped the charter fight would get reporters to pay attention to Rockefeller's generosity. "Even if the bill suffers defeat," he wrote, "it cannot but raise up friends to Mr. Rockefeller."

Murphy drafted the initial bill and Junior sent the draft to John Spooner, the former U.S. Senator from Wisconsin who had recently left politics to practice law in New York City, asking for Spooner's advice on "the wisdom of undertaking to secure a Federal charter." Spooner advised Junior to avoid references to religion because it might spark "covert" opposition. He also suggested some other minor changes and offered to quietly test the waters. Junior continued to press his father-in-law, but no bill was introduced. Meanwhile, the campaign to pick President Theodore Roosevelt's successor heated up and William Howard Taft was elected in November 1908.

With these discussions in the background and the election over, there was some optimism in the Rockefeller office that eventually a bill would be introduced and passed. John D. Rockefeller signed a deed of trust to turn over 72,569 shares of Standard Oil of New Jersey, stocks worth more than $50 million, to a newly created entity to be known as the Rockefeller Foundation. He named three trustees: his son, his son-in-law Harold McCormick, and Frederick Gates. Junior and Gates were appointed as a committee of two "to prepare and present to the Congress of the United States a bill for the incorporation of The Rockefeller Foundation." With the draft of the Act already written, Junior sent it to Aldrich with the

understanding "that you think it will not be difficult to have it acted upon at an early date."

But Aldrich did not make a move, and weeks passed. Because the bill proposed to create the Rockefeller Foundation as a corporate entity in Washington, D.C., Rockefeller's advisors decided to press New Hampshire Senator Jacob H. Gallinger, the Republican chairman of the Committee on the District of Columbia, to sponsor the legislation. Like Aldrich, Gallinger was considered part of the Republican old guard in the Senate. Gallinger promised that he would introduce the bill and call Starr Murphy as a witness to explain and testify on its behalf.

Gallinger introduced the measure on March 2, 1910. The following day, the *Washington Post* headline proclaimed: "Oil King's Money to Aid Humanity." According to the *Post*, the proposed Rockefeller Foundation would become the "Acme of Philanthropy." Rockefeller was "preparing a philanthropic project surpassing anything of its kind ever undertaken in this or any other country." In the world of philanthropy, the Rockefeller Foundation would "become what the Standard Oil Company has long been among corporations."

With a gift of nearly $50 million (more than $1.18 billion in 2013 dollars) in Standard Oil stock (similar to the certificate pictured above), John D. Rockefeller Sr. sought to create the Rockefeller Foundation in 1909. After opposition appeared, he revoked the deed of trust he had signed and waited until the Foundation was chartered in the state of New York to make his first gift. (Rockefeller Archive Center.)

Democracy & Philanthropy

The significance of the Rockefeller Foundation bill was underscored the day after the bill was submitted when John D. Rockefeller Jr. announced that he had retired from the board of Standard Oil so that he could run the Foundation and take charge of his father's philanthropy. In this new arena, according to the press, Junior would "perpetuate the domination so long maintained in the world of industry by John D. Rockefeller Sr. as president of the Standard."

Early newspaper reports on the proposed foundation stressed its innovative approach. As Frederick Gates told reporters, the Foundation would be free to change and adapt to meet the philanthropic needs of the day. The "dead hand" of the donor would not direct the Foundation's activities for generations. "The trustees to whom the details have been intrusted," reported the *Post*, "will grapple with opportunities and problems as they arise, unhampered by red-tapism or any sort of impedimenta, and adequately empowered to meet any emergency with the practically inexhaustible funds in their hands."

The Opposition Organizes

To the dismay of many in the Rockefeller offices at 26 Broadway in New York City, the proposal to create the Rockefeller Foundation did not initially meet with broad approval. Harvard President Emeritus Charles W. Eliot, who would later serve on the board of the Foundation, expressed skepticism. "It is just as possible to throw money away in this manner as in any other," he said, "and many undeserving charities may impose on Mr. Rockefeller's agents." He declared that he was not in favor of "applying the principles of incorporation to such an undertaking, for in my mind that is to commercialize the matter too much." He also feared that the overwhelming scale of Rockefeller's philanthropy might discourage others from giving. Nevertheless, he suggested that the Rockefeller Foundation would ultimately "be a great benefit to all humanity."

Opponents emerged in Congress. The *New York Times* reported that some senators, "especially those from Western States, where suspicion of Standard Oil embraces suspicion of Mr. Rockefeller and about all he does," were leery that "the plan is but a cloak for some device for the advantage of the trusts in which Mr. Rockefeller and his friends are interested." These senators also expressed concern that within a short time the Foundation's assets would grow so large "as to be practically beyond the control of ordinary Governmental restrictions" and "necessitate a great upheaval" to restore the government's authority.

Some people feared that once the Foundation was in place and funded by income from its investments, if the Government brought a case against companies whose stock was in that portfolio – for antitrust activity, for example, "such a chorus of protest against Government action would go up from the beneficiaries of the charity as almost certainly to embarrass the Government's action." Senator Gallinger conceded that this concern needed to be taken seriously. He noted, however, that the General Education Board had received assets worth nearly $53 million from Rockefeller, and none of the beneficiaries of the GEB had risen up to protest the Government's pending antitrust case against Standard Oil.

To many people, the timing of the Rockefeller Foundation bill was suspect. A week after Senator Gallinger introduced the plan, the U.S. Department of Justice filed its one thousand-page brief with the U.S. Supreme Court charging Standard Oil with violating the Sherman Antitrust Act and calling for the dissolution of the company.

Over the next few weeks, newspaper editors also turned against the proposal. The *Washington Post* opined that the Foundation would "be a good thing to those who handle the funds—that much is certain. There will be life positions, easy work, and big pay. The imagination runs forward and sees a swarm of faddists, innovators, reformers, grafters and visionaries buzzing about this pile of money, eager to aid in disbursing it to humanity, including themselves." The *Post* feared the activities of "harebrained reformers." Cynically, they suggested that the effort reflected a "spirit of egotism and selfishness." "The American people as a nation," the *Post* proclaimed, "are not in need of charity from Mr. Rockefeller…If the Rockefeller Foundation should tend to undermine the self-reliance and self-respect of young Americans, it will prove to be a curse."

One Western Republican senator believed that the proposed Rockefeller Foundation was a scheme to indoctrinate young people in favor of the trusts. He noted that Standard Oil's president, John D. Archbold, was a major donor and the longtime president of the board of trustees of Syracuse University and that the Chancellor of the university was now a vigorous defender of Standard Oil and had assailed Theodore Roosevelt and "the idea of Government regulation and control of corporations generally."

Congressmen were also troubled by the open-ended language of the proposed Foundation's mission: "to promote the well-being and advance the civilization of the people of the United States and its territories and possessions and of foreign lands in the acquisition and dissemination of knowledge; in the prevention and relief of suffering and in the promotion of any and all of the elements of human progress." Some feared that the trustees of the Foundation, for example, might determine that the encouragement of manufactures by monopoly constituted an element of human progress and the Foundation would be used to defend or support Standard Oil.

There were also fears that the Rockefeller Foundation would begin to dictate to the nation's charities. A column in the *Springfield Republican* pointed out that "the Carnegie Foundation [sic] tends to exercise control of institutions which accept its financial aid." The *Republican* suggested that this kind of behavior would lead to monopoly in the realm of public charity and "a vast power of dictation in the hands of those who may control the funds."

As debate swirled in the press long before the bill reached the floor of the Senate, rumors proliferated. Murphy had to reassure a *New York Times* reporter that Rockefeller was not going to endow the Foundation with a billion dollars (more than $23 billion in 2013 dollars), an amount far larger than the $694 million federal budget in 1910 and equivalent to 1/65th of the nation's gross domestic product.

A Spirited Defense

Invited to testify before the U.S. Senate's Committee on the District of Columbia, Starr Murphy sought to allay all of these fears. He said first that the proposed charter for the Rockefeller Foundation was essentially modeled after the charter for the General Education Board, which Congress had approved in 1903. Addressing concerns about the lack of specificity in the proposed mission of the Rockefeller Foundation, he suggested that this was a good thing. The GEB's charter also articulated a broad purpose for the organization, which allowed the directors great freedom to address issues as they became apparent. "The charities of the fourteenth century are not the charities of the twentieth century," he said. "[I]t is eminently desirable, it seems to me, that the tendency of philanthropy in the future should be that the dead hand should be removed from charitable bequest" so that decisions "should be left in the hands of living men" who understood the needs of their era. Any effort to narrow the purposes of the foundation would "impose a limitation, which is exactly what he [Rockefeller] seeks to avoid."

Murphy went on to explain why Rockefeller needed to establish the Foundation. Given the volume of requests for assistance and the need for due diligence, Rockefeller simply couldn't keep up without establishing a more formal organization to manage his philanthropy. He described the success of the GEB in the realm of education. He asserted that Rockefeller now wanted to build on that success by creating an organization "which will give to him that same freedom of scope, except that it will not be limited in any way; that wherever there arises a human need this board may be in position to meet it, if that shall seem wise."

Murphy also gently responded to concerns that the Rockefeller Foundation would invade the purview of government. "It is not the purpose of this board to supplant any existing agency," he said. "It has always been the practice of the donor to work through existing agencies, so far as that is possible; never to supplant, but always to supplement." With a few exceptions, including the University of Chicago the Rockefeller Institute for Medical Research in New York; and the Rockefeller Sanitary Commission, created to fight the spread of hookworm, Rockefeller had preferred to support existing institutions rather than create new ones.

Murphy knew that there was great curiosity and concern about how much money Rockefeller intended to give to the new Foundation. He avoided a direct answer, noting only that Rockefeller's pattern had been to start modestly, watch for success, and then provide greater support. This was the pattern with the Institute for Medical Research and the GEB. He did not mention that Rockefeller had already set aside $50 million dollars (equivalent to more than $1.2 billion in 2013 dollars) in Standard Oil stock to fund the enterprise.

Murphy acknowledged that public officials and their constituents were genuinely concerned that the Foundation's assets might be "diverted to uses which will not be beneficial to the public." He responded by pointing out that Congress and the United States Government would continue to maintain ultimate control over the new institution. The Foundation would be required to file annual reports with the federal government. If those reports proved "insufficient or inadequate" the government would have the power to investigate. Furthermore, the language of the bill provided "that this charter shall be subject to alteration, amendment, or repeal at the pleasure of the Congress of the United States." According to Murphy, Rockefeller was glad to see this power vested in Congress, "not merely to protect his wishes, which are solely that this fund shall always be used for the public welfare and for no other purpose, but also that Congress may have the power, if at any time in the future this fund should get into the hands of men who should seek to use it for improper purposes, to exert its authority and bring that fund back again to the uses for which it is intended."

Constructive Criticism

Rockefeller had many enemies in the public sphere and there was little Murphy could do to win over the labor supporters or business interests who felt they had been victimized by Standard Oil's monopoly. But the Rockefeller camp was especially concerned by criticisms raised by people who should have been allies or supporters. In an article in *The Survey*, the leading magazine of philanthropy and social work, Edward T. Devine, a prominent voice in the world of charity, raised three primary concerns. First, he thought that "government should have a voice in the selection of incorporators and trustees." Murphy suggested that this wasn't necessary. Self-perpetuating boards, as proposed for the Rockefeller Foundation, were in widespread use for universities and they had proven to be devoted to the public welfare.

Murphy also asserted that public officials serving on the board would face pressure from their constituents to make certain grants, which would undermine the board's decision making. Fundamentally, Congress didn't need to appoint board members because it held the final authority to revoke the charter.

Devine wanted to require that the Foundation spend its annual income, rather than add the income to the endowment. Murphy asserted that this wouldn't be a problem. With the GEB, the board didn't have the resources to fund all of the good requests it received. The same would be true with the Foundation. Already Rockefeller was receiving 400 to 500 requests a day. They came from all over the world. Down the road, if some board decided to hoard its income, Congress could always step in.

Finally, Devine suggested that the Rockefeller Foundation should have a limited life, and that it should be required to spend its income and principal within a hundred years or more. Murphy did not raise serious objections to this proposal, except to suggest that it didn't serve anyone to force the issue. Rockefeller had given the GEB the power to expend all of its principal and income. He suggested that Rockefeller might do the same with the Foundation. It was all part of a strategy of empowering the board to respond to the needs of the day.

Republican Senator Weldon Heyburn (Idaho) blocked the Senate's consideration of the Rockefeller Foundation charter bill. He told reporters he was concerned that the Foundation was a scheme to "perpetuate the Standard Oil Company." (Library of Congress.)

Devine's concerns did little to derail the bill. But the political environment turned increasingly difficult. When a copy was given to President Taft, he consulted with Attorney General George W. Wickersham, who objected to the idea that Congress would approve the charter while the government was seeking to break up Standard Oil for violating the Sherman Antitrust Act of 1890. Congressmen hostile to Standard Oil raised similar objections, especially when Standard Oil's attorneys filed briefs with the U.S. Supreme Court only a week after the Rockefeller Foundation bill was introduced in the Senate.

Many officials who were suspicious of the Rockefeller proposal focused on the aspects of the concept that were most innovative: the proposed broad charter "to promote the well-being of mankind throughout the world" and the idea that the Foundation might continue in perpetuity with unimaginable resources. Above all, critics were concerned about the lack of public oversight.

"Many newspapers saw the vagueness," writes biographer Ron Chernow, "as a gauzy curtain behind which the evil wizard of Standard Oil could work his mischief." They accused Rockefeller of creating a foundation to buy back the public's goodwill.

At the same time, proponents of business believed that if Rockefeller's fortune was pulled out of the market, capital would be constrained for industrial investment, "thereby appreciably diminishing the prosperity and business progress of the country." To dispel these concerns, Frederick Gates provided a report to the Secretary of the Interior detailing the investments of the General Education Board to show that they were broadly distributed among a host of corporate stocks and bonds.

Murphy had been optimistic following his testimony. He had dined with Secretary Walcott, the head of the Smithsonian Institution, before returning to New York. He later reported to the Rockefellers that the bill had been reported out of committee with unanimous support. But Senator Gallinger was concerned. On March 22, he sent a newspaper clipping to Murphy and noted that the proposal faced serious opposition. "I have grave fears that it will be defeated."

Murphy met with the Rockefellers' toughest opponents. Idaho Senator Weldon B. Heyburn, a Republican lawyer and engineer who was closely associated with big mining interests in Idaho, was a fierce critic of Theodore Roosevelt's efforts to establish and then expand the National Forest System. He opposed the eight-hour day for workers, efforts to pass child welfare laws, and the direct election of senators. Newspapers reported that he opposed the Rockefeller Foundation bill because he believed it would allow the Rockefeller estate to avoid taxation. He also feared that Rockefeller was creating the Foundation simply to "perpetuate the Standard Oil Company." Under this new structure, he believed, Standard Oil would have competitive advantages over other corporations. Heyburn also said he opposed the idea of charities governed by the "dead hand" of the donor. It soon became clear that Heyburn was determined to block the Rockefeller plan. By the beginning of May, barely a month after the bill's introduction in the Senate, false rumors spread in the press that Rockefeller was considering withdrawing his plan.

The Rockefellers recognized that criticisms leveled by Charles W. Eliot and Edward Devine had to be considered. Both had suggested giving the public a greater role in the management of the foundation. Eliot proposed the idea of a Board of Visitors or Overseers that would meet twice a year as a check on the small body of trustees. As a trustee of the Carnegie Endowment for International Peace and the General Education Board, Eliot said he felt the lack of this outside perspective. Harvard had such a board and Eliot thought it was useful.

Sincere in their intent to work with the people's representatives, the Rockefellers decided to make concessions to allay public concerns. Working closely with Senator Gallinger, Starr Murphy drafted a revised bill in 1911. The new provisions considerably strengthened the public's hand. The Foundation's assets were capped at approximately $100 million. The Foundation would be required to spend all of its income to further the purposes of the corporation. Moreover, after 50 years (or 100 years if two-thirds of the directors and Congress approved), the Foundation would be required to spend all of its principal. Meanwhile, new members of the board would be subject to a veto by "a majority of the following persons: the President of the U.S., the Chief Justice of the Supreme Court, the President of the Senate, the Speaker of the House of Representatives, and the Presidents of Harvard, Yale, Columbia, Johns Hopkins, and the University of Chicago. Taken together, these were extraordinary concessions and reflected a sincere desire both to further the public interest and to build public trust.

Junior hoped that with these new provisions the bill would sail through Congress. But he was disappointed. In January 1911, Senator Elihu Root introduced a bill to grant a federal charter to create the Carnegie Endowment for International Peace. With a smaller endowment ($10 million), a bigger and better-known list of incorporators, and more specific language on tax exemption and purpose than the bill to grant a charter to the Rockefeller Foundation, the Carnegie Endowment bill passed both houses of Congress with little debate.

Meanwhile, the Rockefeller Foundation bill languished through the early months of 1911. The unresolved federal antitrust case against Standard Oil played a major role. In February, Attorney General Wickersham wrote to President Taft regarding the Rockefeller Foundation charter bill: "The power which, under such bill, would be invested in and exercised by a small body of men, in absolute control of the income of $100,000,000 or more, to be expended for the general indefinite objects described in the bill, might be in the highest degree corrupt in its influence....Is it, then, appropriate that, at the moment when the United States through its courts is seeking in a measure to destroy the great combination of wealth which has been built up by Mr. Rockefeller...the Congress of the United States should assist in the enactment of a law to create and perpetuate in his name an institution to hold and administer a large portion of this vast wealth." Taft responded: "I agree with your...characterization of the proposed act to incorporate John D. Rockefeller."

Gallinger also reported to Murphy that the changes in the bill hadn't influenced Heyburn at all. He remained stubbornly opposed. And in the face of this opposition, Gallinger was sure that the bill would not be passed and would remain on the Senate's calendar until the end of session.

Charles Walcott, the secretary of the Smithsonian, urged the Rockefellers to follow the pattern set by the Carnegie Institution of Washington, which was first incorporated in the District of Columbia and then sought a national charter. Junior was interested in this proposal but clung to the idea of a federal charter.

In April 1911, John D. Rockefeller Jr., his wife, Abby, and Senator Nelson Aldrich enjoyed a secret lunch with President Taft to press their case for the Rockefeller Foundation. The president suggested that the charter bill stood little chance of passing until the Standard Oil case was decided. Junior left feeling optimistic and later wrote that the president had been "most agreeable and kindly." He followed up by writing to his father-in-law to suggest that, as Taft had proposed, they do nothing more about the Foundation charter until the Standard Oil decision had been handed down.

While Junior negotiated directly with the President of the United States, the Rockefellers' chief advocate in the Senate was caught up in a bitter leadership dispute. Progressive Republicans opposed Gallinger's nomination as president pro tempore of the Senate. They viewed him as a reactionary and aligned with the Senate's old guard. Although Republicans clung to a majority in the Senate, when the Progressives joined with Democrats to support other candidates, Gallinger's election was blocked, undermining the authority of the Senate's old guard.

U.S. Attorney General George W. Wickersham opposed the Rockefeller Foundation bill. He feared that such a concentration of private wealth would invest too much power in the hands of a small group of men. He suggested to President Taft that the Foundation "might be in the highest degree corrupt in its influence" on the government and the nation. (Library of Congress.)

In the meantime, the Rockefellers had their defenders. After Attorney General Wickersham was quoted in the *Chicago Tribune* opposing the charter, the *Chicago Record-Herald* attacked the Attorney General for his objections and urged Congress to approve the measure. After the *New York Times* asked him about this exchange, Starr Murphy said that he remained confident the bill would pass. Serious objections had been addressed with the amendments. "We believe that the nation at large appreciates the service which such a corporation could render, and public sentiment, so far as we know, is practically unanimous on the subject," he wrote. Murphy pointed out that it took years for Congress to pass the charter for the Smithsonian Institution, even given the fact that James Smithson had given the money for the institution directly to the government. "We are by no means discouraged," Murphy continued, "although we should prefer to be able to initiate this great work without so much delay." Following this exchange, the *New York Times* ran an editorial suggesting that the changes in the bill were more than adequate to address the political and public concerns, and that Congress should "realize the significance of this great work of philanthropy."

On May 15, the U.S. Supreme Court ruled that Standard Oil had violated the Sherman Antitrust Act and ordered the dissolution of the company. Following the decision, Junior urged Gates and Murphy to prod the Rockefellers' friends in Congress to reintroduce the bill. Junior wanted it to be clear that the bill had been held back so that it would not be seen to interfere with the court's decision making.

But the Standard Oil decision did not soften opposition to John D. Rockefeller or "the trusts" in the Senate or in the country. In December 1911, Senator La Follette traveled to Ohio to build momentum for an effort by Progressive Republicans to abandon President Taft in the 1912 campaign and nominate La Follette instead. In a speech to Progressives in Cleveland, La Follette blasted the trusts and warned his listeners that the country was in danger.

One Final Effort

As Congress reconvened in the beginning of 1912, Junior pushed for the reintroduction of the Rockefeller Foundation bill. This time, Jerome Greene replaced Starr Murphy as the Rockefellers' chief lobbyist. Greene had come to the Rockefeller offices from Harvard University where he worked closely with the university's president, Charles Eliot. Acting on Gallinger's advice, the Rockefellers decided to look for a sponsor in the House of Representatives instead. On April 11, 1912, the House Judiciary Committee voted unanimously to send H.R. 21532 to the full House of Representatives.

By May, Greene was optimistic. Reaching out to contacts throughout the country, he enlisted friends of the bill to lobby their Congressmen. The campaign seemed to be working. One by one, Greene had received commitments of support. At the end of the month, Greene had sent nearly sixty telegrams urging his contacts to send letters or telegrams to the Speaker of the House urging him to bring the bill to a vote. But still there was no action. Meanwhile, negative publicity against Rockefeller and the trusts continued in 1912 as the U.S. Senate prepared to launch an investigation into efforts by Standard Oil and other big companies to bribe public officials.

Finally, on January 20, 1913, the House of Representatives passed the Rockefeller bill by a vote of 152 to 65. Jerome Greene was elated. Writing to Congressman E.W. Saunders, he said: "I want to thank you once more for the help we received from your wise counsel and leadership in connection with the passage of the Rockefeller Foundation Bill. As I sat in the Gallery and saw you 'on the job' I knew that whether we succeeded or failed, everything would be done that could be done."

Two weeks later, the Sixteenth Amendment to the Constitution of the United States was ratified, clearing the way for federal imposition of an income tax that would target primarily the wealthiest Americans, including John D. Rockefeller. In 1913, it was uncertain whether assets given to charity, including a private foundation, would be exempted from this new tax, but the precedent in American law suggested that it would.

With passage of the Rockefeller Foundation bill in the House, the Rockefellers' attention moved back to the Senate. In mid-February, it was favorably reported out of the Senate Judiciary Committee by a vote of 10 to 4. Jerome Greene also met with President Taft, who now seemed willing to sign the bill if Congress approved it.

With the end of the Congressional session drawing near, Greene was in a race with time. "The Senate is sitting day and night now," he wrote to Starr Murphy. "As the appropriation bills are getting disposed of a glimmer of hope remains that we may get our bill up."

Jerome Greene came to the Rockefeller offices in 1910 to serve as the first business manager of the Rockefeller Institute for Medical Research. With the Rockefeller Foundation bill stalled in Congress, Greene launched a national effort to marshal political support for the bill. The House of Representatives approved the measure in January 1913, but the bill died in the Senate. (Rockefeller Archive Center.)

Greene was negotiating feverishly with the bill's opponents, expressing a willingness to accept further amendments to get it passed.

But in the end, time ran out.

On March 13, 1913, Murphy wrote to Junior to express his disappointment. He suggested that it did not make sense to reopen the matter in Congress. Instead, he proposed taking a new bill to the New York State Legislature. The bill, which was approved by the legislature and signed by New York Governor William Sulzer on May 14, 1913, was modeled after the incorporation of the Russell Sage Foundation (1907) and the Carnegie Corporation (1911). Significantly, all of the concessions made in amendments to the Congressional charter bill were removed. There were no limits on the size of the endowment or the life of the corporation. Congress was not specifically empowered to dissolve or take over the corporation. Leading federal officials were not given veto power over appointments to the Board of Trustees. The people's representatives in Washington had lost their chance to control the world's largest philanthropy.

Had Congress granted the Rockefeller Foundation charter, the history of philanthropy in the United States might have been very different. Government oversight and regulation would likely have been much greater and philanthropy might have become much more politicized. But this did not happen. In some sense, the defeat of the charter bill was a blow to the Rockefellers but a boon to the pluralist society that Tocqueville had praised in 1840.

The legacies of the charter fight would reverberate over the next hundred years as the Rockefeller Foundation, consciously and unconsciously, sought to make important contributions to the vitality of American democracy and support the idea of a pluralistic society. Yet 1913 would not be the last time that it came into conflict with the representatives of American democracy. The role of great concentrated private wealth in shaping the civic culture and public policies of a democracy would be debated many times before the century ended.

CHAP. 488

AN ACT

...Rockefeller foundation.

...1913 with the approval of the
...e-fifths being present.

...ate of New York, represented in
...act as follows:

...ockefeller, John D. Rockefeller,
... Harry Pratt Judson, Simon Flexner,
...eene, Wickliffe Rose and Charles
...ersons as they may associate with
...ors, are hereby constituted a
...The Rockefeller Foundation,
...d maintaining a fund or funds
...ncipal thereof to promote the
... the world. It shall be
...ration to use as means to
...he establishment and mainte-
...eligious, missionary, and
...ncies and institutions, and
...ncies and institutions
...eans and agencies which
...nt to its members or

...d shall have power to
... purchase or lease,
...f its purposes, any
...tation as to amount
... as the legislature
...onvey such property,

and to invest and reinvest any principal, and deal wi...
expend the income and principal or the corporation in...
manner as in the judgment of the trustees will best pro...
its objects. It shall have all the power and be subje...
to all the restrictions which now pertain by law to memb...
ship corporations created by special law so far as the sa...
are applicable thereto and are not inconsistent with the
provisions of this act. The persons named in the first
section of this act, or a majority of them, shall hold a me...
ing and organize the corporation and adopt a constitution
and by-laws not inconsistent with the constitution and laws
of this state. Ths constitution shall prescribe the manner
of selection of members, the number of members who shall
constitute a quorum for the transaction of business at meetings of the corporation, the number of trustees by whom the
business and affairs of the corporation shall be managed,
the qualifications, powers, and the manner of selection
of the trustees and officers of the corporation, the manner
of amending the constitution and by-laws of the corporation, a...
and any other provisions for the management and disposition
of the property and regulation of the affairs of the corporation which may be deemed expedient.

§ 3. No officer, member or employee of this corporation

State of New York
OFFICE OF THE SECRETARY OF STATE } ss.:

B 167

I have compared the preceding with the original law on file
in his office, and do hereby certify that the
transcript therefrom, and...

A split between progressives and conservatives in the Republican Party led to the inauguration of Woodrow Wilson as President in March 1913. Democrats also took control of the House and Senate for the first time in decades. This political sea change made it highly unlikely that a Rockefeller Foundation charter bill would be approved. (Library of Congress.)

CASE STUDIES IN INNOVATION

A Partnership With Government

The boll weevil, an ominous-looking beetle with a snout about half as long as its body and sharp spurs on its front legs, crossed the Rio Grande River from Mexico in 1892, looking for cotton. As it migrated from Texas into adjoining states, it threatened to destroy much of the valuable cotton crop in the American South. Officials at the U.S. Department of Agriculture were concerned. Congress appropriated funds to study and eradicate this new menace. In 1905, the General Education Board (GEB) got involved. Over the next ten years, this Rockefeller philanthropy would help low-income farmers in the South battle the boll weevil. Along the way, the GEB's innovative work would demonstrate a powerful new approach to the idea of partnership between government and philanthropy in the United States.

John D. Rockefeller had endowed the GEB in 1902, tasking it with promoting education in the Southern United States "without distinction of sex, race, or creed." Yet GEB officers soon realized that their work with African-American and white farmers would make little significant impact in the rural South without some improvement in agricultural production. With better farming practices, longtime Rockefeller adviser Frederick T. Gates noted, rural incomes would rise and schools would then "follow as the sequence of greater earning capacity, and should not be planted by charity to become a tax on poverty."

After sending GEB secretary Wallace Buttrick on a survey trip of the United States in search of agricultural education efforts to fund, the GEB began supporting a farm demonstration program that Texas agricultural scientist Seaman Knapp had already initiated with federal funding. Knapp had developed a method

Many African-American children in the rural American South grew up on former cotton plantations where their parents were sharecroppers. At the end of the nineteenth century, few had access to education. (William Henry Jackson. Library of Congress.)

of teaching-by-doing that included cultivation lessons and demonstration plots for farmers. Given his contacts at the U.S. Department of Agriculture (USDA) and his teaching position at Texas A&M, he was a logical choice to lead the government's war against the boll weevil.

Knapp knew that in keeping with the mutual self-help tradition that Tocqueville had observed in the United States in the 1830s, some farmers participated in agricultural societies or clubs where they learned about advances in agricultural science, but many did not. He knew that researchers at the nation's land-grant colleges, supported by the Morrill Act of 1862, were developing new techniques that increased agricultural yields. Knapp sought to extend the benefits of these scientific breakthroughs to more farmers in the American South.

Farm families who were unable to make a living by growing cotton often moved to town. These children were employed spinning thread in the cotton mill in Laurel, Mississippi, in 1911. The General Education Board sought to improve agricultural production so that families could afford to send their children to school. (Lewis W. Hine. Library of Congress.)

Unfortunately many farmers who could benefit from learning how to improve cotton cultivation and control pests like the boll weevil could not participate in Knapp's program because federal funds were only available to states that had already become infested. In April 1906, the GEB and the USDA signed a partnership agreement to extend the demonstration model to Mississippi, a state that had not yet been invaded by the boll weevil. Under the initial agreement, the GEB provided $7,000 to support one agent.

The agreement with the government placed careful restrictions on the GEB's role. The USDA would supervise farm demonstration work, and appoint and control agricultural extension agents all over the country, while the GEB would be limited to paying salaries and costs in the areas it funded. As the concept of agricultural extension or education expanded, the GEB steadily increased its funding alongside its federal partner. The GEB contributed over $100,000 every year after 1909, and reached nearly $200,000 in 1913. Likewise,

CASE STUDIES IN INNOVATION

the USDA gave more than $100,000 in 1909, $200,000 in 1910 and 1911, and $300,000 in 1912 and 1913.

Although they were able to help individual farmers, the GEB and the government were in a race to keep up with the rapidly multiplying insects as they spread throughout the South. As more states became infested, the federal government, acting within its Congressional restraints, could expand its activities. When the federal government took over in a particular state, the GEB moved on to other states that were threatened but not yet under attack. In all, between the spring of 1906 and the summer of 1914, the GEB invested $925,750 in farm demonstration work.

Despite the limited nature of its role, the GEB had a profound influence on the government's agriculture programs. The GEB encouraged Knapp to expand farm demonstration beyond blight prevention and into the realm of more general agricultural education. With GEB support, Knapp promulgated his "ten commandments of farming" to increase the production of a variety of crops. The program's innovative outreach strategies included not only farmers, but also their spouses and children. Knapp organized boys' and girls' clubs as well as women's canning clubs. The USDA would eventually embrace this

To enhance soils that had been continuously cultivated for years, the General Education Board's agents encouraged farmers to plant nitrogen-fixing legumes like cowpeas between rows of corn. The sign posted next to this field in Saltillo, Mississippi, in 1912 helped draw attention to this innovative method and encouraged other farmers to use the new technique. (Rockefeller Archive Center.)

innovative approach and make it a permanent part of the framework for a concept known as agricultural extension.

The GEB's work in agriculture, however, also provided a cautionary tale to philanthropic organizations working with the government. Good intentions in a heated political environment could be misinterpreted. In 1914, public and congressional criticism of the Rockefellers and, by extension their philanthropic endeavors, rose. Shortly thereafter, Congress discovered the memorandum of agreement between the GEB and USDA. Though it had never been explicitly secret, the document had never been made available to the public. Responding to this revelation, some members of Congress accused the Rockefellers of exercising undue influence on the government.

Ironically, this controversy led Congress to assume full responsibility for the program. In 1914 Congress passed the Smith-Lever Act, which created a system of agricultural extension in the United States that included funding research at land-grant colleges and structuring ways for the lessons of agricultural science to flow to farmers through popular education. The law also prohibited GEB collaboration in any aspect of this new program, thus sending a forceful message about the limitations of philanthropic involvement with government.

Nevertheless, the GEB's work with the USDA provided a pioneering example for future collaboration between philanthropy and government in the United States. According to one account, the "very appearance of the southern landscape changed under the impact of Knapp's gospel of clean farming." Meanwhile, the influence of the USDA's Cooperative Agricultural Extension System continues in rural America to this day.

Agricultural extension agents funded by the General Education Board organized clubs for boys and girls. The children learned to grow crops using scientific farming techniques, which they often shared with their parents. This innovative strategy helped accelerate the transfer of new ideas and techniques in rural communities in the American South. (Rockefeller Archive Center.)

CHAPTER II

GOVERNMENT BY EXPERTS

In 1922, twenty-seven-year-old "boy wonder" Beardsley Ruml was hired to take the helm of a comparatively obscure Rockefeller philanthropy, the Laura Spelman Rockefeller Memorial (LSRM). Over the next seven years, the LSRM would grow from being a modest program of social work and charitable almsgiving into a leadership force that would transform the social sciences in America. By the time it became part of the Rockefeller Foundation in 1929, it would challenge basic notions about American government.

At the heart of the American experiment lay the idea that informed citizens are capable of effectively governing themselves. But at the end of the nineteenth century, some Americans weren't sure that the experiment was working. In many cities, corrupt politicians took bribes from streetcar companies and utilities, relying on patronage—giving government jobs to their political friends and allies—to stay in power. Meanwhile, in many state capitols and even in Washington, D.C., railroad companies and other large corporations seemed to control the legislative process. As a result, in many places in the United States, government was ineffective and inefficient.

Activists aligned with the Progressive movement sought to end this political corruption and make government more effective. They sought to fill City Hall with a new cadre of trained, professional administrators who would focus on efficiency. And they wanted policymaking based on the advice of technical experts, people like Beardsley Ruml.

Many Americans could find only irregular employment in the early 1900s. Periodic depressions led to bread lines and protests by the jobless. The Foundation's work in the social sciences sought to smooth the ups and downs of the industrial economy to help the American worker. (Library of Congress.)

Ruml was an applied psychologist who had grown up in the American heartland. His father had been a surgeon and his mother a hospital administrator. Graduating early from Washington High School in Cedar Rapids, Iowa, Ruml earned a bachelor's degree at Dartmouth College in New Hampshire, where he studied psychology and philosophy. He went on to the University of Chicago to complete a Ph.D. in 1917 in the emerging field of applied psychology, which relied on mental testing and statistics to produce insights into the patterns of human behavior. He represented a new phenomenon on the American scene—a man interested in applying the disciplines of the natural sciences to the study of society and government.

Social Knowledge for What?

When the Rockefeller Foundation began its work, the successful combination of capitalist democracy and a protective welfare state was unimaginable. In 1913, employment for most Americans was irregular. There were no income taxes, few labor laws, and no federal social insurance. The Foundation would play a signal role not only in developing social insurance, but also in helping to refine, develop,

Laura Spelman married John D. Rockefeller in 1864. Raised in an abolitionist family with deep social and religious convictions, she was an advocate of women's suffrage. After her death, her husband endowed the Laura Spelman Rockefeller Memorial with nearly $74 million. (Library of Congress.)

and install a modern managerial culture based on scientific rationality, empirical methods, and efficient business practices. By the 1930s, relationships and expectations among individual citizens, private industry, and government were in effect re-imagined and reformed. Each step along the way built upon the last as business culture became American culture, and these changes gained momentum following the unprecedentedly activist government interventions mandated by World War One.

The Laura Spelman Rockefeller Memorial played a critical role in this transformation. Established and endowed by John D. Rockefeller in 1918, following the death of his beloved wife, the LSRM initially focused its grantmaking in arenas that had been important to Laura Rockefeller, who was an avid supporter of Progressive Era social work, relief programs, and reform efforts. At the time he was hired, no one expected Beardsley Ruml to do much more than stay the course at the low-profile fund. But Ruml surprised everyone by crafting an ambitious plan to retool the social sciences in the image of the natural sciences.

Objectivity as the Surest Path

Coming out of the Charter fight in Washington, the trustees recognized that the Rockefeller Foundation had to build a reputation for benevolence and public-mindedness. They had to demonstrate that, despite the dire warnings of the critics, this large cache of private money would not be used for business deals or political string pulling. In 1914, a deadly battle between striking workers and guards at the Rockefeller-owned Colorado Fuel and Iron Company had shocked the nation. A Congressional investigation into the "Ludlow Massacre" followed. In the aftermath of these events, antipathy toward the Rockefellers was high. The Foundation's trustees had to demonstrate that the assets would be used for public good. This controversy put great pressure on the Foundation as it geared up.

Objective and rational decision making became the hallmark of the Foundation's work. The Foundation not only adopted scientific methods for solving social problems at the level of "root causes," it also aimed to soothe public concern that it was merely a tool for furthering vested interests.

Objectivity would connect the Foundation to the democratic values of fairness, equal opportunity, and the greatest good for the most people. A benevolent, disinterested Foundation might even serve a compensatory role, redressing the ills wrought by industrial capitalism using some of the very profits garnered by that system. It would also introduce a new institutional concept—the think tank—to the American political economy.

Large-scale, comprehensive, philanthropic foundations were an unfamiliar phenomenon in the first decades of the twentieth century. As one of only a handful of these institutions in existence in 1913, the Foundation's challenge was to show itself to be an agent of humanitarianism at the very least, and at best an aid to democracy. But the Foundation discovered very quickly that public distrust would make working on issues like labor relations or good government difficult. The Foundation backed away from these arenas and chose to focus on public health and medical education as the surest paths by which it could improve the "well-being of mankind" and stave off further controversy.

While not free of social context, health and medicine were not unduly provocative. Their benefits seemed straightforward, measurable, and universally desirable. As Warren Weaver, director of the Foundation's Division

News of the deaths of women and children during the battle between guards and striking workers at Ludlow, Colorado in 1914 sparked public outcry against the Rockefellers. In Tarrytown, where the Rockefellers resided, members of the International Workers of the World were arrested when they attempted to hold a mass protest. (Library of Congress.)

Democracy & Philanthropy

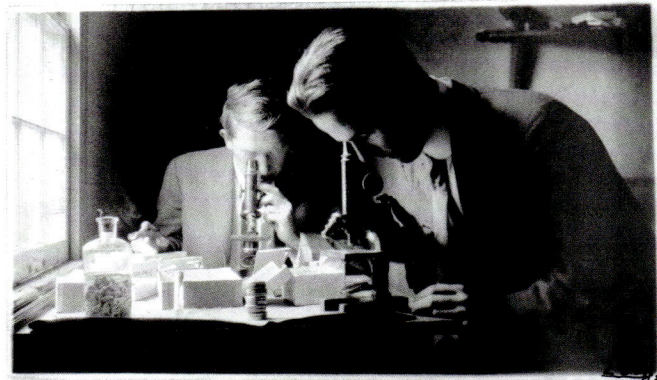

Grants for medical education and public health were far less controversial than projects related to industrial relations or social issues. Some Rockefeller Foundation trustees also believed that investments in this area would ultimately do the greatest good for humanity. (Rockefeller Archive Center.)

of Natural Sciences, would explain some thirty years later, it is not necessary to ask people whether they want to be cured of disease; the answer is always affirmative. "It is, on an exceedingly advanced and competent level, just like having plumbing fixed. Everybody thinks it is a good idea to have plumbing fixed, everybody whose plumbing is bad wants to have it improved, and it is pretty clear how and where you go about finding and making plumbers."

In its first fifteen years, from its founding in 1913 to its first major reorganization in 1928, the Foundation gradually won over a skeptical American public. With its endowment of dozens of medical, nursing, and public health schools at home and abroad, including Johns Hopkins, Harvard, the University of Toronto, and the London School of Tropical Medicine and Hygiene, the Foundation transformed the fields of medical education and research. It launched the first school of public health at Johns Hopkins University. Working with states and municipalities, and carrying on the work of the Rockefeller Sanitary Commission, it set up model public health programs around the country. It funded fellowships in medical and scientific research, moving those fields forward and creating a vast network of health professionals. This work was increasingly enabled by the rise of the modern research university, a movement that the Foundation substantially fostered. When the social sciences were ready to rise to the fore, their growth would rest on the platform of the scientific research university.

The Foundation as an American Institution

While the Rockefeller Foundation's scope was, from the outset, international, it had a special relationship with its home country quite distinct from its work abroad. Outside the United States, the Foundation was careful always to work at the invitation of and in cooperation with other nations' governments. The same basic principle held true in the United States, but here the relationship was more

Founded in 1916 with significant support from the Rockefeller Foundation, the School of Hygiene and Public Health at Johns Hopkins University endeavored to promote research, develop standards for education, and provide training of all kinds in public health. It became a model for the nation and the world. (Rockefeller Archive Center.)

complicated. In other countries, the Foundation sought government cooperation to ensure local support, and to give projects such as vaccination programs or building new medical schools the best chance to succeed. Beyond that, it did not aim to influence forms of government or their administration.

In the United States, however, the Foundation's work evolved against the backdrop of a rapidly developing capitalist, industrial democracy in which the Foundation itself, and a few others like it, were becoming intrinsic to the national landscape. As an American institution, the Foundation served a special purpose. It was able to tackle issues important to government and provide independent support with no obligation to govern or to enact legislation. The Foundation and its sister organizations launched initiatives to increase the productivity of American agriculture, strengthen education, and ameliorate the epidemic of hookworm in the American South. The Foundation could also take on projects designed to give public officials deeper insights into problems related to prostitution, crime, or other social issues.

Early on, the Foundation came to view its role as that of adviser, resource provider, and pioneer. It could afford to pinpoint and endow long-term research efforts not undertaken by any other entity. The government's relationship to both business and public welfare changed dramatically from the mid-1900s through the 1930s, and private philanthropy played a central role in supporting the evolution of that process.

Bringing the Social Sciences to Par

Early on, the Rockefeller Foundation's trustees were reluctant to work in the social arena. Four months after the Foundation made its first grant of $100,000 to the American Red Cross in December 1913, the bloodshed at Ludlow in Colorado prompted Junior to push for a program to study Industrial Relations. The public viewed this initiative with great skepticism, believing that it would lead to a new Rockefeller effort to suppress unions. Although this was not what Junior had in mind, the trustees terminated the effort and focused the Foundation's work on medicine and health instead.

An equal factor in the decision to avoid social issues was the underdeveloped state of the social sciences themselves. In the first two decades of the twentieth century, the social sciences were either armchair, philosophical enterprises that were largely theoretical, or they were enmeshed with social work. Compared to the natural sciences, the social sciences lacked empirical research traditions. They were often tied to social reform efforts, which were inherently partisan and often religious or moralistic, rather than objective, scientific assessments of the "root causes" of social problems. The Foundation took pains to steer clear of altruistic movements that involved private profit, as well as "propaganda which seek to influence public opinion about the social order and political proposals, however disinterested and important these may be."

In 1917, only three years after Ludlow, the trustees selected a sociologist, George E. Vincent, as the Foundation's president. Perhaps surprisingly, Vincent's social science background did not prompt a shift in the Foundation's agenda. In fact, Vincent promoted and guided the development of the Foundation's clear, two-pronged focus on public health and medical education. This did not mean, however, that individuals within the interconnected cluster of Rockefeller philanthropic endeavors were not interested in socially oriented work. John D. Rockefeller Jr., for example, had created the Bureau of Social Hygiene in 1911 to fund research and influence public policy on issues related to sex, crime, and delinquency. While Junior remained its major patron, the Rockefeller Foundation gave the Bureau occasional grants for specific projects.

In these early years, a signal aspect of the Rockefeller philanthropies was their tightly entwined working relationship with each other, marked by close associations among staff and overlapping board memberships among trustees. Although the Foundation formally limited its focus to public health and medical education, the social interests it and the other Rockefeller philanthropies harbored could be designated, for the time being, to the LSRM without being entirely out of the purview of the other entities.

Like the other Rockefeller philanthropies, including the China Medical Board, the General Education Board, and the International Education Board, the LSRM was legally separate from but in constant communication with the Foundation, and its assets were managed by the Rockefeller family office. For the next ten years, under Ruml's direction, the LSRM rather than the Foundation would concentrate on social problems. Given the turn of the entire nation toward managerial culture and the scientific management of social problems, the timing of the LSRM's founding was prescient. It came along on the heels of the war. Its short life spanned the transition from the last days of laissez faire capitalism to the birth of the modern regulated and managed political economy in the United States today.

Sociologist George E. Vincent succeeded John D. Rockefeller Jr. as the second president of the Rockefeller Foundation. An eloquent speaker, he helped to build public trust and confidence in the Foundation and the work of all of the related Rockefeller philanthropies. (Rockefeller Archive Center.)

Following in Rockefeller Foundation Footsteps

When Beardsley Ruml came to the LSRM in 1922, he proceeded to radically change the Memorial's agenda. He mounted a comprehensive program to professionalize the social sciences. This required moving them out of the realm of social work and into universities and independent research institutes.

Ruml and others associated with Rockefeller philanthropy in this era viewed many of society's ills as problems of "social control." Under totalitarian regimes, this idea would take on ominous overtones in the 1930s. To philanthropists in the 1920s, however, the idea was far more altruistic. Alcoholism, domestic violence, juvenile delinquency, mental illness, and a host of other social problems seemed to result from self-destructive tendencies in human nature and society. Developing strategies for social control would empower professionals in government and the growing nonprofit sector to combat these socially destructive tendencies and improve the well-being of all.

Ruml recognized, however, that many Americans were suspicious of these initiatives because they smacked of coercion and threatened to collide with the country's democratic values. He and his colleagues at the Rockefeller Foundation sought to balance the role of expertise with the processes of democracy by working to improve society's understanding of social issues. Increased knowledge would inevitably lead to enhanced "social control" by virtue of inevitable, rational selection on the part of the country's citizens and elected representatives.

Ruml was careful to eschew tactics geared "to secure any social, economic, or political reform." When it came to controversial issues—and social problems were invariably controversial—the scientific objectivity of empirical research promised protection from partisanship, moral quandaries, and political pitfalls. Properly and dispassionately conducted, social science research could make inroads on social issues without stirring up controversy. The "essence of the situation," Ruml explained, was "not whether a problem is controversial, but rather whether it is studied by men of competence in a spirit of objectivity and thoroughness with a freedom of inquiry and expression." Not only did the LSRM approach fit well with the Foundation's approach to health and science, it offered the Foundation a template for later investment in the social sciences.

To inform its decisions about what and where to invest, the Rockefeller Foundation traditionally began by conducting a thorough survey. Scientific surveys served to quantify problems, verifying their existence beyond armchair speculation, so that methodical solutions could be developed. Over the years, the Foundation surveyed public health problems, public schools, patterns of disease, urban living conditions, and the state of medical education, to name only a few. Surveys were an important tool of the Progressive Era. In an increasingly bureaucratic society whose hallmarks were large urban populations, complex organizations, mass production, mass consumption, and mass distribution, the Foundation recognized that social problems required systematic information-gathering on a macro-scale. Surveys helped new, richly endowed, broadly purposed organizations like the Rockefeller Foundation, the Carnegie Corporation, and the Russell Sage Foundation to move beyond charity to "scientific philanthropy" and target the underlying "root causes" of problems, rather than merely treat symptoms or distribute scattered relief. Empirical research, reliable data, quantitative analysis, and efficient management underpinned the Rockefeller Foundation's approaches to solving complicated health issues. Ultimately, this scientific, rational method would extend beyond actual physical disease to encompass social and economic maladies as well.

As Ruml set out to transform the social sciences, he hired economist Lawrence K. Frank to survey the field. Frank visited universities, the private sector, and independent institutions. He assessed graduate training, career trajectories, and the quality of research and publications. In his report, Frank noted that training in the social sciences was inconsistent, with minimal course work in research methods and very few dissertations based on empirical work. There were no research fellowships and very few publishing outlets. There were hardly any graduate students enrolled in Ph.D. programs—in fact, faculty outnumbered students almost two to one.

If Ruml and others hoped that the private sector might have higher standards for empiricism and relevance in social science research, they were disappointed by Frank's report. Business organizations lured potential scholars away from universities, offering higher salaries and better facilities to would-be social scientists to study management, internal organization, forecasting, and business cycles. Yet as Frank crucially pointed out, industry-led research was

The era of prohibition (1920-1933), when the United States banned the sale, production and transportation of alcohol, has been called an unsuccessful experiment in social control. Proponents hoped the law would diminish domestic violence and lead to working-class financial stability. (Library of Congress.)

The National Bureau of Economic Research, founded in 1920 with support from the LSRM, sought to help policymakers avoid boom and bust economic cycles. By providing reliable data on the economy, NBER leaders hoped to promote a scientific approach to policymaking. (Rockefeller Archive Center.)

inevitably biased. As he put it, "the men who do the actual research work are subordinate to the executives of their organization and this frequently produces a conscious or unconscious tendency toward bias in order to 'please the boss.'" Furthermore, industry-led research was not openly disseminated, and tended to serve private rather than public interests.

Frank conducted his survey at a crossroads moment in American business and higher education. Graduate schools of business and commerce were just beginning to emerge in universities, upending economics departments as the traditional home for the study of supply and demand, wages, pricing, and commodities. But business schools were geared toward professional development rather than the increase of scholarly knowledge. At the same time, American business was becoming increasingly corporate. The face of entrepreneurialism had significantly changed since the unfettered conditions under which John D. Rockefeller made his fortune. With the development of large, multi-divisional corporations, the well-being of many American workers was linked directly to the fortunes and practices of big business. One academic scholar, for example, encouraged the LSRM to support scientific economics out of a sense of responsibility to the general public. He argued that economics was more and more important to the average American because "we are all employees now."

Universities, traditionally uninvolved in and distant from political and business affairs, were deemed the most suitable arena for building the social sciences. Plus, the Rockefeller philanthropies already placed great faith in the research university as a forum for scientific problem solving and progress. The LSRM moved to shore up social science departments in universities throughout the United States and Europe, distributing over $40 million ($532 million in 2013 dollars) in ten years. It aimed to create a network of institutions working in shared technical language and engaged in common approaches, much as the Foundation had done in the natural sciences.

Taking its cue from the Foundation, the LSRM concentrated its giving on a core group of the strongest existing institutions, attempting to "make the peaks higher" and thus to influence entire fields. Major grantees included the

Statistics played an increasing role in government, especially after the Bureau of the Census was permanently established in 1902. Data such as these being collected by clerks in the Vital Statistics Section, was analyzed by social science experts funded by the LSRM and the Rockefeller Foundation. (Library of Congress.)

University of Chicago ($3.4 million), Columbia University ($1.4 million), the London School of Economics ($1.25 million), and Harvard University ($1.2 million). University departments could produce studies that government might use, but could also make forceful social arguments, which even well-staffed, government-sponsored research bureaus could not. A government bureau might be able to obtain vast amounts of statistical information, but analyzing such information ran the risk of partisanship. Furthermore, as many of Ruml's advisers noted, the individuals who were well qualified to run government programs were often not comparably well qualified to interpret complex economic data.

A Tool for Democracy

The University of Chicago, the Memorial's most substantial beneficiary, exemplifies the type of politically engaged yet "objective" research the LSRM sought to promote. It was home to the paradigm-changing work of sociologists Robert Park and Ernest Burgess and political scientist Charles Merriam. With LSRM support, the so-called "Chicago School" transformed sociology and political science through methods including

64

Henry Ives Cob

Endowed by John D. Rockefeller, the University of Chicago played a pivotal role in the emergence of the social sciences. Grantees of the LSRM and the Rockefeller Foundation, including Robert Park and Charles Merriam, helped develop modern sociology and political science that sought to understand American democracy. (Rockefeller Archive Center.)

observational fieldwork and quantitative analysis of demographic and statistical data. The city of Chicago became their social science laboratory.

At Chicago, Park, Burgess, and their colleagues created a new, urban sociology concerned with social stability and what disrupted it. They described and predicted processes of urban growth and decay, ethnic group assimilation to the mainstream, and inter-group competition and conflict. They developed a model that used metaphors drawn from biological science to describe the city as an ecological (and thereby rational) system, a system that underwent predictable cycles and stages of growth and change. Merriam and the political science faculty addressed voting patterns, the city's political institutions, public administration, political movements, and the psychology of public opinion. Chicago School sociology and political science rejected the dominance of armchair theorizing and advocated practical approaches, grounded in research, which would encourage a more harmonious and pluralistic society. Merriam in particular envisioned social scientists as technical advisors to political leaders, blurring the distinction between research and application and framing the social sciences as an essential tool for promoting efficient and effective government that would serve a pluralistic democratic society.

Independent Research Institutes

While Ruml and the LSRM began with the intention to simply build fields in the social sciences, external forces increasingly put pressure on researchers in these disciplines to help policymakers solve problems. By the 1930s, responding to the crisis of the Depression, the Foundation would come to encourage such applied efforts. But throughout the 1920s, continuing to eschew policymaking and political controversy, the LSRM instead created and positioned independent research institutes as a means of tackling issues neither it nor the Foundation could afford to work on directly. These institutes could go beyond the departmentalized academic research of universities to do interdisciplinary work, thus targeting complex social issues holistically.

Although one of the LSRM's goals had been to separate social science from social work, it did not aim to wipe out social welfare organizations—quite the contrary. It wanted merely to promote scientific research that was not tied to welfare programs and objectives. But always in mind was the larger idea that social welfare organizations (as well as business, industry, and government) required knowledge of social forces if they were to combat the social problems of the age. Independent research institutes, using trained academic specialists, could aggregate, produce, and disseminate that knowledge. At the close of World War One, government officials and social scientists who had worked in wartime agencies predicted a need for commissions and bureaus dedicated to postwar readjustment. The war had fundamentally changed American habits, markets, and ambitions. Agencies such as the War Industries Board or the Central Bureau of Planning and Statistics offered models of the comparable peacetime usefulness of the social sciences.

Research Institutes as Intermediaries: The Social Science Research Council

The Social Science Research Council (SSRC), founded in 1923 by Chicago's Charles Merriam, was among the most prominent of the independent entities the LSRM supported and shaped. Its member organizations were the professional associations of seven social sciences: political science, sociology, economics, statistics, psychology, anthropology, and history. The SSRC served not only as an intellectual center for scholars by distributing LSRM-backed grants, initiating cross-disciplinary research projects, and issuing publications, but also as a proxy for exploring LSRM and Rockefeller Foundation interests. The Council worked through committees organized around specific topics. Key examples from the 1920s and 1930s reflect the domestic policy and empirical priorities of that generation: "the Eighteenth Amendment," which prohibited the manufacture and sale of alcoholic beverages; "Interracial Relations"; "Corporate Relations"; and "Consumption and Leisure." The SSRC's annual summer conference in Hanover, NH, became a much-anticipated event. Foundation officials, SSRC staff, university administrators, and accomplished scholars gathered for several weeks each August to present and discuss research and to target emerging issues. The Hanover conferences in effect set the national research agenda for the following year in American social science.

The SSRC became a de facto arm of the LSRM and, later, the Rockefeller Foundation. In 1950, looking back at the Council's first quarter century, SSRC President Pendleton Herring described it as "an intermediary agency" between Foundation funding and academic specialists "upon whom the foundation must rely to achieve its purposes." The value the SSRC placed on objectivity, scientific credibility, and the advice of trained experts resonated with Rockefeller Foundation values. Much like the Foundation, the SSRC considered itself responsible for acting in the public's interest. As Herring emphasized, "the men of public affairs who serve on foundation boards get, through the Council,

Riots, lynchings and discrimination provided harsh evidence of the abiding problems related to race in the United States. After the Social Science Research Council (SSRC) was established in 1923, with critical support from the LSRM, "interracial relations" became a focal area for one of the SSRC's many working committees. (Walker Evans. Library of Congress.)

the best judgment of men of research affairs, given in the same spirit of public responsibility that motivates all trustees of integrity."

Perhaps the SSRC's most pragmatic contribution was its role as preliminary investigator on issues important to the LSRM and the Foundation. As Herring described, "Foundation officials have learned that proposals for grants will be made by someone on almost any subject in which the foundation is known or rumored to be interested. The real task, however, is to find those problems upon which something of significance can be done and the imaginative and responsible specialists who are prepared to carry through the project." The SSRC subjected research ideas to scrutiny and helped researchers develop them into feasible proposals, thus saving Foundation officers' time and energy. And, as Herring astutely noted, the SSRC also spared the Foundation from researchers' assumptions that initial interest was a guarantee of financial support. As a kind of "first-pass" filter for the Foundation's potential investments, the SSRC enabled the Foundation to concentrate on its central concern: "What are the leads which, if pursued, will open up new facts and theories that will result in later applications of great social utility?"

The LSRM, and later the Rockefeller Foundation, increasingly relied on the SSRC to assess social issues, especially those that reflected a changing American government. In the 1930s, the Foundation heavily funded the SSRC committees on Social Security and Public Administration. Social Security played a major role in designing the implementation of the 1935 Social Security Act and in tracking its effect on the public and the economy. Public Administration measured the growing need for a new kind of trained civil servant within the federal government as well as new forms of management developing within the civil service.

Research Institutes as Providers of Data: The National Bureau of Economic Research

Founded in 1920 by Edwin Gay of the Harvard School of Business and Wesley Mitchell, a Columbia University economics professor, the National Bureau of Economic Research (NBER) aimed, more expressly than the scholarly SSRC, to cooperate with governments in generating social science knowledge. Where the SSRC studied government programs, the NBER offered statistics and analysis to government programs. Mitchell, an early founder of quantitative economics, had worked for the War Industries Board during World War One, and later the Central Bureau of Planning and Statistics. He had hoped the bureau would continue, but the Wilson administration ended its tenure in the belief that "spirited businessmen and self-reliant laborers" would handle the nation's postwar readjustment through their individual initiatives.

Mitchell felt that statistics offered information for future planning rather than merely serving to describe present conditions or to record the past. Like other social scientists recruited to the war effort, Mitchell was convinced by his experience that statistical data were needed for sound planning and efficient economic management during peacetime, especially to ensure the harmony of social relations within modern capitalism, given its inherent disparities of wealth and income. The government's wartime interventions in the American economy had proved stunningly effective in a time of crisis, and revealed how productive the U.S. economy could be. But wartime research also revealed the immaturity of the social sciences before the war, and how inadequate the existing knowledge of the national economy was. Mitchell feared that careful planning would fizzle out in peacetime without sufficient knowledge of the causal processes that shaped the economy. Social behavior and economic growth might then return to a random pattern of fits and starts. Economic statistics, he felt, could lead to "the guidance of public policy by the quantitative knowledge of the social fact." A rational technocratic planning process offered an alternative to more radical social reform movements. As Mitchell saw it, "agitation or class struggle is a jerky way of moving forward. Are we not intelligent enough to devise a steadier and more certain method of progress?"

Mitchell directed the NBER in projects across a matrix of complex factors, including income distribution, national income, pricing, credit, business cycles, and unemployment. The Bureau saw itself not as a policymaker, nor even a lobbying body, but as a provider of quantitative data to policymakers. Its aim was to foster consensus on sound policies through the provision of disinterested scientific studies. Furthermore, the Bureau could conduct the kinds of studies essential to government and industry that the American government itself could not support.

Facts and Values

Like the rest of the growing movement of empirically oriented social scientists the LSRM was building, the NBER believed that factual evidence could be separated from value judgments and from pre-existing agendas. Action plans, therefore, would logically emerge from the objective ground that quantitative data provided, especially when analyzed by rational, well-trained experts. Not everyone, however, adopted the technocratic vision. Particularly troublesome to its opponents was the field's acceptance of corporate capitalism as a permanent feature of American life.

Social scientists often viewed the social costs of capitalism as the result of ignorance, poor management, or lack of information, but they believed the ship could be righted through the increase and application of knowledge. To them, corporate capitalism was flexible and could be molded to accommodate all, with a minimization of inequities and slumps. Many economists, business leaders, and foundation officers during the 1920s saw the business cycle's downturns not as inherent features of capitalism, including periods of overproduction and the accumulation of surplus labor, but rather as irregularities that could be stabilized with proper planning.

Labor organizers felt differently, as did settlement house workers whose direct provisions of relief and reform were being challenged by the rise of bureaucratic, scientific management. Social justice movements competed with a rising, professionalized middle class of salaried specialists in economics, agriculture, education, and social work. As historian Camilla Stivers points out, the two impulses of the era were never entirely distinct, as "the warmest-hearted reformer's concern for the poor recognized the need to help

At the Henry Street Settlement house, where Raymond Fosdick began his career, immigrant children learned useful skills like knitting. A precursor to scientific philanthropy, the settlement house movement sought to improve material conditions for the poor through interaction with the middle class. (Lewis Hine. Library of Congress.)

efficiently, while the most calculated plan to improve accounting methods was in aid of some social betterment goal." But the new professional networks of educated experts, situated between the truly wealthy and the struggling masses, ultimately eclipsed grassroots efforts as the primary tool for ameliorating social suffering and systemic inequality.

The Rockefeller Foundation demonstrated from the beginning its faith in scientific, efficiently managed, institutionally based problem solving, and the funding strategies of the Rockefeller philanthropies had much to do with this shift. The danger inherent in the new order of scientific management of public policy, however, was that meaningful outcomes might fall victim to policymakers' fascination with efficient procedures for their own sake. And by privileging elite experts in debates over social policy, the authority of the voters in a democracy might be undermined.

Fortunately for the cause of pluralism in the ever-changing cauldron of American politics, other interests learned to appropriate the work of the social sciences to make their own compelling arguments to policymakers and the electorate. Labor organizers, far from being eclipsed by the new marriage of social science statistics and managerial business practices, began to find common ground with economists who encouraged business leaders to keep wages high as a means of promoting a consumer economy. While the American Federation of Labor (AFL) had struggled against management in bread-and-butter negotiations before the war, it now found itself on somewhat common turf with municipal efforts to clean up corruption and inefficiency, wipe out loan sharks and pawnshops, and support industrially favorable strategies like consumer credit and installment buying. Union opposition to wage reduction during the short recession of 1920-21, combined with relatively flat population growth and extreme drops in the prices of consumer goods, provoked economists, including the NBER's Mitchell, to advocate for higher wages and higher consumption as a means for controlling the business cycle. But prosperity on this model would prove to be short-lived.

Transition on the Horizon

By the late 1920s, the signs were becoming increasingly evident that industrial capitalism was entering a cataclysmic crisis. Industrial unrest, high inflation, and international conflict were forerunners to the 1929 stock market crash and subsequent worldwide Depression. In the United States, agriculture was hit hardest and earliest, already flailing even as the urban industrial complex of business, government, and technocratic expertise manipulated price and wage data to encourage consumer-driven prosperity. Notably, agriculture already occupied a slot in the roster of issues studied by the SSRC in the 1920s, even before deeper levels of devastation struck in the 1930s.

Herbert Hoover had encouraged a decade-long experiment between research and policy as secretary of the U.S. Department of Commerce from 1921 to 1928. As president, Hoover continued to favor voluntary cooperation among business, government, and labor as a means of regulating the economy. Historian Ellis Hawley has described this as the "associative state," featuring a small federal apparatus, with economic reforms based on persuasion

Trained as an engineer, Herbert Hoover embodied the Progressive faith in expert-led public policymaking. As U.S. Secretary of Commerce, he promoted the ideal of the "associative state," which promoted voluntary cooperation among business, government, and community organizations and looked to academic experts as leaders in economic and social reform. (Library of Congress.)

rather than regulation, and private groups, including trade associations and community organizations, rather than the federal government at the center of policymaking activities.

Research Institutes as Brokers of Social Knowledge

One key private institution influencing policymaking and public administration was the Brookings Institution, created in 1927 by merging three existing organizations: the Institute for Government Research (IGR), the Institute of Economics, and the Robert Brookings Graduate School of Economics and Government. The LSRM had long supported the IGR, and it was this organization that the reconstituted Brookings most resembled. Similar to the NBER but with a less-exclusive emphasis on economics, Brookings aimed to strengthen the operations of government and effect a closer alliance between social theory and political practice. The SSRC often studied government programs and social issues, but its emphasis was interdisciplinary academic research and its findings remained confined to the broad community of scholars and foundation program officers.

Brookings was expressly policy-oriented, claiming to be the first such organization to look at public policy on a national level. Unlike the SSRC, it had policy objectives in mind when shaping its research. Unlike NBER, it went beyond the mere provision of facts to make recommendations to government agencies. The SSRC and the NBER were each concerned with understanding the problems and processes of democracy. Certainly neither was anti-democratic, but they did aim to develop programs and policies that they believed were impartial and unbiased by politics.

The Brookings Institution, on the other hand, was overtly focused on strengthening American democracy. In its early years, it sought to strengthen systems for public administration and enhance the training of public servants. It also aimed to contribute to domestic social and economic security, increase American prosperity, and from time to time would even oppose government programs if

Economist Edmund Day became the first director of the Rockefeller Foundation's newly created Division of Social Sciences in 1928. He also served as an officer of the General Education Board. In 1937, he left the Foundation to become president of Cornell University. (Rockefeller Archive Center.)

Work Pays America!

PROSPERITY

WORKS PROGRESS ADMINISTRATION

it judged them harmful to the economy. It was the nation's first true "think tank." Eventually, however, the American notion of voluntary participatory democracy would have to change to accommodate emergency measures when the associative state failed to stabilize an economy in free-fall. Brookings and the other LSRM-supported private institutions were expressly designed to be independent and adaptable, and thus they were ideally suited to make the transition toward working more openly with an expanding federal government after the crisis hit.

America Changes and The Foundation Expands

In 1929, the Rockefeller Foundation absorbed the LSRM and established its own Division of Social Sciences under the direction of Harvard-trained economist Edmund E. Day, who was also an early supporter of the NBER and a former SSRC treasurer. Beardsley Ruml went on to a stint as Dean of the Social Sciences at the University of Chicago and later served as Chairman of R. H. Macy & Company. In 1942, he proposed the pay-as-you-go federal income tax system, which led to payroll withholding. His work and career illustrate the increasingly close cooperative relationship that was evolving among academia, the federal government, and the Foundation, enacted through informal networks of scholars, foundation professionals, and policymakers.

By the end of its tenure as an autonomous Rockefeller philanthropy, the LSRM had expended over $50 million in grants to universities and research institutes. It had successfully differentiated rigorous social science research from social work and professionalized entire fields. Meanwhile, the Rockefeller Foundation had gained confidence from its successes in public health and medical education and was ready to branch out. But as economic and social crises seemed to unfold endlessly in the early 1930s, the Foundation's desire to work actively in social fields became more than mere readiness for expansion. As longtime trustee and eventual Rockefeller Foundation President Raymond Fosdick described, the Foundation also realized something was missing. "Public health and medicine," Fosdick explained, "even when supplemented by the biological sciences and pointed toward a fuller understanding of human behavior, do not constitute a rounded program for an organization whose concern is the well-being of men."

The LSRM's success in cultivating and professionalizing the social sciences gave the Foundation a strong

During the Great Depression, policymakers often relied on patriotism to encourage business leaders, workers and farmers to restore the nation's economy. Rockefeller Foundation grants to the social sciences reflected a deep desire to support the great American experiment at a time when it was threatened by economic and social instability. (Vera Bock. Library of Congress.)

institutional matrix to tap into when it decided to expand beyond health and medicine. At first the Foundation's new Division of Social Sciences (DSS) did little more than follow through on existing commitments it had inherited from the LSRM, commitments that tended to be for broad, open-ended, general support. But by 1934, spurred by mounting concerns about the Depression, the Foundation wanted to play a more forceful guiding role in determining lines of research. The movement toward social science as a direct and practical tool had come to fruition. The Foundation now sought to respond to the fact that, as Fosdick explained, "it was obvious something was fundamentally wrong with a society in which raw materials were plentiful, workers were eager to apply their productive capacity, adequate industrial plants and equipment were at hand, and yet the whole enterprise was halted, and millions were out of work."

The Foundation contemplated its future path against a social, economic, and political landscape that had transformed unimaginably within a span of only two decades. In 1913, the government had just begun to assume a regulatory role. But even by World War One, the Foundation still out-spent the federal government in relief. The experience of the war, however, helped usher in a new era of federal planning. From 1900 to approximately 1920, American businesses had begun to practice what is often termed "industrial paternalism," that is, measures of care and benefits for workers intended not only to protect workers as a resource, but to forestall both radical labor unionism and legislatively mandated reforms. But World War One had shown the advantages of federal intervention in the national economy. The federal government had experimented with new, quantitative testing methods to assess the skills and proper placement of hundreds of thousands of soldiers and marshaled the talents of data-driven economists to manipulate pricing and productivity. Furthermore, the war effort had prompted unprecedented cooperation between management and labor. In the 1920s, during the Coolidge and especially the Hoover administrations, policymakers hoped that voluntary

The Rockefeller Foundation collaborated closely with experts and policymakers in the development of the Social Security Act of 1935. Foundation grants worth $761,000 ($12.9 million in 2013 dollars) to the SSRC played a pivotal role in implementing the new law. Government workers used innovative machine readable, key-punched card systems to track wage reports. (Library of Congress.)

cooperation among industry, government, and private research would solve social problems and address the needs of workers, thus keeping the actual federal apparatus small. Data supplied by trained experts would enable business to make the right choices, to predict and compensate for its own periodic downturns, and keep workers adequately provisioned. After the 1929 stock market crash, it seemed increasingly and exceedingly unlikely that the American industrial crisis would be able to stabilize itself and provide for American workers without government intervention. In this new era the Foundation and the research institutes it had helped establish entered into a much closer relationship with government, providing advice, shaping programs, and assessing the growing needs of the emerging welfare state.

The social and economic crisis of the Depression spurred the Foundation to seek useful applications for the so-called "pure" research it (and the LSRM) had supported for over 15 years. As an influential trustee and soon-to-be president of the Rockefeller Foundation, Raymond Fosdick urged the Foundation to play a more active role in developing better social scientific means to combat the increasing complexity of modern life. He emphasized that this did not mean relinquishing research as a method, but rather that the Foundation should avoid research as an end in itself. "We are interested in it," he explained, "as a means to an end, and the end is the advancement of human welfare."

Setting New Goals

On the advice of the trustees, Edmund Day set three priorities for the new Division of Social Sciences: economic stabilization, community organization and planning, and international relations. These represented the most acute concerns of the crisis: The U.S. economy was in apparent free-fall, American communities were beset with social stressors, and conflict loomed in Europe. The DSS would accomplish its work in each of the three areas through the accumulation and dissemination of knowledge. In fact, the Foundation at this time adopted "the advancement of knowledge" as a new maxim for all its divisions and programs.

In social science, the axioms of the Foundation now became "social planning," "social control," and "social intelligence." While it recognized that even the best scientific fact-finding would not produce easy or immediate "cures" to complex problems—no "road to Utopia," as its 1937 annual report cautioned—the Foundation nonetheless maintained faith in the eventual, even inevitable, benefits of combining expertise with objective research. It aimed to "increase the body of knowledge which in the hands of competent technicians may be expected in time to result in substantial social control."

As the 1930s wore on, open inquiry became more and more correlated to the preservation of a democratic society. With collectivism and statism looming on the European front as frightening repressive alternatives, the Foundation redoubled its commitment to objectivity and the scientific method. Moreover, it increasingly linked the idea of intellectual freedom, a basic construct of the scientific method, to the cause of democracy. "To abandon the attempt," the Foundation asserted in its annual report in 1937, "would betray the liberal tradition upon which democratic society depends, and consign social development to ignorance and partisanship." With such high stakes, no longer was open-ended institution-building the best use for the Foundation's funds; it needed to make practical interventions in the mounting national crisis, and Day's three areas of focus aimed to do just that.

From Stability to Security

The area of economic stabilization—one of the three DSS priorities—initially comprised research on business cycles, wages and prices, and economic history studies as a means for understanding the present—very similar to the types of research the LSRM supported throughout the 1920s. But the convergence of the stock market crash, a global economic downturn, and unprecedented levels of unemployment spurred the Foundation to seek broader definitions of stabilization and recovery, including how Americans could be protected if recovery was not fully achieved.

In 1935, after the Social Security Act was signed into law, the trustees changed the name of this program from "economic stabilization" to "social security." The revised program would focus not only on prevention but also on protection. It continued to support "the description and measurement of cyclical and structural change" in the economy—the thrust of the business cycle research—in order to predict (and potentially prevent) catastrophic fluctuations. But it also explored the "development of more adequate protection against the main hazards that confront the individual, such as sickness, accident, old age dependency, and unemployment through improved provision for social insurance and organized relief."

Up until this point, the Foundation had sought to solve economic problems through planning and administration. Now it grappled with the possibility that the deeply entrenched crisis of the 1930s might not be readily controllable. Overproduction, high unemployment, falling price levels, and recurring recessions all seemed to indicate, as Day put it, that "the afflictions of modern competitive society appear to be essentially organic in character." If stabilization could not be achieved, if chaos was to some extent inevitable in modern capitalism, then individuals would have to be protected in different ways than ever before to ensure the continued functioning of a democratic society.

The Foundation provided several grants, totaling $761,000 ($12.9 million in 2013 dollars) to the SSRC to fund the work of a Committee on Social Security. This committee's initial report highlighted the fundamental changes that most concerned the Foundation. The prolonged and intense depression had created "virtually a new problem in the United States." The thousands of cases appearing on the relief rolls did not "belong in the old categories." While some relief had always been necessary, in the past it had gone to the physically and mentally incapacitated and to "widows and orphans." The crisis of the 1930s, on the other hand, affected otherwise capable breadwinners and intact families in such significant numbers (one-third of the American population) that the entire national economy was impaired.

Treasury Secretary Andrew Mellon told President Hoover that the Depression would "purge the rottenness" out of the economy. Mellon proudly supervised the physical expansion of the government into new buildings on the Capitol Mall. Social scientists and public administrators trained in programs funded by the Rockefeller Foundation and the SSRC staffed many of these agencies. (Library of Congress.)

The sheer magnitude of the crisis prompted the Foundation's response, especially because the situation had so clearly "shaken confidence in the effectiveness of national institutions." In 1933, when Franklin Roosevelt became president of the United States, banks were failing across the country, bread lines stretched from soup kitchens, and some people privately hoped for a dictatorship to get the nation's factories going again.

The Foundation's embrace of what might appear, on the surface, to be the very relief measures it had long rejected in favor of a focus on "root causes" was motivated by this democratic crisis. And the Foundation, like others in the United States, began to acknowledge that the American system must expand to protect its citizens, not only for humanitarian reasons but to ensure the survival of the system itself.

At the same time, these new, seemingly inorganic "social control" measures were difficult to parse in a free society. The Foundation navigated this tension by suggesting that, although "the individual must be protected in the interest of political and social stability," there was some sense that these efforts would be temporary, "pending adequate understanding of the causes of disruptive change." The Foundation was quite accustomed to taking the long view. It had always been skeptical of quick fixes. Public health networks and entirely new institutions in science and medicine had not sprung up overnight. Its continued assertion that economic and social stability were ultimately, but not immediately, attainable reflected its moderate character. Much rested upon this attitude of moderation. Sticking to the path of social scientific inquiry, guided by experts, would create the means for managing institutional mechanisms, means that would ultimately empower an informed citizenry. Increasingly, scientifically based social improvements were held up as nothing less than the prerequisite of democracy. As the Foundation and the American government were acutely aware, the alternatives to modern capitalism, clearly on view abroad, included national socialism, fascism, and communism.

Oppositional Voices

While New Deal reforms rested in large part on inroads made during the years of the voluntary "associative state" in the 1920s, not all businessmen were in agreement with the federal government's next steps. To many conservative businessmen, not only did federal redistributive and protective measures usurp the primacy of business in the American economy, they undermined human nature itself by removing risks these businessmen saw as "natural." Some leaders of private industry also lamented the difficulty of maintaining a good staff of workers when people were lured away to work for government-sponsored public works projects.

The relative (if shaky) prosperity of the 1920s, not to mention the success of the rising paternalistic bureaucracy in repressing more radical, anarchistic movements, had helped remove Americans' hostility to big business. The fledgling consumer-driven economy, including higher wages, cheaper goods, and employer-granted benefits, meant that many individual workers now saw themselves as potential economic winners, through wage-earning or stock market investing.

After the crash, Roosevelt's New Deal reforms positioned the government and its expert advisers, not captains of industry, as the heroes of the age. Conservative business executives organized to try and combat what they viewed as the encroaching welfare state through organizations like the Liberty League and the National Association of Manufacturers, but as historian Kim Phillips-Fein chronicles, their efforts would largely go underground, not to emerge in full until after the liberal political cycle, with its Keynesian stimulus plans, ended some 40 years later.

Yet the New Deal was never entirely opposed to business or free enterprise. In fact, as the SSRC study of the need for social security helps illustrate, its measures were enacted to preserve capitalism by protecting private property, encouraging back-to-work programs rather than relief, and creating scores of government jobs as a means of staving off high unemployment and more socialistic political movements. At this historical moment, the previous decade's surge in professionalization and managerial thinking found an ideal venue for enactment in the emerging field of public administration.

From Community Planning to Public Administration

Public administration focused on the efficient management of government organizations and systems. The program evolved as it became increasingly clear that the Depression was a problem on a national scale, and as federal bureaucracy expanded to address the situation. The national crisis would not be effectively ameliorated solely through city or state governments, which varied widely in their resources and administrative infrastructure. At first, the Foundation's community planning initiatives focused on grants to city and regional organizations, including the Welfare Council of New York City, the Community Council of Philadelphia, and the New Hampshire Foundation, all of which essentially served as central coordinating agencies for a widely scattered array of social services. Soon, however, federal work-relief and economic adjustment programs began to supplant the haphazard efforts of city councils and public and private local agencies. The expansion of federal programs during the first years of the Roosevelt administration created an unprecedented demand for trained administrators and bureaucrats, and called for graduate-level education in administration as well as retraining programs to give new direction to the careers of existing federal employees.

As described earlier, the Foundation, through the LSRM and its public health programs, had a long record of developing excellence and expertise in public administration. Foreseeing the boom in federal employment, the Foundation established schools of public administration, much as it had established schools of public health a generation before. Key institutions included Harvard, Syracuse, Chicago, Cincinnati, Minnesota, Virginia, and the University of California at Berkeley. While responding to urgent New Deal administrative challenges, the Foundation was also building a new academic field. Nowhere was this more evident than at Harvard, where faculty members in the School of Public Administration received funds to plan the curriculum, organize fieldwork for students, and develop the graduate degree program. Significant funding also went to American University in Washington, D.C., the logical place to offer supplemental training to employees already in the federal workforce.

Beyond classroom education, the Foundation wished to ensure that aspiring civil servants received on-the-ground field experience. After all, public administration was perhaps the most obvious arena in which the Foundation chose to enact its growing commitment to shift the pursuit of "pure" social science research toward more directly practical ends. Through the National Institute of Public Affairs, the Foundation designed and underwrote public administration fellowships, granted to the most outstanding students in the discipline. In 1937, for example, a dozen interns were assigned to the Office of Indian Affairs in a model training program. These first Washington interns spent an additional year after coursework shadowing government officials, legislators, and administrators to learn the ropes firsthand.

Keeping Government Useful

Much as the NBER had believed the data it supplied to be value-neutral, so too did the Foundation and its grantees in public administration believe that efficient procedures were separate from politics. Chicago's Public Administration Clearinghouse (initially funded by the LSRM as the Government Research Exchange) was described as "government disconnected from its electioneering phases and considered as a science of administration." The Clearinghouse served as a physical location for governors, mayors, city managers, and municipal workers to meet. It distributed literature on governance and dispatched experts to consult with cities, counties, and states seeking administrative guidance. For its part, the Clearinghouse claimed to advocate no particular political plan or form of organization to remedy administrative ills, but simply to supply factual material to those in a position to make decisions.

Ironically, the expansion of the federal government during the Roosevelt administration helped reverse public apprehensions about the Foundation and Rockefeller money in general. In the 1910s, the Foundation had been suspect for its vested interests and scrutinized by the government on behalf of the public. By the 1930s, the apparently neutral institutional infrastructure fostered by the Foundation, with social sciences operating as objective organizers of information and insight for policymakers, positioned the Foundation as a trusted public resource.

In this era, the Foundation often underwrote studies focused on new government activities; for example, it gave almost $300,000 to the Brookings Institution's review of the National Recovery Administration and the Agricultural Adjustment Administration from 1933 to 1935. The Foundation funded these investigations not from a skeptical or oppositional point of view, but as a partner who could help the government improve its performance. Moreover, through publications, the Foundation and its grantees aimed to help citizens understand New Deal programs "as they are related to our whole economic and social system."

In its 1935 annual report, the Foundation called the increased reliance on the expert and the technical adviser by governmental authorities "the most significant development of the past decade." By the late 1930s, the program in public administration made a full circle to focus on local bureaus of government research once again. Training in public administration had become so successful and widespread that the Foundation feared redundancy at the local level, with funds pouring in from public and private sources, including official, tax-supported research units. The Foundation gave the SSRC one million dollars in 1937 to figure out how to avoid duplication, marveling that "a field of operation which only a few years ago was being actively discouraged by American universities is now being rediscovered. It is conceivable that as much harm may result from future overemphasis as from past neglect." The Foundation had not only launched a new field, but had helped inculcate a new way of thinking about American government and society that was, above all, bureaucratic, administrative, and procedurally efficient.

CASE STUDIES IN INNOVATION

Self Determination and the Office of Indian Affairs

They were the continent's first inhabitants, but citizens of the United States only since 1924. Resilient over generations in the face of unknown diseases, military suppression, and assimilationist policies that removed children from their parents and undermined traditional practices of self-government and land management, American Indians in 1928 were fighting for their natural rights, when the Rockefeller Foundation agreed to help.

For decades the federal government's Office of Indian Affairs (later renamed the Bureau of Indian Affairs) had been known for corruption and inefficiency. In the 1920s, when the government threatened to take away land from the Pueblo people in New Mexico, a broad coalition of native people and white reformers came together to protest. With Rockefeller Foundation support, the Institute for Government Research (later Brookings Institution) conducted a study led by Lewis Meriam. Published in 1928 as *The Problem of Indian Administration*, the report detailed the failures of the government's forced assimilation policies. Although it did not advocate for change, the study provided the framework for a fundamental shift in Indian policy based on the ideas of cultural pluralism, sovereignty, and self-determination.

Boarding schools for American Indians, often run by missionaries, were criticized by the Meriam report in 1928 for failing to provide a high-quality education. Funded by Rockefeller philanthropy and developed by the Foundation-supported Institute for Government Research, the report recommended educating younger children in community schools near home. (Marquette University Libraries.)

John Collier was one of the social reformers who pushed the government to ask for the Meriam Report. Appointed commissioner of Indian Affairs by President Franklin Roosevelt in 1933, Collier set out to reshape federal policy and fundamentally reform the Office of Indian Affairs. With the President's support, he pushed through the Indian Reorganization Act (IRA) of 1934—sometimes called the Magna Carta for Indians—which stopped the sale or allotment of Indian lands and encouraged the revitalization of tribal government by providing incentives to tribes to draft and adopt constitutions that would give them federally recognized, autonomous governments. It thus represented an effort to support the functions of democratic government and recognized the diversity in the American system that responded to a pluralistic society.

To reform the Office of Indian Affairs, Collier turned to the Rockefeller Foundation for assistance. Unlike other federal posts, work in the Office of Indian Affairs required expertise in almost every area, from agriculture to education, public health administration, land management, and unusual forms of credit administration. To cultivate this kind of expertise and professionalism, Collier and the Rockefeller Foundation developed an innovative internship program that not only helped the Office of Indian Affairs, but also set a precedent for internships that have become ubiquitous in Washington, D.C.

The program was modest in scope. In 1937 the Foundation appropriated $54,000 ($876,000 in 2013 dollars) for the National Institute for Public Affairs

President Franklin Roosevelt appointed John Collier (at left, wearing glasses) to lead the Office of Indian Affairs. Hoping to rid the agency of its reputation for corruption, Collier implemented various staffing reforms, including an innovative professional internship program developed with the Rockefeller Foundation. (Harris & Ewing. Library of Congress.)

CASE STUDIES IN INNOVATION

With the passage of the Indian Reorganization Act (IRA) in 1934, Bureau of Indian Affairs officials met with tribal leaders, including these Navajo in Pinon, Arizona, to explain the provisions of the new law. Based on the recommendations of the Meriam report, the IRA was intended to promote tribal unity and self-government. (Winfrid Stauble. Marquette University Libraries.)

(NIPA), a Rockefeller Foundation-sponsored entity focused on improving public administration. With these funds, the Office of Indian Affairs launched an experimental initiative in the Navajo and Pueblo areas of the American Southwest. Eight to twelve university graduates were hired as interns each year over the course of the three-year grant. The selection process was arduous compared to other NIPA internships. Candidates had to show an enormous degree of cultural sensitivity, because many Native Americans were suspicious of the interns and thought they were government spies.

Working with a specially appointed director of training, the interns were rotated through various departments "to test their abilities, draw out their potentialities, and give them administrative experience in the field." The interns also participated in ongoing professional development led by the University of New Mexico and other academic institutions. The program was structured to provide a path to permanent Civil Service employment based on performance. According to the Foundation, careful records were kept to measure the effectiveness of the program, and the Civil Service monitored the entire effort as a potential model for the rest of the federal government.

DEMOCRACY & PHILANTHROPY

For the Rockefeller Foundation, working with the Office of Indian Affairs laid bare the questions of democratic participation, pluralism, and government intervention with which all Americans grappled in the 1930s. Collier hoped to resolve American Indian resistance to, or lack of engagement in, tribal politics. He said that many American Indians, like white Americans, who "openly, or by the refusal to serve as an effective part of the electorate, invite the substitution of dictatorship for democracy."

Indeed, Collier feared that the lack of American Indian engagement with tribal government threatened to prolong what he saw as internal dictatorship on American soil—the longstanding, previous dictatorship of the Office of Indian Affairs. In his mind, public administrators were not effective as dictating forces, but rather as information providers and efficient managers who would actually facilitate democratic political participation. As Collier put it, "Leadership is fundamental in all government, Indian and white alike." Public administration was designed to be value-neutral, encouraging political participation rather than any particular politics.

The democratic reforms in Indian country that were sparked by the Meriam Report—made tangible by the Indian Reorganization Act of 1934 and embedded in the Civil Service through the NIPA's internship program—helped to transform the relationship between the government and American Indian tribes. Subsequent federal administrations would retreat from many of these initiatives, and American Indians would later be highly critical of the paternalistic role of the federal government that was codified by the IRA. But the innovations funded by the Rockefeller Foundation in the 1920s and 1930s transformed the legal and administrative framework for Indian policy and helped bolster the importance of tribal sovereignty and cultural deference.

Pueblo Indian leaders traveled to Washington, D.C., in 1923 to appear before a Senate committee. Carrying canes presented to the Pueblo nation by President Abraham Lincoln, the delegates helped spark public support for Indian land claims. Under public pressure, the Secretary of the Interior authorized a study of conditions on American Indian reservations. (Library of Congress.)

CHAPTER III

PHILANTHROPY AT WAR

Raymond Fosdick was deeply troubled. For nearly two decades he had given much of his life to promoting peace and international understanding. Having witnessed the horrors of World War One battlefields, he had agreed to serve as under secretary general of the League of Nations in 1919 because he hoped the League would prevent future conflicts and ensure world peace. When the United States Senate refused to approve U.S. membership in the League, however, Fosdick resigned his position. For years afterward he traveled throughout the United States and Europe giving lectures and lobbying in support of U.S. membership. Fosdick had agreed to become president of the Rockefeller Foundation in 1936, in part because he believed the Foundation's efforts to develop the science of human behavior would temper humanity's individual and collective tendency toward violence and self-destruction.

Fosdick never escaped the shadows of his past, but by 1936 he had recovered his equilibrium enough to be described by *Newsweek* as "a good conversationalist, genial, witty and generous." He was also persuasive and "brought an air of 'crispness' to the foundation headquarters," according to his biographer Daryl Revoldt. With his hair neatly parted on the side and combed in a wave across his large forehead, he had sharp penetrating eyes. His years as a diplomat had enhanced his natural ability to foster a cooperative spirit among colleagues. Division of Natural Sciences Director Warren Weaver described him as, "from the point of view of the operating officers,

Raymond Fosdick became president of the Rockefeller Foundation in 1936. The former under secretary general to the League of Nations was a long-time advocate for international cooperation. With the rise of totalitarian regimes in the Axis nations, Fosdick struggled to interpret and define the Foundation's mission and role in a world at war. (Rockefeller Archive Center.)

an ideal president. He was warm, friendly, and full of stimulating questions."

But Fosdick had become president at a time when he and the Rockefeller Foundation were forced to reconcile the American and the international qualities of the institution. Fosdick was perhaps the ideal person for the job. Closely affiliated with John D. Rockefeller Jr. since 1913 and on the board since 1921, no one knew the Foundation's values and culture better. In fact, as a trustee Fosdick had been the architect of the Foundation's 1928 reorganization, as well as one of three members of a special emergency committee appointed in 1934 to respond to the urgent needs of the Depression in the United States. He was no stranger to the need for calm, decisive, yet visionary responses in a crisis.

While the Rockefeller Foundation had not been established expressly to promote international peace (as had the Carnegie Endowment for International Peace, for example), the founder and his advisors believed that efforts to address the root causes of humanity's problems and to promote the well-being of humankind would inevitably increase international understanding and reduce conflict in the world. As Fosdick would write in 1940, the Foundation strove for decades "to carry on its work regardless of flags or boundary lines." And as he acknowledged, "There is a sense, of course, in which the Foundation's entire program is aimed at the single target of world peace." But in an ideological world, torn by nationalistic ambitions and international competition over resources, peace was an elusive goal.

During World War One, the Foundation's humanitarian relief for millions of people facing starvation was motivated by empathy, but was also deeply troubling to many of its leaders. John D. Rockefeller Sr. had hoped that his money would lead to permanent solutions rather than temporary assistance. After World War One, some of the Foundation's leaders quietly resolved that they would not be drawn into the business of relief again. They clearly wanted to maintain a distance from political tensions that might hamper their efforts to find long-term or permanent solutions to humanity's problems, or that might use up their considerable, yet still finite, resources.

The faith of both Fosdick and the Foundation in reason as the best means to promote humanity's well-being was profound and essentially international.

"Achievement in science," Fosdick wrote in the 1939 annual report, "more often than not, is the result of the sustained thinking of many minds in many countries driving toward a common goal. The creative spirit of man cannot successfully be localized or nationalized. Ideas are starved when they are fenced in behind frontiers."

All too soon after World War One, events that would culminate in World War Two worried Fosdick and the staff and trustees of the Rockefeller Foundation. In Asia, for example, the Foundation was funding projects in health and medicine in both China and Japan prior to the Japanese invasion of Manchuria. On the very day that Japanese bombs fell on the Rockefeller Foundation-funded Nankai University in July 1937, the Foundation had written a check for $74,000 in partial fulfillment of its pledge to provide $1 million for a new public health institute in Tokyo. Fosdick asked, "Has Japan written herself out of the orbit of our interests?" Similar issues were provoked by Germany, Italy, and the Soviet Union. Grants from the International Education Board had helped to build up one of the world's greatest centers for mathematics at the University of Göttingen in Germany, but as Fosdick noted with chagrin, "This center has been practically destroyed by the anti-Semitic policies of the Nazi regime." The Foundation now questioned the appropriateness of "relations with countries whose political and social policies seem to clash with those widely accepted in this country." Yet the Foundation had always taken pains to avoid shaping the politics or governments of other nations. Just as important, it had been careful to maintain an almost flawless record of fulfilling its financial pledges once they had been made.

As the Foundation reduced its grantmaking to institutions in countries governed by totalitarian regimes, Fosdick carefully explained in 1937 that the Foundation was not taking sides in an international conflict or interfering in the domestic politics of other nations. "We have declined to make appropriations not because of our disapproval of the totalitarian philosophy, but because that philosophy makes impossible the kind of scientific research that we want to support."

Fosdick acknowledged that the Foundation had done valuable work in "countries whose governments have won wide condemnation." The issue at stake was the Foundation's ability to hold onto its "reputation for disinterestedness and impartiality." That reputation had garnered worldwide respect and trust for the Foundation. But the fascist and totalitarian governments

The American Red Cross received the Rockefeller Foundation's first grant in December 1913. The $100,000 gift ($2.36 million in 2013 dollars) "to commemorate the services of the women of the United States in caring for the sick and wounded of the Civil War" helped the Red Cross purchase property for its headquarters in Washington, D.C. (Hayden Hayden [Howard Crosby Renwick]. Library of Congress.)

spurring this second world war would challenge the Foundation's ability to remain impartial, for it was the very objectivity of scientific inquiry which these governments repressed and threatened to destroy.

Long before Fosdick wrote these words, the Foundation had committed itself to supporting intellectual freedom in the face of totalitarianism. With Hitler's rise to power in Germany, leading Jewish scholars and scientists had been expelled from Germany's universities and research institutions. Many feared for their lives. As early as 1933, the Foundation began providing fellowships to help refugee scholars move to institutions in countries where they could be safe and productive. After Germany's invasion of Poland in September 1939, applications for these fellowships nearly overwhelmed the staff. Some insiders argued that the program should be ended because the moral tension bound up in the decision to save lives based on intellectual contributions was untenable, but Fosdick asserted that the Foundation had to do what it could.

Forced to choose among applicants, the Foundation established selective criteria that factored in the eminence of the applicant, his or her age, and the seriousness of the threat to the applicant's productivity and his or her life. For scholars desiring to come to the United States, the Foundation also weighed their potential contributions to the intellectual life of the nation and whether places could be secured for them.

Germany's invasion of Poland and the subsequent outbreak of war in Europe forced the Foundation to clarify its position vis-à-vis the rise of totalitarianism even further. At the time, the Rockefeller Foundation had 110 different grants worth more than $4 million ($67.15 million in 2013 dollars) open in 22 countries in Europe. That week, Raymond Fosdick met with the staff to consider the Rockefeller Foundation's options. Fosdick was adamant that the Foundation should not be drawn into relief work. The Foundation kept a small "token" office open in Paris, but reduced grants to Europe dramatically. In an ominous section of the Foundation's annual report in 1940, Fosdick lamented on behalf of the board and staff that "In the shadows that are deepening over Europe the lights of learning are fading one by one.... Everywhere the exigencies of the war have erased the possibility of intellectual and cultural life as that term was understood a few years ago."

With the outbreak of war, Fosdick and others who had prided themselves on their internationalist perspective reaffirmed the liberal, Western, and especially American values at the heart of their work. "It is only in an atmosphere of freedom that the lamp of science and learning can be kept alight," Fosdick wrote in 1940. "It is only free men who dare to think, and it is only through free thought that the soul of a people can be kept alive."

As the war spread, the Foundation's activities in Europe came to a virtual halt, and work in China and Japan slowed as well. Fosdick and other leaders thought about suspending the Foundation's activities altogether. Instead, they looked to other parts of the world, including Mexico and Latin America, for potential new areas of work. They also focused on providing support for the cause of freedom and democracy.

Victory for the Allied forces was essential, but Fosdick was acutely aware of a risk that the Allies, in an all-out effort to win the war, might sacrifice their ideals. "The crisis presents us with a problem of delicate balance: how to win the war and at the same time preserve those intellectual ideals and standards, those 'great things of the human spirit,' without which a military victory would in the end be nothing but ashes." Fosdick worried that war cultivated the psychology of hate, "but

Joseph Willits was the director of the Division of Social Sciences when the Nazis threatened France in June 1940. He urged the Foundation to help leading scientists and scholars find refuge in the West. His memo, "If Hitler Wins," anticipated concentration camps and an end to freedom of expression in occupied countries. (Rockefeller Archive Center.)

Democracy & Philanthropy

the insistent voice of reason tells us that violence and hate cannot serve as foundation stones with which to build a new world."

As it turned out, much of the Foundation's support for the war effort in the United States represented a natural extension of its prewar efforts to promote the humanities, social science research, and international understanding. On the home front, particularly in the humanities, the Foundation redoubled activities that helped Americans to understand themselves, including an appreciation for their very diversity. This kind of thinking fit well with the rhetoric of the Roosevelt administration, which was also consumed by promoting America's diversity as its strength.

As the conflict in Europe deepened with the fall of France in the spring of 1940, Americans began preparing for war despite strong support for isolationism and neutrality. In a fireside chat in May, President Franklin Roosevelt asserted that the physical defense of the nation depended on

In radio speeches, President Franklin Delano Roosevelt exhorted Americans, from the home front to the battle lines, to work together to win the war. Though he did not always agree with the president, Raymond Fosdick admired him. The two were friends and had worked together on various projects. (Library of Congress.)

"the spirit and morale of a free people." The ideological conflicts at the heart of World War Two reawakened the fundamentally American character of the Rockefeller Foundation and strengthened its relationship to the American polity, while inspiring the Foundation to deepen and disseminate an understanding of the regional, cultural, and ethnic variety within the nation and the common values that united it.

A Foundation for the Fight for Democracy

As the nation's factories were converted from peacetime to war-related production—and as men and women across the country enlisted in the Armed Forces—the Foundation increasingly looked for ways to use its resources and experience to support the war effort. This new attitude was not simply a reflection of patriotic or nationalist sympathies on the part of trustees and officers, who were nearly all Americans; it also reflected a profound belief in the ideals of the American experiment with democratic government.

The Foundation's efforts to support the Allied cause were increasingly reflected in its grantmaking. The Foundation funded Princeton University's surveys of American attitudes toward entering the war, for

Language training became an important element in the Foundation's grantmaking in the humanities in the 1930s. Research in basic linguistics led to innovations in instruction. Using curricula developed with Foundation support, the U.S. Army taught soldiers to understand and speak Japanese and Chinese as well as other Asian languages. (Rockefeller Archive Center.)

Democracy & Philanthropy

example. And in the two and a half years between January 1, 1939, and June 30, 1942, six percent of all funds appropriated for the Humanities went to new projects that benefited the government in its war efforts. Of the Foundation's total expenditures, meanwhile, 24 percent "sustained projects that now parallel and supplement governmental activities."

Just as important, initiatives long supported by the Foundation became important to the government in the context of the war. For example, government planners focused on winning the war were extremely interested in the work of scholars and linguists researching China, Japan, and other Asian countries. Many of these academics were associated with the American Council of Learned Societies (ACLS) and had been supported for years by the Rockefeller Foundation. Meanwhile, Foundation fellows trained in Far Eastern languages or communications research were recruited into government services. Foundation-funded language training programs in Chinese, Japanese, Russian, and Portuguese were repurposed for military and diplomatic initiatives as well as for theoretical work to help accelerate the pace with which people learned another language. Foundation grants also ensured the protection and dissemination of knowledge and ideas. Grants to the American Library Association (ALA) between 1939 and 1944 helped the ALA ship books and periodicals not only to Allied soldiers but also to citizens of occupied nations abroad.

Technological advances in microphotography were generously supported in the 1930s by the Rockefeller Foundation's Division of Humanities. When German bombing raids over Great Britain threatened historic archives at Windsor Castle, the Foundation provided a grant to microfilm this material and make copies available to American scholars. (Rockefeller Archive Center.)

In yet another area, the Foundation played a major role in promoting the technology of microfilm, establishing university training centers and purchasing cutting-edge equipment. This effort reflected the Foundation's recognition of the serious losses to cultural expression posed by the war. As the monthly confidential bulletin to the trustees put it, "The lost cannot be recovered, but let us save what remains; not by vaults and locks which fence them from the public eye and use in consigning them to the waste of time, but by such multiplication of copies as shall place them beyond the reach of accident." The Foundation's pioneering efforts would be useful to government intelligence agents, but also to librarians in Europe who were rushing to copy important historical manuscripts and drawings for architectural monuments, all threatened by falling bombs. The Foundation also subsidized microfilming in the Public Record Office of London of "over 900 years of British history." These reels, along with microfilmed versions of holdings in the U.S. Library of Congress, were shipped around the world to keep lines of intellectual communication open.

As the war progressed, the Foundation married its efforts to protect what Fosdick called the "intellectual capital" of humankind to the Allied military strategy. The Foundation provided resources to prepare detailed maps of the locations of cultural monuments in Europe—libraries, museums, galleries, palaces, and churches—and these maps were provided to the bombing headquarters of the U.S. Army in advance of military operations. Years later, Fosdick wrote that the maps undoubtedly saved a number of treasures from destruction, although they were not able to prevent the war from engulfing landmarks like the city of Dresden or the famous monastery at Monte Cassino in Italy.

American flight crews reviewed maps of German rail lines in Italy before embarking on bombing missions in 1944. With funds provided by the Rockefeller Foundation, world-famous museums and churches were marked on maps of Florence and other Italian cities so that precision bombers could try to avoid important cultural landmarks. (Library of Congress.)

Democracy & Philanthropy

Even support for community theater assisted in the nation's defense, providing a stable of trained personnel to organize entertainment for the troops to boost morale. The speed with which the government appropriated personnel from communities and colleges startled the Foundation's program officers. "Automatically, then, the role of any non-governmental agency alters," wrote John Marshall, the associate director of the Division of Humanities, in October 1942. "It has now wisely to follow and to supplement what government does. And its first success in this situation will depend on the close co-operation of its effort with government initiative." Actors and musicians deployed as soldiers helped establish orchestras, glee clubs, and theatrical troupes, "putting on plays in the jungle," as one of the Foundation's trustees' bulletins reported. On the home front, by 1943 the National Theatre Conference, a consortium long supported by the Foundation, reported that 83 of its member theaters in 34 states had given shows in 191 army camps in 38 states.

Writing about the Foundation's work in the Humanities, Marshall also outlined the larger role for the Foundation's war efforts in all of its programs. Many of the organizations supported by the Foundation in the past were now stepping up to wartime activities—such as the ACLS training linguists and the ALA planning to help restore or rebuild libraries in postwar Europe

The American Library Association, with funds provided by the Rockefeller Foundation, purchased approximately 350 scholarly journals—ranging from the American Economic Review to Cancer Research and Art Quarterly—to resupply European libraries once the war was over. (Rockefeller Archive Center.)

and Asia. The ALA was also keeping copies of periodicals to replenish the devastated holdings of Europe and Asia. These activities increased overhead costs for the organizations at a time when they were already short on personnel because of the draft. Marshall suggested that the Foundation could help "with a special readiness to meet overhead costs which the war imposes on them." While such grants were generally not the Foundation's practice, making them was in reality a contribution to the long-term viability of these organizations. Ironically, emergency grants for overhead were actually providing the kind of permanent impact the Foundation sought, not just temporary relief that would dissipate quickly.

For the duration of the war, work usually associated with peacetime activities was examined from new points of view and found to have unanticipated applications. A grant given by the Humanities Division to Professor Harold Burris-Meyer at the Stevens Institute of Technology in New Jersey, for example, was intended to support research in the control of sound and light for theatrical performances, including those at the Metropolitan Opera in New York. The Navy took over this project during the war, and Burris-Meyer became a lieutenant commander doing research on a secret effort to develop a sound-and-light production that would fool enemy forces into thinking that a beach landing was being staged.

Physicist Ernest Lawrence relied on Rockefeller Foundation funding to build the world's largest cyclotron at the University of California, Berkeley. For his work on the cyclotron, Lawrence was awarded the Nobel Prize in 1939. (Lawrence Berkeley National Laboratory.)

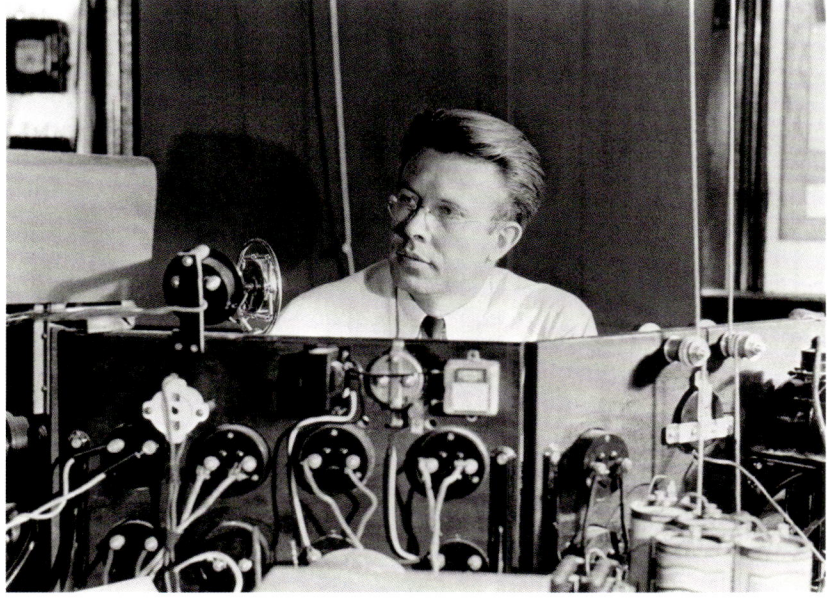

After Pearl Harbor the Foundation provided an emergency grant to expedite installation of the cyclotron's magnet. According to Lawrence, the grant reduced the time needed to develop the atomic bomb and thus shortened the war. The trustees received this news with mixed emotions. The Foundation was glad to be recognized for helping the war effort, but was deeply troubled that the investment in science had unleashed such destruction. (Donald Cooksey. Rockefeller Archive Center.)

The Foundation's decades-long effort to promote public health and medical research also provided benefits to the Allies. In its laboratories in New York, the Foundation's Max Theiler had developed the vaccine for yellow fever shortly before the war, which earned him the Nobel Prize. During the war, the Foundation manufactured 34 million doses of yellow fever vaccine, which were supplied to Allied forces fighting in North Africa and other tropical regions. Teams of Foundation-supported doctors were sent to Naples to battle a typhus epidemic that erupted soon after the Allies took control of the city. And the Foundation provided critical funding to Dr. H.W. Florey at the University of Oxford, whose work—performed while the bombs were falling during the Battle of Britain—led to the clinical development of penicillin. Even the Foundation's support of research-oriented science proved to have direct applications to health work in wartime. Harvard University biologist Edwin Cohn's highly theoretical research on molecular weight provided a breakthrough in fractionating (separating) blood, enabling longer storage times and more efficient uses of blood proteins, which further stretched much-needed transfusion supplies.

"A more diversified and less technical task," wrote one Foundation staffer, "is to aid citizens of the United States to understand intimately the varied life of this continent and to apply that understanding in daily life." John Marshall suggested that the Foundation could play a useful role in the war effort by helping Humanities scholars to focus on developing what amounted to a practical and ideological understanding of the differences between American culture and the cultures of other nations involved in the war. Marshall believed that the Foundation should also help in the dissemination of this knowledge to a mass audience through university extension services, agricultural organizations, radio, and film. A 1941 grant to the American Film Center enabled the organization to use the relatively new medium for making Hollywood-quality educational shorts. Produced by professional writers, directors, and actors, these films explored important topics in an entertaining way, including "Nutrition," "Community School," "Liberación del Hombre" (depicting mechanical invention as a civilizing influence), "Our New Farm," and "I Am Williamsburg." The Foundation also funded the first feature documentary on black education in the United States, entitled "One Tenth of Our Nation."

The war also forced the Foundation to rethink its own relationship to national life. As Marshall noted in a memo in October 1942, many people who had thought of themselves as scholars in the prewar years would likely return to the postwar society with "a quickened sense of what the Humanities can be in a vastly different world." They would put a premium on relevance and utility, and on the consequences of ideas.

The U.S. at War and the Atomic Bomb

The Japanese bombing of Pearl Harbor on December 7, 1941, added a new dimension to the Foundation's attitude toward war. Five days after the attack, according to biographer Daryl Revoldt, "Fosdick restated his opposition to relief and suggested that the foundation concentrate on post-war reconstruction. The foundation should not get swept up in the urgencies of a long and bitter struggle." Once again, in October 1942, he asked the staff whether the Foundation's work should be suspended for the duration of the war. Or should the Foundation join the war effort in some way?

Fosdick struggled to find a moral path for the Foundation. The world had become an "insane asylum." As Revoldt explains, "The waste of human life appalled him. Yet Hitlerism was also the very antithesis of everything he valued with its threat to individual liberty and intellectual freedom. He thus believed that to resist totalitarianism, America might be compelled to suppress its own civil liberties." Fosdick also recognized that "the most gigantic war humanity has ever known" might force people of conscience to make very painful choices. For Fosdick and Warren Weaver, the director of the Division of Natural Sciences, these choices would have momentous consequences.

One of the greatest moral tragedies of the war, for the Rockefeller Foundation, was the perversion of science to support slaughter and destruction rather than the well-being of humanity. By 1940, as one government official noted, for both the Allies and the Axis powers "Science can now have but one object: to help win the war." While the Foundation's contributions to the American war effort through the humanities were substantial, investments in scientific research—many made long before the outbreak of the conflict—proved crucial to winning the war.

The Foundation had begun supporting physics research by funding fellowships in cooperation with the National Research Council in 1919. It was the first program of its kind in the United States. Through the International Education Board, the Foundation also provided institutional support to laboratories and universities in Europe and the U.S., helping to make the California Institute of Technology, for example, into a world-renowned center for quantum physics research.

As a board member in the 1920s, Fosdick understood the theoretical possibility that unlocking the secrets of the atom might unleash destructive forces. "In California at the present moment," he told college audiences, "a combined attack, financed and equipped on a huge scale, is being launched on the problem of the structure of matter." Physicists now understood that "in atoms of matter there exists a store of energy incomparably more abundant and powerful than any over which we have thus far obtained control." This energy could be used to power machines. It also had the potential "to blow a modern city into oblivion."

The Foundation's support for basic research in physics in the 1920s and 1930s led to pivotal discoveries and insights. Twenty-three physicists who would later play a pivotal role in the atomic bomb project developed their expertise with the help of Rockefeller Foundation fellowships—including Oppenheimer, Lawrence, Fermi, Allison, Condon, Teller, Smyth, and Compton.

The Foundation also played a critical role in developing the equipment needed to produce the bomb. Years earlier, the Foundation had provided funding for Leó Szilárd, the man who first conceptualized the cyclotron. (Szilárd later received Rockefeller Foundation support to flee Nazi Germany under the refugee scholar program.) The Foundation then supported Ernest Lawrence, the University of California physicist who first built one. When Lawrence came to the Foundation in 1939 seeking funds to build the largest cyclotron ever constructed, the Foundation agreed to support basic research with an enormous contribution of $1.15 million ($19.3 million in 2013 dollars) toward the estimated total cost of $1.4 million.

The cyclotron was initially embraced for its potential role in radiation cancer therapies. But it proved to have other uses in war, including the ability to separate weapons-grade uranium-235. The cyclotron had not been completed before Pearl Harbor, but an emergency grant of $60,000 enabled the installation of its magnet. That made the extraction of U-235 possible, and Lawrence's demonstration of U-235 directly aided the progress of the Manhattan Project. Although Fosdick, Weaver, and the trustees understood

Cyclotron researchers in Berkeley in 1940 identified plutonium, which became the fuel for the atomic bomb. This research was transferred to the University of Chicago, where physicists Norman Hilberry (left) and Leó Szilárd worked with Enrico Fermi to engineer the world's first self-sustained chain reaction on December 2, 1942. (U.S. Department of Energy.)

what the cyclotron would accomplish, everyone held out hope that an atomic bomb would never actually need to be used. Tragically, they were wrong.

After the war, debate within the Foundation (as in America) centered not on whether the bomb should have been developed—scientific knowledge rendered that virtually inevitable—but on whether the bomb had to be dropped. In partnership with the University of Chicago, Fosdick and the Foundation played a leading role in convening the era's foremost atomic physicists to discuss the ramifications of and responsible uses for atomic energy. Implicitly, the Foundation was also forced to come to terms with its own role in the development of the bomb as a consequence of its commitment to democratic values and the advancement of scientific knowledge.

Four long years of war profoundly influenced the culture and economy of the United States. They also affected the work of the Rockefeller Foundation. Remarkably international from the outset, the Foundation had faced a fundamental challenge with the outbreak of World War Two. How should the Foundation balance its patriotic duties with its mission to serve the well-being of all mankind? American officials and grantees working on war-related research pressured the Foundation to support initiatives that would help the cause. Foundation-funded research helped to protect American soldiers from disease and provided insights that were critical to applied problems in weapons. But the Foundation stopped short of surrendering its resources and mission to the national effort to win the war. Defining the limits of patriotism in philanthropy and crisis reflected a self-conscious effort on the part of the Foundation to remain at arm's length from the needs of the government in a time of war.

CASE STUDIES IN INNOVATION

EXPORTING IDEALS: THE ROCKEFELLER FOUNDATION AND THE COLD WAR

During the Cold War, the Rockefeller Foundation launched an innovative but politically perilous effort to offer ideas and information about the United States and its political economy to other nations. Some of these countries were struggling to form and stabilize new governments in the wake of failed totalitarian Axis regimes. Others were seeking to establish themselves as independent nations following the collapse of the colonial order. The Foundation's goals paralleled those of the U.S. State Department and the federal government. This alignment brought the Foundation dangerously close to losing its reputation for intellectual and institutional independence.

When Dean Rusk assumed the Foundation's presidency in 1952, after serving as a trustee since 1950, he came from the U.S. State Department, where he had been a rising star and an Asian specialist. The Foundation was striving to understand several seismic world changes during this time: the apparent permanence of the so-called "Iron Curtain," the "loss of China" to communism, and the extreme monetary inflation that was transforming a "Western world which thought in terms of millions of dollars to one which thinks in terms of billions."

The Foundation felt keenly the obligation to contribute to a peaceful world order. The shifting geopolitics of the era, however, brought an unprecedented urgency to understanding the role of the United States, not only in terms of political power and responsibility, but on moral, philosophical, and cultural levels as well.

To its already established programs in international relations, economics, and public administration, the Division of Social Sciences added a program entitled "The Functioning of American Political Democracy." This initiative built on ten years of Foundation funding in the field of American Studies, but the new effort was not limited to United States institutions. Equally important was the development of centers for pursuing the serious study of American culture abroad. The first major grant in this arena was given to Munich to help develop the Amerika-Institut.

A small but crucial grant enabled the Salzburg Seminar to continue when its budget had nearly been depleted. Founded by young Harvard graduates in 1947 to demonstrate American culture in war-ravaged Austria, especially to young Europeans, the Salzburg Seminar recruited a changing roster of visiting faculty

DEMOCRACY & PHILANTHROPY

from American colleges and universities. Early instructors included anthropologist Margaret Mead, economist Wassily Leontief, and literary historian F. O. Matthiessen. The seminar was not intended to be propagandistic, or to foster American cultural imperialism. As Matthiessen told participants the first summer, "none of our group has come as imperialists of Pax Americana to impose our values on you." Accordingly, the seminar would consider not only the strengths of American democracy, but also its "excesses and limitations." The seminar's driving goal was to facilitate communication across otherwise daunting, even threatening ideological divides.

American Studies was but one arena within the larger field of what would come to be called Area Studies, an initiative modeled on the wartime Army Specialized Training Program (ASTP). Foundation funding also enabled the American Council of Learned Societies (ACLS) to develop language programs adaptable to military training, and the Social Science Research Council (SSRC) to support the wartime Ethnogeographic Board, which utilized scholars across disciplines and geographic specialties to assemble research portfolios on countries of interest.

Rockefeller Foundation President Dean Rusk had served in the U.S. Department of State from 1945 until he came to the Foundation in 1952. In the years after World War Two, he was deeply concerned about the welfare of former European colonies in the developing world as they sought to establish their own governments. (Yoichi Okamoto. Lyndon B. Johnson Presidential Library.

CASE STUDIES IN INNOVATION

The Pacific conflict, especially, had drawn U.S. forces into engagement with myriad non-Western peoples whose cultures were not well-known to Westerners. After the war, the Foundation sought to build on this work. The first development in the field was an exploratory conference convened by the Rockefeller Foundation in 1944, which brought together its own officers with representatives from the Carnegie Corporation, university scholars, and "area men" with experience in wartime military training programs. Beginning with the founding of Columbia University's Russian Institute in 1946, the Foundation also steadily underwrote new programs in Eastern European, Asian, African, and Latin American studies at major U.S. and foreign universities throughout the 1940s and 1950s.

The development of both the American and Area Studies initiatives presented a potential risk to the Foundation's work abroad. Over three previous decades, the Foundation had earned widespread respect for its independence and objectivity, but the bilateral polarization of political ideology that characterized the Cold War was something new. In the context of the Cold War, the American and Area Studies initiatives were seen by some as efforts to promote American propaganda. While Area Studies was modeled on wartime activity, however, the Foundation was adamant that, in peacetime, such work should possess broader scope, deeper academic legitimacy, and the genuine pursuit of cross-cultural understanding. The ultimate objective of Area Studies was to bridge the ideological chasms that divided the world in the postwar era, but it also helped train students for the increasing number of foreign service and foreign policy posts, thus strengthening the Foundation's link to the U.S. Department of State.

More than any previous Foundation president, Dean Rusk worked closely with the U.S. government. Secretary of State John Foster Dulles had been chairman of the Rockefeller Foundation in 1952 and played a leading

The Rockefeller Foundation helped pioneer the field of "area studies" in the 1930s to promote an interdisciplinary approach to the study of regions of the world. In Lebanon in 1949, for example, faculty at the American University of Beirut helped students expand their knowledge of the language, culture, and history of Arabic nations. (Rockefeller Archive Center.)

DEMOCRACY & PHILANTHROPY

John Foster Dulles (front row right) served as President Dwight D. Eisenhower's Secretary of State. Prior to his appointment, while chairman of the Rockefeller Foundation, he led the committee that selected Dean Rusk to be the Foundation's president. (Thomas J. O'Halloran. Library of Congress.)

role in Rusk's selection as president. Despite this close relationship, however, Rusk resisted the blurring of lines in the implementation of the American and Area Studies programs. And when Dulles's brother Allen, the director of the CIA, suggested that Rusk share the confidential field diaries of Foundation staff officers working abroad with the government's spy agency, Rusk, with the support of John D. Rockefeller 3rd, refused. Rusk also blocked the government's efforts to use the Foundation's education development programs to promote U.S. foreign policy interests.

Throughout the Cold War era, the Foundation responded to and sought to educate an American public that was learning about new parts of the world and coming to view itself in new ways. As an American institution, it worked with the government and the private sector to promote democratic values at home and abroad. Critical historians have sometimes asserted that the Foundation and others in the philanthropic field gave up too much of their autonomy in this period to promote American ideals. The remarkable lesson, however, is that Rusk—who was so closely associated with the State Department—and others in the Rockefeller Foundation were guided by the deep cultural values of an organization that prized intellectual freedom above all.

THE ARTS, THE HUMANITIES, AND NATIONAL IDENTITY

For decades, science and education paved the main road of Rockefeller philanthropy, but some staff and trustees believed that the Rockefeller Foundation should not only heal the body, but also lift the spirit. In 1915 Jerome Greene, who served as the Foundation's executive secretary, wrote a letter to former Harvard University president and Foundation trustee Charles Eliot suggesting that "It may be true that contributions to health through medical research and preventive medicine are the surest means of doing an unqualified good to the human race, but it seems to me that there can be no better application of philanthropy than in efforts to promote the intellectual and spiritual life of the human animal." With Eliot's support, he hoped to encourage the trustees to use as much as half of the Foundation's income to promote Arts and Letters and to improve public appreciation for architecture, painting, sculpture, music, and drama.

Greene's concern reflected a long-standing anxiety in American culture. The "gross materialism" that he believed was rampant in New York was "typical of American tendencies." Compared to Europe, the United States seemed to lack a developed sense of high culture. This young nation, not even to the halfway mark of its second century when Greene wrote to Eliot, had been more consumed with settlement and agriculture, as well as building industries and new forms of government, than it had with the relative luxury of artistic expression. As a result, great artists, fine poets, and celebrated writers seemed

Vaudeville and early movie theaters offered entertainment for the working classes, while affluent philanthropists supported concert halls and museums for symphonies and fine art associated with Europe. Straddling this tension between low and high culture, many Rockefeller Foundation grants in the 1930s supported theater and literature that explored American identity and culture. (Library of Congress.)

to be far more rare in the United States. This was troubling to some champions of democracy, for it suggested that artistic and cultural accomplishments might depend on aristocratic patrons and a frame of mind that put artists—along with kings, queens, and saints—on a pedestal above the masses. These cultural critics hoped that Alexis de Tocqueville had been wrong when he wrote, "If a democratic state of society and democratic institutions were ever to prevail over the whole earth, the human mind would gradually find its beacon-lights grow dim, and men would relapse into a period of darkness."

Frederick Gates did not share Greene's concerns, and opposed his proposal. Gates was afraid that even a fortune as great as John D. Rockefeller's could be dissipated by grantmaking in too many fields—a phenomenon he called "scatteration." To Greene's dismay, the majority of the board agreed. Except for a single $100,000 grant to the American Academy in Rome in 1913 for

Democracy & Philanthropy

classical studies, the Foundation did not make grants for the humanities or the arts during its first decade of existence. For years to come, however, the trustees would struggle with a lingering sense that science could only do so much to promote the well-being of humanity, and that the Foundation would play a role in supporting American culture.

First Steps

Edwin Embree, who replaced Jerome Greene as secretary to the Rockefeller Foundation, revived Greene's proposal in 1922. He wrote to President George Vincent to suggest that the Foundation should help to stimulate and develop the arts as a "great benefit to this country." At a meeting of the officers of the General Education Board (GEB), Embree asked, "Of what good is it to keep people alive and healthy if their lives are not to be touched increasingly with something of beauty?" Embree suggested a fellowship program for promising American artists, dramatists, and musicians. He also proposed grants for non-commercial production companies offering theater, opera, or music; for traveling art exhibitions; and for the establishment of art centers in a number of cities throughout the country. "By such means," he said, "the Rockefeller Foundation might greatly affect the cultural development of America during the next

Grants from the Rockefeller Foundation's International Education Board, along with personal gifts by John D. Rockefeller Jr., helped finance excavations and study at the site of the ancient Agora in Athens—the public square and marketplace of the ancient city where ideas were debated during the golden age of classical democracy. (Rockefeller Archive Center.)

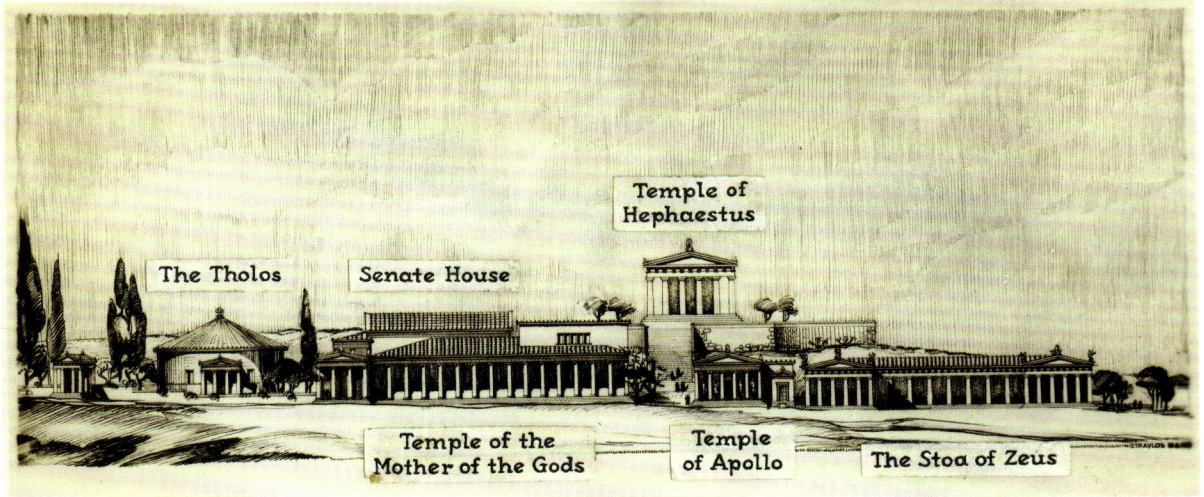

century." Embree's appeal was echoed by Abraham Flexner, a board member whose report on medical education in the United States had revolutionized the field. "A well-developed civilization requires humanistic as well as scientific culture," Flexner told the GEB officers.

The General Education Board, which Flexner served as secretary, did begin making grants in the humanities to universities in 1924, and the International Education Board (IEB), which was a subsidiary of the Rockefeller Foundation, followed suit. Most of these awards were for projects relating to archaeology, art history, or classical studies. In many ways, they reflected the continuing ethnocentrism of American elites who believed that high culture was rooted in the European past, and did little to alleviate anxiety about American culture or change the European-dominated artistic paradigm. Years later, the GEB would be criticized for supporting academic work with little relevance to the needs of modern society. And at least one trustee, Anson Phelps Stokes, grew frustrated with the limited scope of the program. He wanted the field of the humanities to be defined much more broadly "to include art, music, education, literature, sociology, etc."

General Education Board Secretary Abraham Flexner urged board members to provide support for the humanities. A leading proponent of education reform in the United States, Flexner went on to found and direct the Institute for Advanced Study in Princeton, New Jersey. (Rockefeller Archive Center.)

The reorganization of the Rockefeller philanthropies in 1929 resulted in a greater commitment to the humanities. The Laura Spelman Rockefeller Memorial (LSRM) was closed, as was the IEB, and the work and assets of both institutions were combined with the Rockefeller Foundation. The GEB would continue as a separate legal entity under its federal charter, but its endowment would be liquidated as soon as possible and any additional funds would come from the Rockefeller Foundation, making it effectively a subsidiary organization. At the same time, the Foundation established a Division of Humanities to carry forward the work of the IEB and the GEB. With these structural changes, the Rockefeller Foundation also adopted a new subsidiary mission statement: "the advance of human knowledge."

In the early years of the Division of Humanities, funding was directed primarily to American universities, with a continuing focus on classical studies and Europe, but the program suffered from a lack of consistent leadership. While these efforts contributed to the Foundation's goal of advancing knowledge, they fell short of Jerome Greene's vision of a program that would counter the "gross materialism" of American society and uplift the spirit. The early efforts also fell short of building the ethical and political consensus that Raymond Fosdick had called for in speeches around the country during the 1920s, a consensus he believed was necessary to respond to advances in technology. Moreover, among the trustees and even within the staff, there was ongoing resistance to the idea of a humanities program. When Max Mason succeeded George Vincent as president of the Rockefeller Foundation in 1929, the humanities were low on his priority list.

The Rockefeller Foundation was not alone in giving only modest support to culture. Trustee Anson Phelps Stokes, for example, was taken aback when he opened the *New York Times* in 1931 and found a report on giving by all private foundations in the United States. Of the nearly $52.5 million granted ($806 million in 2013 dollars), less than $1 million had been given in the humanities and only $1.39 million had been granted for a category the report dubbed "Aesthetics." In a letter to Mason, Stokes conceded that "medicine, general education, and the sciences represent especially fruitful fields." However, he noted, "if the Humanities are put into the background in American education, the nation will ultimately suffer in its idealism and its culture." Stokes urged Mason to get on with the business of finding someone who would lead and invigorate the Division of Humanities. Stokes was supported by Jerome Greene, who had rejoined the Rockefeller Foundation's board of trustees in 1928, as well as by fellow trustee Raymond Fosdick.

In 1932, Mason recruited David Stevens to direct the division. Stevens, like Mason, had come from the University of Chicago where, as a professor of English and as a dean, he had worked closely with Mason. A vice president of the General Education Board since 1930, Stevens made a natural transition to the Rockefeller Foundation two years later. In turn, he hired John Marshall to serve as deputy director of the division.

As Stevens and Marshall began to explore the framework of their program, they shifted away from the Foundation's earlier focus on ancient civilization. With the onset of the Great Depression and the rise of Hitler in Europe, the world seemed suddenly

As director of the Division of Humanities, David Stevens led the Rockefeller Foundation into new arenas, including drama, radio, film, linguistics, literature, and history. He believed "the function of the humanities is to make the individual a citizen of the world in matters of the spirit—to create within him his own forms of mental, emotional, and spiritual freedom." (Rockefeller Archive Center.)

incomprehensible, even threatening, and the American people struggled to understand the seismic and dark changes taking place around them and what they might mean for society and democracy. Some trustees felt the Rockefeller Foundation should aid this effort. As Ernest Hopkins, the president of Dartmouth College, wrote to fellow trustee James Angell, the president of Yale, "The Rockefeller Foundation's work has become too largely an investment in remote futures with an attendant policy of ignoring the present to such an extent that civilization may never reach the future."

Stevens and Marshall embraced this challenge. Working with the American Council of Learned Societies (ACLS), the Rockefeller Foundation pioneered new initiatives in international cultural relations that were less Eurocentric. These programs included grants for the study of language and culture in Asia, the forerunner of the Foundation's later path-breaking support for "area studies" that focused on an interdisciplinary approach to the history, language, culture, and political economy of a region.

Stevens and Marshall also believed that American culture was alive and worthy of study. They sought to discover "the ways in which the American public now gains its culture" and to combat the idea that "culture" was something Americans had to import from Europe. They wanted "to foster 'a larger appreciation of those elements in American life that constitute our national heritage.'" In this line of thinking, Stevens and Marshall were not alone; American universities were also beginning to legitimate the study of American culture, history, and literature. The first program in American civilization was launched at Harvard University in 1937, and the Foundation would become an essential partner to the emergence of American Studies nationwide within the next ten years.

Community Theater

Like Tocqueville, who suggested in the 1830s that drama was the literary form most suited to democracy, Stevens believed theater offered rich opportunities to cultivate artistic and humanistic sensibilities while contributing to the effort to strengthen American culture. A great renaissance in community theater had taken place in the United States in the 1920s, and would flower even further throughout the 1930s. Inspired by Progressive ideas, leaders of the community theater movement believed that theater and the arts relieved social stress and provided a forum for uniting a community around shared values and traditions.

The Rockefeller Foundation supported this movement. Grants to university and college theater programs sought to foster broad community participation

and make the dramatic arts "a strong social force." The Foundation worked to complement the community theater programs launched by the Depression-era Federal Theatre Project and the Works Progress Administration (WPA). One beneficiary of this new initiative was the Carolina Playmakers at the University of North Carolina. The group performed new plays by regional authors who incorporated regional folk tales and local culture into their work, including the plays of Paul Green, whose pageant *The Lost Colony* would run for decades. The Carolina Playmakers also traveled and performed in high schools, community centers, and festivals throughout North Carolina, bringing drama to communities that had no theater. To maintain the vitality of the community theater movement, encourage institutions to learn from one another, and promote theater education, the Rockefeller Foundation also provided grants to the National Theatre Conference to help it become a national organization. For more than four decades the conference played a pivotal role in connecting theater professionals to one another, and in encouraging new theater training programs in American universities.

Community theater offered Americans an important arena for exploring social issues. Adapted from Sinclair Lewis's 1935 novel, the play *It Can't Happen Here* imagined the United States in the hands of a dictator. Sponsored by the Federal Theater Project, which received support from the Rockefeller Foundation, the play opened in 21 theaters in October 1936. (Library of Congress.)

The Foundation continued this interest in community theater into the 1940s. In Montana, for example, it funded an interesting and far-sighted experiment in arts-based community engagement. Fearing that small towns in rural Montana would be decimated by the out-migration of soldiers and factory workers during the war, community leaders looked for ways to organize citizens to articulate and build on the existing strengths of their communities. The Montana Study brought people together to discuss and portray the history, culture, and character of their communities. One distinctive product of the initiative was theatrical productions that engaged communities and explored the meaning of place. The Montana project also represented an early effort to use the arts as a vehicle for community development, a theme the Foundation would return to in subsequent decades.

American Studies

When the United States was barely half a century old, Tocqueville had suggested that there were essential elements to the American character. He and others emphasized the tension between individualism and mutualism, or cooperation, that ran deep within American culture. Later, in 1893, historian Frederick Jackson Turner famously asserted that the essence of American character had been formed by the Europeans' encounter with the frontier American landscape. These formulas sought to bolster the idea of pluralism by suggesting that common experiences forged a shared identity despite differing national origins. However, they failed to include the heritage of groups like African Americans, American Indians, and Hispanic Americans. They also tended to smooth over real tensions in values and perspectives that made the realities of a pluralistic society so challenging.

In the context of the 1930s, as the nation strained under pressures brought about by the economic crisis, the Division of Humanities sought to help Americans understand themselves and their history more fully. The Foundation's first grants in this area were made to the Universities of Texas, Oklahoma, and New Mexico for studies of American culture, including research on the American Indians of the Southwest. Grants were also given to the Library of Congress and music historian Alan Lomax to record the songs of African-American laborers in the South. According to historians Joel Colton and Malcolm Richardson, these grants aimed to "uncover authentic local traditions, or local cultures, which contributed to the mosaic of American life."

In 1942, the trustees agreed to help fund a study of the teaching of the humanities at universities and colleges in the United States. The study was to be aligned with "a going inquiry into ways of interpreting the history and contemporary meaning of life on this continent" (including not only the U.S. but Mexico and Canada). The content-wide focus reflected the Foundation's growing awareness that the entire hemisphere shared overlapping, if not completely identical, concerns in the face of totalitarianism in Europe and the Soviet Union. One result of the humanities study was the creation of a new program called Regional Studies of American Life. Under its auspices, the Foundation held conferences in the Great Plains, New England, and the Maritimes in Canada. A conference in Saskatoon led to the creation of a Canadian-American committee that developed a curriculum

Frederick Koch founded the Carolina Playmakers at the University of North Carolina in 1919. An English professor who taught playwriting, Koch encouraged his students to write "folk plays" based on the culture of ordinary people in the region. The Carolina Playmakers became a model for the Federal Theater Project and received support from the Rockefeller Foundation. (Rockefeller Archive Center.)

for exploring "the common values and problems of life in this region of both Canada and the United States.

After World War Two the Foundation continued to invest in scholarship that preserved and enhanced the American people's understanding of their past. Several grants in 1947 helped support the publication of President Abraham Lincoln's papers. This work led to projects documenting the lives and philosophies of other fundamentally important American leaders—including Alexander Hamilton, James Madison, Woodrow Wilson, Franklin Roosevelt, and Booker T. Washington—as well as non-Americans who contributed to the development or understanding of the American experiment, such as Alexis de Tocqueville. For example, with substantial support from the Rockefeller Foundation, the writer Dumas Malone completed his landmark six-volume study of Thomas Jefferson. To be sure, all of these projects accounted for only a small portion of the Foundation's grants in the humanities, which were international and multicultural in scope. But the projects in American culture represented

Alan Lomax and his father John recorded the folk traditions of American song for the Library of Congress. Grants from the Rockefeller Foundation and the Carnegie Corporation helped pay for their recording equipment. Alan made this picture of writer Zora Neale Hurston (left) with musicians Rochelle French (center) and Gabriel Brown (right) in Eatonville, Florida, in 1935. (Alan Lomax. Library of Congress.)

signal interventions in the existing Eurocentric framework. The projects also contributed greatly to public appreciation of the American past during the Cold War era, and laid essential groundwork for enhancing national identity and self-awareness.

Support for Creative Expression

During World War Two, however, the intellectual search for fundamental insight into American culture also prompted renewed interest in supporting cultural expression. In 1944, economist Walter W. Stewart, chairman of the Foundation's board of trustees, wrote to Raymond Fosdick suggesting the need to consider support for creative artists in literature, music, and the visual arts. "In our secular society with its scientific habit of mind, and the consequent accent on specialization, we should continue to search for ways of supporting those who are interested primarily in the

The forced relocation of Japanese Americans to internment camps during the war troubled defenders of civil liberties. Concerned that intolerance might lead to the ill treatment of other minorities in the future, the Rockefeller Foundation joined several other foundations to fund sociological research in the camps by a team of U.C. Berkeley social scientists. (Dorothea Lange. Library of Congress.)

To support the work of new and emerging writers in the United States, the Rockefeller Foundation provided grants to literary magazines like the *Kenyon Review*, which was edited by writer and critic John Crowe Ransom (seated). (Rockefeller Archive Center.)

interpretative, the critical and the creative. It is a venturesome field, but since it is one in which the market does not function effectively, I believe it to be especially appropriate to a Foundation organized on a non-profit basis." Stewart's comment about the market encapsulated issues that had troubled the Foundation ever since Greene's proposal was rejected by Gates in 1915, namely, that "results" in the arts were difficult to quantify, and work in the arts might never become fully self-supporting.

Stewart's suggestion percolated within the Foundation after the war, in part because the war seemed to prove, once and for all, that science alone would not provide all the solutions to humanity's problems. In literature, the Foundation made grants to a number of small literary magazines so they could increase their payments to authors as a way to support the work of emerging writers. John Marshall then proposed that the Foundation offer fellowships "to creative writers and critics of exceptional promise." He envisioned that these awards would be on a par with those offered by the John Simon Guggenheim Foundation. Similarly, the Foundation contemplated fellowships in contemporary music.

Still, the Foundation was not yet entirely comfortable with the idea of funding individual creative work as its primary instrument for supporting the arts. In 1950, in the shadow of the Cold War, Charles Fahs of the Humanities Division suggested that communist countries had effectively recruited or coerced individual writers to "manipulate the subconscious attitudes and beliefs of a nation." Wary of promoting propaganda since its earliest days, the Foundation was concerned that its support for individual writers might seem to be equally coercive. To Fahs, therefore, the answer in a pluralistic society was to fund independent criticism as well as expression, to guarantee that a wide range of dissenting, diverse voices would be heard.

The Foundation's experience with the literary arts sparked further interest in the role of the arts, broadly construed, in American culture. In 1953 the Foundation began to look at establishing a wide-ranging program of support. This was admittedly a move beyond the bounds of its earlier experience, but in keeping with the postwar resurgence of what some historians have called "high culture" in American society. Dean Rusk, who came from the U.S. State Department to become president of the Foundation in 1952, explained that the program was aimed primarily at the United States, where the role of the arts in society seemed to be changing and where new "patterns of support for the arts" were emerging. In particular, Rusk suggested that the increasing affluence of the middle class was leading to a democratization of the arts. Museums and symphonies were no longer the sole province of the wealthy elite. Cultural institutions were turning from dependence on patronage to more democratic systems of support, including broad public membership and even tax dollars.

Rusk linked the rise of the arts and culture in the United States to the success of the American experiment. "The American democracy is one of rising standards of living, great total productivity, and, in almost all parts of the community, an ample surplus above the requirements of minimum subsistence." Economic success increased discretionary income and provided more free time, enabling greater support for the arts and piquing the public's interest through new media—from the latest magazines to radio to the nascent technology of television. The expansion of educational opportunities through the G.I. Bill would further broaden the audience for culture by introducing an entire generation of soldier-students to American poetry, literature, visual art, and music. The Foundation, likewise, could now afford to look beyond subsistence. Whereas the Foundation had been compelled during the 1910s and 1920s to address pressing problems of a practical, physical nature—from economic cycles to bodily health—it too could now think about the other types of elements that comprised the American fabric.

Rusk praised the democratic character of the arts and culture in the United States, highlighting the proliferation of local symphonies, community theater, dance schools, and opera workshops. Echoing other cultural pundits, he noted that the sales of high fidelity records had "grown enormously, undoubtedly representing an interest stimulated by many years of music broadcasting and greater attention to music in the schools." But Rusk did not merely echo the pundits from a distance; the Foundation had been instrumental in fostering the emerging capacities of radio throughout the 1930s and 1940s, and had funded studies of the "condition, maintenance and utilization of music records" in the schools since the early 1950s.

The Foundation recognized that artistic organizations were generally not equipped, from a management standpoint, to handle the expansion of their role in society. Nor did the Foundation have the resources to underwrite the annual deficits of every major symphony in America or to subsidize a level of activity that could not be sustained. The tradition of the Foundation emphasized building strong groundwork and attacking root causes, and therefore the trustees felt it was better, in the long run, to help the arts establish new patterns of support.

Philosophically, the Foundation articulated a belief that success in the arts reflected a blend of tradition and inspired creativity, and committed to supporting efforts in both areas. Funding the American Shakespeare Festival Theatre and Academy, for example, supported the contemporary revival of classic drama, while another grant to the Louisville Philharmonic for $500,000 ($4.29 million in 2013 dollars) provided for the commissioning of new music. In 1959 the Foundation also launched an initiative to strengthen the field of fine arts conservation in the United States, so that museums could provide adequate care for their collections. These holdings represented the artistic heritage of the nation, and the Foundation's conservation grants enabled museums to make art "an ever more intimate part of the life of the individual American." The centerpiece of this initiative was a multi-year $500,000 challenge grant to the Conservation Center at the Institute of Fine Arts of New York University.

Further reflecting an organizational desire to preserve and innovate, the Foundation asserted that it was interested in supporting established organizations as well as new entities on the cultural scene. Its program in the late 1950s and early 1960s also demonstrated an abiding interest in America's distinctively pluralistic culture. Noting, for example, that American Indian artists were often isolated from "the mainstream of an open society" by the reservation system, the Foundation provided a major grant to the University of Arizona for training that would allow traditional American Indian artists to take advantage of new techniques and materials for creative expression. Along

At the groundbreaking ceremony in New York City on May 14, 1959, President Dwight Eisenhower praised the public-private partnership that would make the Lincoln Center for the Performing Arts a reality. It symbolized "an increasing interest in American cultural matters," he said, and addressed one of the nation's most pressing problems—urban blight. (Bob Serating. Rockefeller Archive Center.)

After he became president in 1961, J. George Harrar initiated a review of the Rockefeller Foundation's programs. Five new or redefined programs emerged from this process, including "Aiding Our Cultural Development," which sought to help cultural activities "take root more deeply in the communities of the nation." (Rockefeller Archive Center.)

the same lines, the Foundation supported the American Craftsmen's Council's efforts to document the rich expressions of American folk culture embodied in the handicraft created by artist-craftspersons from around the country.

All of these efforts, as Rusk stated in 1959, represented a new approach to philanthropy for the Rockefeller Foundation and raised issues about the role of philanthropy within America's creative sector. Rusk had acknowledged in 1956 that there was a growing call for public funding for the arts, but some people on the Foundation's board—as in the rest of the nation—opposed this idea. Given the strength of the American economy, they believed, government support was not necessary. If the arts were worth supporting, they would find paying customers. Moreover, government aid might lead to political control, which would be anti-democratic and ultimately unhealthy for the free expression that artistic excellence required. The concept of a public-private partnership in the arts was appealing to other trustees, however, who believed it could be consistent with the Foundation's past work with government in public health, education, and agriculture.

Philanthropy's potential for partnering with government to develop cultural infrastructure in the United States represented a key element of the changing pattern of support for the arts in the late 1950s and 1960s. In New York City, the Foundation provided a critical $50,000 grant to the Metropolitan Opera Association to help fund the Exploratory Committee for a Musical Arts Center. This grant was followed by a $10 million gift to support the construction and development of the Lincoln Center for the Performing Arts. The Foundation hoped that Lincoln Center would be more than a venue for performance. With the inclusion of the Juilliard School of Music and plans to support public education in the arts, the Foundation believed that Lincoln Center would "encourage the flow of creativity which alone can bring innovation and change on the one hand and the perfection and strengthening of vital traditions on the other." Several years later, the Foundation reaffirmed its support for the development of national performing arts centers with a $1 million contribution toward the construction of the National Cultural Center in Washington, D.C. (later renamed the John F. Kennedy Center for the Performing Arts). The Foundation also added to its support for Lincoln Center with a $5 million gift in 1963, bringing the Foundation's total contribution to $15.05 million (more than $114.7 million in 2013 dollars).

Some historians have noted the ways in which this resurgence in the arts in the United States supported the country's Cold War ambitions. In 1959, for example, C. D. Jackson, the director of Lincoln Center, reveled in the idea that "culture today is emerging as a great element of East-West competition" and that the word itself had become "of immense worldwide political significance." Seen in this light, according to the Center's board of directors, "The Lincoln Center for the Performing Arts can be the greatest cultural development of our times that would not only symbolize cultural maturity to American citizens, but announce America's cultural maturity to the world."

Though framed in Cold War terms, Jackson's excitement over Lincoln Center reflected not only the nation's continuing anxiety over democracy's ability to cultivate high standards and innovation in cultural

Rockefeller Foundation funding helped preserve American folk music, including cowboy songs, and support the development of new symphonies that integrated folk traditions. Founded in 1975 with grants from the Rockefeller Foundation, New World Records produced a 100-disc anthology of American music for use in educational and cultural institutions around the globe. (Russell Lee. Library of Congress.)

expression, but also a growing confidence. Far from being extraneous to American politics, culture was now intimately linked to it. As one in-house report prepared by the Rockefeller Foundation explained, "New York is the cultural capital of America and the nearest that exists to a capital of the world. The performing arts are an essential part of the enriching and integrating forces of human culture. We must achieve a greater measure of cultural eminence if we are to maintain the political leadership which we now enjoy." In the 1960s, the Rockefeller Foundation would look for new ways to support artistic contributions to the continuing evolution of American identity and culture.

The Challenge of a New Era

In the early 1960s, the focus of the Foundation's work in the arts and humanities shifted in tandem with its work in agriculture and university development abroad, which concentrated on building local institutional capacity. With Dean Rusk's departure for Washington, D.C. to become U.S. Secretary of State, J. George Harrar became president of the Foundation in 1961. Harrar was an agricultural scientist who had played a leading role in the Foundation's efforts to dramatically increase food production in developing nations in Latin America and Asia. In 1962 he told the public that the Foundation would no longer concentrate on supporting performances or specific works of creative expression. Instead, much as it aimed to do in higher education, the Foundation would look for new ways to encourage institutional development anchored in broad public support.

In the fall of 1963, the Rockefeller Foundation trustees reorganized the Foundation's programs. Their report, entitled "Plans for the Future," envisioned the consolidation of the Foundation's work into five thematic, mission-driven programs: Toward the Conquest of Hunger, The Population Problem, Strengthening Emerging Centers of Learning, Toward Equal Opportunity for All, and Aiding Our Cultural Development. Of these five program areas, two were focused particularly on the United States—Equal Opportunity and Cultural Development. Articulating the rationale for continued work in culture, the Foundation reflected the tenor of the times. With the Depression and World War Two fading from memory, the mass media and American advertisers were celebrating an age of prosperity that seemed to encompass broad segments of the American population. In this context, arts and culture became a commodity for consumption in an increasingly affluent post-industrial society. As George Harrar explained in the 1963 annual report, "With the advance of American technology the

Democracy & Philanthropy

pattern of life has changed dramatically." Automation was decreasing the need for hard manual work, leaving more people with more time and energy for leisure, including cultural pursuits. As Harrar put it, "Today the American citizen seeks expression for the additional time which he can call his own."

Within the framework of its redefined cultural program, the Foundation articulated a broad goal to help "cultural activities take root more deeply in the communities of the nation." Building on its long-standing interest in theater, the Foundation provided grants to the Actors Studio in New York and the Guthrie Theater in Minneapolis to help develop new plays and playwrights. The Foundation also extended support to symphonies, encouraging them to engage with local colleges and universities by rehearsing and performing on college campuses as well as recording new or seldom-heard American music.

Audience development also became a major theme in the Foundation's efforts in the 1960s, underlying its grants both to institutions and creative artists. According to the Foundation, the "democratization of the arts" had widened the gap between the artist and the audience. As artists explored new media, audiences needed to be educated in order "to foster receptivity to new forms of expression." In service of this goal, the Foundation funded programs to bring new performers to high school and college students. And in 1966 the Foundation provided grants to Theatre in the Street in New York and the Free Southern Theatre in New Orleans, to mount performances for inner-city neighborhoods as well as poor rural African-American communities in the Mississippi Delta. To support broad cultural education in music, the Foundation helped fund a program at the University of Southern California to train music critics.

As television became a ubiquitous part of American life, new artists emerged in the field of video and other rapidly changing recording technologies. In the mid-1960s, the Foundation launched an innovative program in media arts led by Howard Klein. He was an avant-garde musician who came to the Foundation in 1967 from the *New York Times*, where he had been a music reporter and critic. Aware of Natural Sciences Director Warren Weaver's remarkable efforts to nurture the development of the field of molecular biology from the 1930s to the 1950s, Klein also hoped to support the development of an emerging field. He believed that video represented a new art form and over the next two decades he cultivated the field and the artists within it. During this time the Foundation provided critical support to video artists—including Nam June Paik, Bill Viola, Kit Fitzgerald, and John Sanborn—and worked with public television stations to build audiences for this unknown and highly experimental form of expression.

At the time of the nation's bicentennial, the Foundation recognized the contribution of yet another cultural form to the success of the American

experiment. A major grant to New World Records helped to produce a 100-disc anthology of American music to be distributed at cost to schools and libraries. The recordings demonstrated the remarkable variety of American music, from Civil War ballads to Cecil Taylor jazz, including cowboy songs, American Indian drum music, ragtime, country music, and folk. Initiatives like these built on decades of work by the Foundation to explore and nourish pluralistic forms of expression that acknowledged the tensions as well as the rich diversity in American culture. These efforts would become the major theme of the Foundation's work in humanities and the arts in the era ahead.

Project Row Houses, which began in 1993 in Houston, is a catalyst for change in the historically African-American Third Ward. The project combines arts and culture with neighborhood revitalization, low-income housing, education, historic preservation, and community service. (Carol M. Highsmith. Library of Congress.)

In 1979 the Rockefeller Foundation redefined its cultural program to include the goal of enhancing "the country's pride in its diversity as well as its unity by encouraging humanistic research on minority groups…to foster the study of our national heritage and its cultural pluralism." Through this new initiative, the Foundation sought to more explicitly help Americans embrace the nation's multicultural heritage. In 1988 the Foundation furthered this goal with the creation of the Multicultural Arts Project, a performing arts initiative "to promote the understanding of diverse cultural heritages through innovative new works that comment on, and perhaps even change, the way we see the world." The Foundation often carried forward this emphasis on diversity within its support for traditional arts media. According to the program's director, Joan Shigekawa, it was "interested in building and maintaining a theatre culture in the United States," which included the ongoing development and production of new works.

Defending Freedom of Expression

Freedom of expression, a value that lies at the heart of the humanities and the arts as well as the American experiment, was for generations a core value of the Rockefeller Foundation in its grantmaking and daily operations. During World War Two, Raymond Fosdick suggested that such freedom was fundamental to the advancement of knowledge in all spheres of human activity. In his Congressional testimony in the 1950s, Dean Rusk had reaffirmed this principle. In 1990, however, the Foundation found itself defending the idea in an American court for the first time.

A series of controversial art exhibitions funded by the National Endowment for the Arts (NEA) in the late 1980s, including a major exhibition of the work of photographer Robert Mapplethorpe, had sparked a raging culture war between those opposed to public obscenity and indecency and those who supported artistic free expression. Reacting to this debate, Congress passed a law, signed by President George H.W. Bush in October 1989, that imposed content restrictions on art funded by the NEA. To implement this new law, the NEA began to require grantees to certify that they would not promote, disseminate, or produce materials that could be construed as obscene.

The Rockefeller Foundation believed that the NEA's certification process would have a chilling effect on artistic production. After the Bella Lewitzky Dance Foundation and the Newport Harbor Art Museum filed suit against the NEA, arguing that the certification was unconstitutional and violated free speech rights, the Rockefeller Foundation submitted an *amicus* brief with the court in support of the plaintiffs. The outcome of these suits represented a victory for champions of free expression. One court, citing the Foundation's brief, held for the grantees. The litigants in the other court settled in a way that cleared the constitutional objections. As President Peter Goldmark exulted in the Foundation's annual report for 1990, "We supported the effort of various groups to re-affirm the principles of freedom of expression and restraint upon the power of the state that is central to this country's traditional values."

Ethnographic recordings made of traditional Blackfoot music at the end of the nineteenth century continue to find new audiences through the Smithsonian Global Sound web site and library subscription service, which was funded in part by the Rockefeller Foundation. (Library of Congress.)

American Culture and International Understanding

By the early 1990s the Foundation's attention to and investment in arts and culture was increasingly linked to one of its longest-standing commitments: the promotion of international understanding. The Foundation was interested in "the flow of art and knowledge between developing world cultures and the United States" and in focusing attention on the history and culture of American ethnic groups with roots in the

developing world. In this way, the Foundation's international and domestic work in the arts and humanities were increasingly interwoven.

The ongoing evolution of what had become the Foundation's Arts and Humanities Division also reflected the challenges raised by the collapse of the Soviet Union and the end of the Cold War. As new states in Eastern Europe struggled to redefine their basic systems of government, they sought models for free expression as well as for citizen participation and enfranchisement. Václav Havel, the poet and president of Czechoslovakia, reminded the world that "The best laws and the best-conceived democratic mechanisms will not in themselves guarantee legality or freedom or human rights—anything in short for which they are intended—if they are not underpinned by certain human and social values." In this context, the American faith in a pluralistic society increasingly became an internationally held value. In 1993 the Rockefeller Foundation redefined the focus of Arts and Humanities to reaffirm its decades-long support for this value by launching a new initiative known as "Understanding Diversity in Changing Societies."

Throughout the 1990s the Rockefeller Foundation sustained the Arts and Humanities Division because "the root causes of societal change play themselves out in the arts and humanities in ways that interact with government, science or economics. The result is a unique perspective on the human condition." Lessons learned from funding diversity initiatives sparked a national conversation related to strengthening civil society. Programs like Partnerships Addressing Community Tension (PACT) sought to preserve traditional culture as a way of promoting dialogue among different racial groups. PACT's projects ranged from indigenous communities in Alaska to Asian Americans in Minnesota. Meanwhile, funding for Project Row Houses in Houston, Texas, preserved historic architecture as a means of preserving working class history. The project transformed a neighborhood of old "shotgun" row houses by developing creative spaces for art exhibitions and supporting vital services such as childcare centers. The grantee in this project captured the Foundation's attention with the idea that "You have to revitalize the souls and spirits of people if neighborhood revitalization is to have real meaning."

Through the end of the millennium and into the early years of the twenty-first century, the Rockefeller Foundation deepened its exploration of the relationship between creativity and economic vitality, especially in communities where poverty and social instability seemed to undermine the civic culture that sustains not only a satisfying quality of life, but also a healthy democracy. One major initiative launched in concert with the Urban Institute, a Washington, D.C.-based think tank, sought to measure these relationships through the development of the Arts and Culture Indicators Project (ACIP). The project resonated with the Foundation's work in the humanities as far back as the 1930s by linking cultural expression with community development. It also took an innovative approach by recognizing that what counts as culture may vary significantly from community to community. Measuring and supporting cultural expression and vitality was part of an attempt to account for these differences, especially in low- and moderate-income communities, communities of color, and immigrant communities.

By 2006 the Rockefeller Foundation's engagement with the arts and humanities had come full circle. Judith Rodin, a former president of the University of Pennsylvania, had succeeded Gordon Conway, to become the first woman to serve as president of the Rockefeller Foundation. As with many of her predecessors, Rodin and the trustees used the moment of leadership transition to evaluate the Foundation's existing programs and realign its approach to a new era. The strategy that emerged built upon the trajectory of nearly three decades of work. As the Foundation faced the urgency of addressing the challenges and opportunities of globalization and its impact on poor and vulnerable populations around the world, support for the arts and humanities was channeled in more specific ways. For example, in 2006 the Foundation delivered a $3 million grant to help fund a new national organization, United States Artists, devoted to supporting and recognizing America's finest living artists in a variety of disciplines and to representing the diversity and vibrancy of the nation's population. The Foundation also completed a significant grant to National Video Resources Inc., to help make independent films more widely available. And in New York City, the Foundation's "hometown," it established the Rockefeller Foundation New York City Cultural Innovation Fund. In this sense, the city has remained a laboratory for new initiatives as well as insights into the relationship between inspiring the soul and protecting the basic economic security of the poorest and most vulnerable in American society.

The deep tensions that Alexis de Tocqueville identified in American culture in the 1830s inspired much of the Rockefeller Foundation's work in the arts and humanities over the last century. In a society that celebrates both the freedom and responsibilities of the individual, as well as the ideal of social and political equality, abiding inequities rooted in historic patterns of racism and discrimination have historically led to a continuing discomfort with any notion that there is a universal American culture or character. The Foundation's investments in the arts and literature—from Lincoln Center in New York City to community theaters across the nation—enable Americans of all backgrounds to continue to explore the meaning of American democracy.

CASE STUDIES IN INNOVATION

LOUISVILLE SYMPHONY ORCHESTRA

In the mid-1950s, the *Wall Street Journal* reported a curious statistic. Sales of classical music records were skyrocketing. In less than ten years, their share of the market had risen from 15 to nearly 40 percent, grossing more than $70 million. Yet even as the demand for symphonic music boomed, support for living composers languished. In Europe, public funding for the arts helped promote new work, but in the United States the lack of funding threatened the long-run vitality of symphonic music.

The Rockefeller Foundation's first major grant in the arts sought to address this gap. On April 7, 1953, the Foundation announced a $400,000 award to the Louisville Philharmonic Society for an ambitious project supporting contemporary commissions and recording. Musicians, conductors, composers, and symphony fans were stunned by the size of the award and the fact that it had been given to an institution that was not in New York, San Francisco, or one of the country's other cultural capitals. Moreover, the project's champion was not a famous conductor, but rather the city's mayor, Charles Farnsley, who had conceived and developed

Conductor and composer Robert Whitney co-founded the Louisville Orchestra with Charles Farnsley in 1937. He led the orchestra for 30 years, until his retirement in 1967. (James N. Keen. Rockefeller Archive Center.)

the plan in collaboration with the Louisville Philharmonic Society.

Foundation leaders and the proposal's reviewers saw promise in Louisville, however. Elected in 1948, Mayor Farnsley had decided to focus on culture. He had organized the Louisville Fund for the Arts, "a community chest for the arts," to benefit fourteen cultural organizations, including the Louisville Philharmonic Society. He also encouraged the symphony to cultivate and perform new music, and since 1948 the society had commissioned and staged five new works a year during its concert season. Although some proposal reviewers were concerned about the project's ambitious nature, they recommended funding, one "with all flags flying." Composer Otto Luening, for example, while conceding that it seemed like a "crazy idea," believed Mayor Farnsley's record of accomplishment in Louisville was "little short of extraordinary." He said the Louisville Orchestra represented "all I hoped for as a model of honest artistry in our grand and sprawling America."

Columbia Records engineer (seated) with Louisville Mayor Charles Farnsley in 1953. New music performed by the Louisville Symphony was recorded by Columbia with support from the Rockefeller Foundation as part of an effort to reach new audiences. (Rockefeller Archive Center.)

With Rockefeller Foundation support, over the next four years the Louisville Philharmonic Society commissioned more than 40 new pieces a year. The society also commissioned five additional works each year from its own funds. Established and emerging composers, including Aaron Copland and Lou Harrison, as well as students, received commissions. These new compositions were performed every week, except during the summer months, and each piece was performed on four occasions.

The Louisville Philharmonic Society's project also emphasized geographic and compositional diversity. Roughly two-thirds of the composers were American, while the remaining one-third came primarily from Europe and Latin America. The compositions included chamber music, symphonies, and operas.

Recording and distributing the performances of this new music was a key element of the society's plan. The Foundation provided an additional grant of $100,000 to support this part of the project. The recordings were released on a subscription basis at the rate of six discs a year, which helped the composers market their work to other conductors and orchestras as well as to home audiences.

When the grant ended in 1958, the Louisville Philharmonic Society and the Rockefeller Foundation sought to measure the impact of the project on the production of new music, the expansion of audiences for this work, and the increase in financial support for its composers and performances. Nathan Broder, a critic, scholar, and musicologist who also had extensive experience in the business of classical music, wrote an evaluation for the Foundation's trustees that focused on both the quality of the new work and its impact on the business of concert music in America.

From an artistic standpoint, based on Broder's own assessment and the critics' reviews, roughly 20 percent of the works released by July 1958 were "good, substantial or highly imaginative pieces." Another 69 percent were "well-made" but not overly impressive. He deemed 11 percent to be failures. Broder thought this was a reasonable outcome, representing a normal distribution for artistic production.

Critics of the grant often focused on Louisville's small size, compared to New York or Chicago, and therefore its limited potential to attract a large audience for this new work. Indeed, attendance at the project's Saturday afternoon concerts averaged only 200 people. Given the lack of a broad popular following for most new symphonic music, Broder felt that even in New York these concerts might not have attracted significantly more people.

Most important, Broder asserted in his evaluation, the grant, concerts, and recordings brought increased attention to new music, and the project played a significant part in helping to strengthen the field. According to John Marshall, the associate director of the Humanities Division, no other major foundation had provided funding for composition prior to the Rockefeller Foundation. After the Louisville project was announced, however, other foundations, including Ford, began to provide support to composers and orchestras interested in bringing new symphonic music to American audiences. Meanwhile,

DEMOCRACY & PHILANTHROPY

Tenor Farrold Stevens meets with Conductor Robert Whitney, composer Lukas Foss, and Columbia's musical director Howard Scott in preparation for the Louisville Symphony's performance of Foss's 1953 work "A Parable of Death." (Rockefeller Archive Center.)

the Rockefeller Foundation provided additional support for symphonic music and audience development with grants to the American Symphony Orchestra League, New York's City Center of Music and Drama, Young Audiences New York, and the American International Music Fund.

With the growth of this support—from foundations and audiences throughout the country—the Rockefeller Foundation chose to exit the field in the 1960s. As Humanities Division program officer Robert July wrote in 1962, "The original idea seems to have caught on, there is ample foundation activity and interest, [and] avant-garde composition appears to be thriving."

DEMOCRACY & PHILANTHROPY

CHAPTER V

FOUNDATIONS UNDER FIRE

In the hot summer of 1951, Congressman Edward Eugene Cox rose to deliver a scathing criticism of American foundations to the United States House of Representatives. The 71-year-old Georgia Democrat had been a member of the U.S. Congress for more than a quarter of a century. Nicknamed "Goober" because peanuts were the major crop produced in his district, Cox preferred to be known as "Judge Cox." He had trained and practiced as a lawyer and served as a judge and mayor of the small town of Camilla before his election to Congress. By 1951 he was one of the most powerful men on Capitol Hill.

A fierce opponent of organized labor and an anti-communist, Cox warned that private foundations in the United States were engaged in "un-American and subversive activities." He chastised the Rockefeller Foundation in particular for providing grants and fellowships that aided individuals whom he said had communist sympathies. He suggested that the Foundation's investment of $45 million in China over 32 years had supported the "student and teacher element" that led the communist revolution there. In summary, Cox claimed, foundations had "become a powerful and unregulated factor in our national life, enjoying Federal subsidy through tax exemption.... They should be investigated and exposed to the pitiless light of publicity, and appropriate legislation should be framed to correct the present disquieting situation."

Cox's speech was delivered against the backdrop of growing Cold War fears. In 1949 the U.S. State Department had revealed that the Soviet

Following the victory of the Chinese Communists in 1949, the U.S. State Department and the Truman Administration were blamed for having "lost China." Congressman Edward Eugene Cox insinuated that the Rockefeller Foundation's investments in the Peking Union Medical College and other educational initiatives in China had indirectly aided the communists. (Rockefeller Archive Center.)

Union had acquired the knowledge of how to build an atomic bomb. Meanwhile, the communist victory in China that year was used by some Americans to incite fear that the United States would soon be under attack. Widespread concerns that communist sympathizers in the government were passing secrets to the nation's enemies fueled anti-communist rhetoric.

These anxieties seemed to be confirmed by the House Un-American Activities Committee's investigation into Alger Hiss, a former State Department official who was president of the Carnegie Endowment for International Peace when the House began its investigation. The revelation that Hiss had been a communist, along with his conviction for perjury in January 1950, encouraged Wisconsin Senator Joseph McCarthy to launch a full-throated campaign against alleged communist sympathizers in the government the following month. Cox's speech to the House in August 1952 came at the height of McCarthy's five-year attack.

For his speech, Cox borrowed from an article entitled "Rockefeller Fortune Backed British Socialism," published by the Constitutional Educational

League in a tract entitled *Headlines*. He was encouraged by a number of individuals and groups who believed that any efforts to promote international cooperation, or "internationalism," were inherently subversive to American interests. Although Cox's criticism came from the most conservative corner of American politics, in its substance it echoed the critique leveled by Progressives and labor advocates 40 years earlier during the Foundation's charter fight. According to Cox, private foundations were guiding public policy in ways that contradicted the interests of the nation, without the authority of the country's democratically elected representatives. They should be feared, rather than encouraged.

In the spring of 1952, with support from Republicans and conservative Democrats, the House approved Cox's plan and established the Select Committee to Investigate Tax-Exempt Foundations and Comparable Organizations, which was empowered to identify those institutions that were using their resources for purposes other than those for which they were established and, specifically, institutions that were "using their resources for un-American and subversive activities or for purposes not in the interest or tradition of the United States." With this vote, private philanthropy's role in a democratic society would once again be put on trial in Washington.

With a shifting focus, and led by various members of Congress, this trial would continue for the next 18 years. The Rockefeller Foundation would play a critical role in the defense. In 1969, however, the investigation would end with a sweeping reform of tax laws in the United States that would impose far greater government controls on the operation of private foundations. Initially, the Foundation was dismayed by these changes, but over time, the Foundation's leaders embraced this new paradigm and, in the process, helped restructure the relationship between philanthropy and democracy.

The Cox Committee Investigation

The "Cox Committee," as it was known in the philanthropic world, hired Chicago attorney Harold M. Keele to lead the investigation in the summer of 1952. As historian James Allen Smith writes, many in the foundation community were wary and unresponsive as Keele began his work, but they soon discovered that Keele was an honest and fair investigator. "I will not be a tool or instrument of hatchet work on behalf of or for any political party, creed or belief," he promised. In fact, he worked

QUESTIONNAIRE

SUBMITTED BY THE

... of the House of Representatives

OF THE

... of the United States

Created by House Resolution 561,
... Second Congress, Second Session,
... Investigate Tax-Exempt Foundations
... and Comparable Organizations

SECTION B

in the policy of your organization in relation thereto, and, if so, the date and reasons therefor.

B–13. If the answer to question 9 is in the affirmative, state whether the results of such investigations were reduced to writing or if any memoranda were made in connection therewith.

B–14. If the answer to question 13 is in the affirmative, state whether such writings or memoranda (a) were extant as of January 1951, (b) are extant now, and (c) if extant, the person, firm, corporation, or organization in whose possession or custody they are.

B–15. If the answer to question 9 is in the affirmative, state whether any such investigation revealed any person hired or employed by or affiliated with your organization who at the time of the investigation had or prior thereto had had any affiliations with communist front organizations.

B–16. If the answer to question 15 is in the affirmative, state the name or names of such person or persons.

B–17. If the answer to question 9 is in the negative, state whether such investigations were ever considered or discussed by your organization or the trustees, board of directors, or officers thereof, and, if so, by whom and the basis of any decision reached in connection therewith.

B–18. If the answer to question 15 is in the affirmative, state what action was taken by your organization with reference to such person or persons.

B–19. What steps, if any, have been or are being taken to prevent infiltration of your organization by subversive persons?

B–20. If the answer to question 19 is in the negative, state whether you think it necessary or advisable to initiate procedures to prevent possible infiltration of subversives into your organization; and, if so, whether you intend to do so and the general routine of the intended procedures.

3

... Attorney General of the United States influences you in the making or withholding of grants, gifts, loans, contributions, or expenditures either directly or indirectly to organizations so listed.

D–8. If your answer to question 6 is in the negative, state the reasons therefor fully.

*List of organizations designated by the Attorney General as within Executive Order No. 9835 according to the classification of ...
the Executive Order.

---

9. Do you consider it your duty or re... to consider the possible effects of g... loans, or contributions to organiza... have been so listed by the Attor... of the United States?

Has your organization made any g... loans, contributions, or expendit... directly or indirectly through ot... izations to any organization so li... Attorney General of the United S... any individual, individuals, or or... considered "subversive" as you ha... that term in answer to question 1?

If your answer to question 10 is in ... ative, list the recipient and date of ... grant, gift, loan, contribution, or ex... and the amount and nature thereo...

If your answer to question 10 is in t... tive, state whether you knew su... ation had been so listed by the ... eneral or was considered "subve... e time you made such grant, gift, ... ibution, or expenditure.

... your answer to questions 10 an... th in the affirmative, state your rea... king such grant, gift, loan, cont... expenditure.

... your organization made any gra... n, contribution, or expenditure ... indirectly to any individual, ind... up, organization, or institutior... nt, gift, loan, contribution, or expe... recipient has been criticized or ... Un-American Activities Committe... ed States House of Representa... Subcommittee on Internal Securit... iciary Committee of the United ... te?

... ur answer to question 14 is in the ... list the recipient and date of ea... , gift, loan, contribution, or expe... and the amount and nature thereof.

D–16. Does your organization consult the "G... Subversive Organizations and Publica... House Document No. 137, prepared a ... leased by the Committee on Un-Am... Activities, United States House of Repr... atives? If so, for what purpose and to ... effect?

closely with F. Emerson Andrews, the director of philanthropic research at the Russell Sage Foundation, to prepare a comprehensive questionnaire that would provide the Committee with insight into the operations of the leading foundations in the United States.

The Rockefeller Foundation received the questionnaire in October 1952. Raymond Fosdick had retired, succeeded for a brief period by Chester Barnard, a management guru and former telephone company executive, before Dean Rusk became president on July 1, 1952, just as the Cox Committee was getting started. Rusk worked with the staff to develop the Foundation's response to the Committee's sweeping request. In addition to basic information about a foundation's operations, assets, and governance, the questionnaire asked whether the organization conducted an investigation into the background of all persons responsible for planning the distribution of the foundation's funds. The Committee wanted details on the process for conducting these investigations. Did these investigations reveal "any affiliations with communist front organizations?" Did the foundation think it necessary to take active steps to prevent possible infiltration by subversives? Did the foundation consult with other agencies or governments when it made gifts or grants? Did it make grants to subversive individuals or organizations? In the process of grantmaking, did the organization consult the "Guide to Subversive Organizations and Publications" promulgated by the Committee on Un-American Activities of the United States House of Representatives?

The questionnaire also included questions that went beyond the specific focus on communist and subversive organizations and individuals. The Committee asked foundation executives to express their opinion as to whether tax-exempt philanthropic foundations should be allowed to finance or sponsor projects that might influence public opinion in the field of politics, economics, education, international relations, religion, government, and public administration. Detailed questions followed about ways in which the foundation might be involved in influencing public opinion or public policy. The Committee wanted to know if the foundation contributed directly to individuals or organizations "for political purposes." The Committee also asked about the foundation's work in foreign countries, and whether the foundation consulted with the U.S. Department of State on this work.

Near the end of the questionnaire, the Committee raised enduring questions about the role of philanthropy in the United States. What needs were these institutions filling? "Could the functions of foundations be effectively performed by government?" They also asked whether the public had a direct interest in tax-exempt foundations. "Is some form of governmental regulation of foundations necessary or desirable?" Should foundations be allowed to include broad mission statements in their charters, or should they be required to spell out the specific purposes for which they were established? And like the congressmen of 1910, when John D. Rockefeller first sought to create the Foundation with a federal charter, the Committee asked whether there should be limits on the size of a foundation's endowment, its legal life, or the right of its trustees to spend the organization's capital funds.

The Rockefeller Foundation was among 54 large foundations that returned the questionnaire to the Cox Committee (only one refused). The cooperation from the foundation community seemed to soften the chairman's attitude. When he opened hearings in November 1952, Cox made it clear that the investigation would not seek to "smear or whitewash" the foundations and their work. As the hearings progressed, 40 witnesses testified, including including both Rusk and board Chairman John D. Rockefeller 3rd. The tone remained generally fair and balanced, even as the questions zeroed in on potentially controversial grants to individuals and organizations

John D. Rockefeller 3rd and Dean Rusk both testified before the Cox Committee in December 1952. Over a period of 40 years, Rusk said, the Foundation had made 28,753 grants worth $470 million. Only two organizations and 23 individuals on that list of grantees had been criticized by the Committee. Rusk called this a pretty good "batting average." (Rockefeller Archive Center.)

that might be deemed by some to be subversive or un-American. In the end, very few controversial grants were uncovered. Out of 29,000 grants made by the Rockefeller Foundation, only two organizations and 23 individuals were considered questionable by the committee.

The Committee's staff rushed to complete a final report at the end of 1952. Their work was interrupted by the sudden death of Congressman Cox on Christmas Eve. Nevertheless, the final report was issued on January 1. As historian James Allen Smith notes, "The report's language teetered back and forth, attempting to strike a balance between those members who wanted to scold foundations and others who wanted to absolve them of wrongdoing." In the end, the report affirmed

Editorial cartoonists around the country satirized the Reece Committee's investigation into the activities of private foundations, suggesting the inquiry would do more to undermine freedom than protect it. (Rockefeller Archive Center.)

the important role that foundations played in American society by promoting research and education. "The foundation, once considered a boon to society, now seems to be a vital and essential factor in our progress."

The hearings made good headlines, and sparked considerable public reaction. The Rockefeller Foundation received letters criticizing its grantmaking. One writer, for example, proclaimed, "It is inconceivable that requests for aid to undertake studies in the area of American culture were not honored, while it did not seem too difficult for communist groups to receive assistance." This writer suggested that, given the hearings, it would be difficult for many Americans to continue to believe in the Foundation's "high purposes." To fix the public relations problem, the author suggested, the Foundation should "grant assistance to as many projects dealing with American life or culture that warrant it, and to give these grants the widest publicity possible."

This kind of criticism did not reshape the pattern of Rockefeller Foundation grantmaking, but the hearings did force the Foundation once again to confront an element in American culture that perceived "internationalism"—or, as one newspaper editorial called it, "globalissimo"—as inherently anti-American. In January 1953, a memorandum was developed on "Officer procedures for avoiding grants to subversive individuals." Meanwhile, the investigation reinvigorated an awareness deep within the Foundation's culture that public officials and the general public cared about what the Foundation did, and that it needed to be accountable, as Starr Murphy had pointed out during the charter fight, to the elected representatives of the people.

Representative Reece Continues the Campaign

Congressman B. Carroll Reece, a Republican from Tennessee, was not happy with the results of the Cox Committee. He had been a member, but attended only one of the 18 public sessions. Reece had also been chairman of the Republican National Committee in 1952. He was a supporter of Robert Taft for the Republican nomination for president, and he hoped that a further investigation would tar Dwight Eisenhower, another leading candidate and president of Columbia University, with the internationalist label.

Reece insisted that the Cox Committee's work had been rushed, and neglected important topics. In particular, Reece wanted to know if foundations and other tax-exempt organizations were actively lobbying the government or trying to shape the outcome of elections. He was also troubled by funding provided by the Rockefeller Foundation to Dr. Alfred Kinsey's studies of sexual behavior. At Reece's request, the House of Representatives authorized another investigation in July 1953.

The Reece Committee staff proved far more interested in attacking foundations than learning from them. After the Committee launched its hearings, it heard from only five witnesses and three members of the Committee's staff before abruptly terminating its investigation in July. Those witnesses, however, had asserted that the United States was drifting toward socialism and collectivism aided by a "diabolical conspiracy of foundations and certain educational and research organizations."

Dean Rusk and the presidents and staff of other leading foundations were extremely frustrated by the Reece Committee. The Rockefeller Foundation spent hundreds of hours preparing its responses to the Committee's questionnaire and the testimony, but had not been allowed to rebut the charges made by the witnesses. Rusk sent a telegram to Reece noting the "charges and innuendoes" made against the Rockefeller Foundation and the General Education Board, and saying that the Foundation would submit a sworn statement to the Committee and provide copies to the press and the public.

Fortunately for the foundations, the Reece Committee was divided by the proceedings and in its findings. Three of the five members filed a final report with fourteen key findings, including an assertion that foundations wielded so much power and influence that they might control a large part of the U.S. economy. The report suggested that while foundation work in health and the natural sciences was of great benefit, work in the social sciences was insidious because it focused on "empirical" research, which the Committee members believed would lead to "a deterioration of moral standards and a disrespect for principles" in the United States.

While the Reece Committee's anti-communist concerns about the subversion of morals and principles were not taken seriously by a majority in Congress, the Committee did raise important points about government supervision of private foundations. Specifically, the Committee recommended that the Internal Revenue Service (IRS) should watch foundations more closely. The public should have full access to foundations' annual tax returns (known as the Form 990). Private foundations should be barred from political activity and lobbying. The life of a private foundation should be limited to ten to twenty-five years, with mandatory requirements for distributing income along the way. Moreover, the government should limit the ability of corporations or entrepreneurs to run their businesses from within the tax shelter of a private foundation. But Congress took little action on these recommendations.

Foundations generally emerged from the Cox and Reece investigations with renewed support from the media and those citizens who paid attention. An editorial in the *Buffalo Courier-Express*, for example, under the headline "Foundations Foster American Way of Life," noted that the American "social and governmental system" was "sustained in large part by the fruits of free enquiry in colleges, laboratories and other testing places endowed or supported independently of the government." Philanthropy, they said, played a large role in funding this exploration. "If the day should come when these foundations were brought under government control and compelled to support only such educational scientific and cultural activities as followed a 'party line' laid down by dominant elements in Congress— well, then 'the promotion of Socialism and collectivist ideas' would have been accomplished, not by the foundations, but by the politicians and the witch-hunters." One noted observer expressed concern that the investigations might have a long-run deleterious effect on philanthropic work in the United States. When asked if he feared that foundations might become too radical, the eminent jurist Roscoe Pound replied, "No, my sole fear is that they will become sterile."

At the Rockefeller Foundation, the conclusion of the Cox and Reece investigations left staff and trustees feeling a sense of accomplishment. The investigations could have turned the public against the philanthropic community and particularly the Rockefeller Foundation. Instead, as a committee of trustees wrote in their five-year review and appraisal of the Foundation's work, "the Foundation came out of both investigations stronger than it went in—stronger internally, stronger in the opinion of the Congress and stronger in the public judgment." The experience had been a trial by fire for Rusk, especially. But it had also immersed him deeply in the Foundation's history, mission, and program.

Many of the Reece Committee's recommendations did not relate to the Rockefeller Foundation. Ever since it was founded in 1913, the Foundation had provided the public with detailed annual reports on grantmaking and the membership of the board of trustees and the staff. These annual reports provided a model to the sector. But the Foundation did concede that the evidence suggested that the foundation community in general could do more to satisfy the public trust. Specifically, the Foundation recognized a need for some regulation, and articulated two core principles: 1) the collection and submission of reports demonstrating that individual foundations satisfied the conditions for nonprofit status, and 2) the preparation of public reports that would allow the general public to be fully informed on the activities of private foundations. In the short run, leaders at the Rockefeller Foundation seemed confident that they were doing the right thing.

As it turned out, Congress was not finished. In the early 1960s, a new crusading congressman emerged to pick up where Cox and Reece had left off. Unlike his predecessors, Congressman Wright Patman, a Texas Democrat, was a populist rather than an anti-communist. He was aware that thousands of new private foundations were being created in the United States, many as a tax dodge for wealthy entrepreneurs who nested ownership of their companies within the tax-free structure of a foundation. As chairman of the House of Representatives Select Committee on Small Business, Patman hoped to do something about the situation.

Patman began what would become a long campaign in the spring of 1961 when he made a speech in the House of Representatives entitled "A Fresh Look at Tax-Exempt Foundations," criticizing the "disproportionately rapid growth" of foundations. Echoing the Reece Committee critique, he warned of "the astounding growth and the power and influence wielded by the giants of the foundation world.... The fact is that the foundations have become a force in our society second only to that of Government itself." He warned Congress that the number of tax-exempt foundations had increased 367 percent between 1952 and 1960—from 12,295 to 45,124—and that many of these foundations were closely integrated with privately held businesses.

Over the next several years, as he sought to build support for his crusade, Patman focused on a number of key issues: foundation influence on corporate activity, speculative investment in the stock markets fueling volatility, the accumulation of income rather than spending it for the public good, engaging in non-charitable activity, competing with for-profit enterprises while enjoying tax advantages based on their nonprofit status, hurting small business by redirecting productive capital, and increasing the tax burden on the public by not paying income taxes.

Although many of Patman's concerns applied to the proliferation of new foundations, the Rockefeller Foundation did not escape his attention. In speeches to the House and to his constituents, Patman reminded audiences that his concerns had deep roots. He quoted senators who had spoken against the Rockefeller Foundation charter bill to bolster his arguments.

After succeeding Dean Rusk as president in 1961—when Rusk was appointed Secretary of State by newly elected President John F. Kennedy—J. George Harrar was forced to respond to Patman's charges. Harrar noted that foundations performed a vital service to the public, and without this work many services would have to be provided by the government. Government would not be as economical, efficient, or impartial as private foundations.

The Rockefeller Foundation also disputed Patman's statistics, pointing out that he had lumped private foundations together with all tax-exempt organizations, including hospitals, welfare organizations, museums, and similar institutions. According to the Foundation Library Center, the actual number of private foundations and trusts appeared to be less than 12,500, and less than half of these institutions had assets worth more than $50,000 or expenditures of more than $10,000. Furthermore, foundation assets represented only a small share of U.S. assets, and their total value, relative to the stock market, was diminishing.

Despite his tendency to exaggerate the facts, however, Patman had identified a significant problem. High tax rates during World War Two and afterwards had fueled a dramatic increase in the formation of private foundations as tax advisors encouraged entrepreneurs to use foundations as a way to prevent the forced sale of their businesses to pay inheritance taxes. Many of these new organizations were family foundations and tightly controlled by a family group. Others were corporate foundations created to receive substantial contributions in profitable years, to be used for corporate giving regardless of the economic cycle. Both of these types of organizations tended to have minimal permanent assets. Instead, the founders took a pay-as-you-go approach, funding the organization with surplus cash that was likely to be heavily taxed or when some charitable need arose that they wanted to contribute to.

Patman's campaign struck a chord with the press. An editorial in the *New York World-Telegram*, for example, bluntly stated: "Tax exemption is the same as a subsidy. Those who do pay taxes have a right to know, in detail, why others don't."

The U.S. Treasury Department, which was responsible for supervising the IRS, responded to Patman's concerns by investigating the situation. Their report, issued in 1965, exonerated most private foundations, but acknowledged that there was evidence of "serious faults" in the system. Treasury recommended to Congress a series of reforms focused mainly on financial abuses, including prohibitions against self-dealing, stronger limits on income accumulation, and restrictions on foundation business activity and financial transactions unrelated to charitable functions.

The House Ways and Means Committee held hearings in 1965 to consider Treasury's proposals. Testimony reflected a continuing ambivalence about the nature of private foundations. Charles L. McClaskey, the president of the National Association of Foundations, objected to Treasury's plan to limit family membership on the board of a family foundation after 25 years. "The right of control is one of the essentials of ownership," McClaskey said. "Thus, any attempted abridgement by law of the retained right of a creator of a private foundation to control and manage it would be…unconstitutional."

This was, of course, not the argument that the creators of the Rockefeller Foundation had offered to Congress in 1910. It hardly reflected the spirit of compromise that characterized their negotiations with the country's elected representatives. And it ignored the basic premise that the assets of a private foundation represented an irrevocable gift by the donor to the foundation. Moreover, a significant portion of those assets included foregone tax revenues held in public trust.

The Decisive Year for Reform

As chairman of the Rockefeller Foundation and as the informal philanthropic leader of his family, John D. Rockefeller 3rd emerged as a major defender of private foundations during this period of attack. He began this defense with a speech in October 1964, saying, "At the outset, let me affirm my personal faith in private philanthropy as a unique feature and a vital strength of American society." Acknowledging the criticisms being leveled against the field, Rockefeller called on philanthropists to be more innovative and to partner with government. He also called for greater collaboration within the foundation world.

Over the next several years, as both President Lyndon Johnson's administration and Congress considered various tax reform proposals, Rockefeller frequently went to Washington to make the case for private philanthropy. But as the administration's wars in Vietnam and on poverty in the United States increased federal spending, the pressure grew to find new sources of federal revenue. To try and resolve many of the issues facing the philanthropic community, John D. Rockefeller 3rd helped form the Commission on Foundations and Private Philanthropy, known as the Peterson Commission, a blue-ribbon committee organized to make policy recommendations regarding the philanthropic sector.

Creation of the Peterson Commission, however, lagged events in the public sector. Following Richard Nixon's inauguration as President in January 1969, the Treasury Department released its Tax Reform Studies and Proposals, a four-volume report developed during the Johnson administration. Shortly thereafter, the House Ways and Means Committee, under chairman Wilbur D. Mills, held hearings on tax-exempt organizations. Wright Patman laid down the gauntlet in his opening testimony, announcing his intention to cure the problem once and for all by introducing a bill "to end tax-exempt status of private foundations."

Action on tax reform stalled during the presidential campaign in 1968. Candidate Richard Nixon (appearing with his wife Pat and New York Governor Nelson Rockefeller) did not focus on tax reform. Shortly after Nixon's inauguration and the beginning of a new session in Congress, momentum began to build for a fundamental revision of the tax laws affecting private foundations. (New York State Archives.)

The House Bill Emerges

By the late 1960s, the critique of private foundations had expanded beyond the realm of taxes. As political activism increased in the 1960s, foundations, including the Rockefeller Foundation, had become more deeply involved with government, raising issues related to the free speech rights of charitable organizations. The Carnegie Corporation, for example, had funded a massive lobbying effort—criticized by some in Congress—in support of the legislative program of the National Urban Coalition. The Sierra Club had been forced to change its tax status from 501(c)(3) (tax-exempt) to 501(c)(4) (still non-profit, but allowed to use less than half of its resources for political activity) because of its legislative activities. Meanwhile, the Ford Foundation, the Rockefeller Foundation, and others had supported efforts to register African Americans to vote. To some congressmen, especially those who opposed civil rights, this kind of political activity was an anathema. To others, it reflected a basic right to free speech.

Scheduled to testify with other major foundation leaders in mid-February, George Harrar confessed to the Foundation's staff that he was worried. The public seemed deeply divided on the proper role for private foundations in the arena of advocacy, concerned that foundations were "either too much or not enough involved in action for social change." Harrar asked staff members to think about this issue so that the Foundation could

McGeorge Bundy, president of the Ford Foundation during the hearings related to the Tax Reform Act of 1969, had served as National Security Advisor to Presidents Kennedy and Johnson. Bundy was a key figure in battles with Congress over the role of private foundations. (Yoichi Okamoto. LBJ Presidential Library.)

see its way forward. Meanwhile, he and John D. Rockefeller 3rd were working with other major philanthropic organizations to explore self-regulatory concepts that would allow the philanthropic sector to police itself or have state governments monitor foundations rather than have the federal government establish a separate agency to do the job.

On the day of his testimony, Harrar and other major foundation leaders expressed general support for efforts to curb abuses of the tax code. They also supported the idea of transparency and requiring foundations to issue annual reports. But questions from members of the House Ways and Means Committee underscored their continuing concern, especially following the testimony of Ford Foundation president McGeorge Bundy, a lightning rod for political controversy. Bundy had served as National Security Advisor to Presidents Kennedy and Johnson before becoming president of the Ford Foundation in 1966. Brilliant and outspoken, he antagonized some of the Committee members as they questioned him about the Ford Foundation's ownership of company stock, as well as what historian Eleanor Brilliant calls "its politically suspect grantmaking."

The questions to all of the foundation leaders reflected a remarkable transformation that had taken place during the postwar years in the role of government and its relationship to philanthropy, as government became more involved with social welfare and undertook a huge expansion in its support for basic research. A number of Committee members suggested that philanthropy's day had come and gone. Moreover, given the burden imposed on ordinary citizens who were paying for this expansion, the idea that pools of money might go untaxed and undirected by the people's representatives seemed to some congressmen grossly unfair.

Harrar tried to respond to this critique, highlighting the fact that philanthropy still bet on riskier ideas. He also noted philanthropy's greater ability to be flexible and to meet the needs of local situations. But he clearly had no desire or even ability to speak for the field. The Rockefeller Foundation had little or no contact with the thousands of smaller, more local foundations that were proliferating around the country.

In the end, Harrar felt that he and the leaders of the other major private foundations had not mounted a strong enough defense before the Ways and Means Committee. As historian Eleanor Brilliant says, the hearings seemed to make it clear to Congress and the public that private foundations were not like other public charities and that they were "worthy of suspicion."

Indeed, foundation leaders were disappointed when, at the end of May, the Committee tentatively approved three proposals. The first would prohibit private foundations from engaging in activities intended to influence the outcome of an election or the decision of any governmental body. The second would bar private foundations from making grants to individuals for travel, study, or similar purposes. And the third would impose a tax on the net investment income of foundations.

The bill that ultimately came to the floor of the House—HR 13270, otherwise known as the Tax Reform Act of 1969—was indeed tough on private foundations. It sought to eliminate self-dealing between them and their largest contributors. If a foundation was a major owner of a business, it would be required to divest its equity in the business over a ten-year period to eliminate its control. The bill banned grassroots lobbying and other activities designed to influence legislation, while grants to individuals would be restricted unless they were made by some objective and nondiscriminatory procedure. The House bill also proposed a seven-and-a-half-percent tax on investment income, including capital gains. This tax, combined with the payout requirement, would effectively limit the life of a private foundation, forcing it to spend itself out of existence.

HR 13270 was deeply troubling to private foundation leaders. Although the Nixon administration lobbied to reduce the tax to two percent—arguing that the government, having granted tax-exempt status, shouldn't capriciously come back and tax the income of charitable organizations—the administration supported the measure. It suggested that a two-percent tax was reasonable since it would help pay for the cost of auditing private foundations.

Clearly, as the bill went to the Senate, leaders of the nation's largest private foundations feared they were losing in the court of public opinion. The public and Congress were willing to support charitable organizations that provided direct services, but they increasingly distrusted institutions with great wealth and no visible operations.

After World War Two, public funding for medical research increased dramatically, leading some in Congress to wonder about philanthropy's continuing role in the field. The newly created National Institutes of Health (NIH) took the lead in public funding for health sciences. At the Rocky Mountain Laboratories, a part of NIH, the government took over the production of yellow fever vaccine, which had been discovered by Rockefeller Foundation scientists before the war. (U.S. National Library of Medicine.)

In the Senate, a Second Chance

When the Tax Reform Act of 1969 moved to the Senate in the fall, leaders in the foundation community tried to coordinate their testimony and present a unified front. They continued to oppose a tax on foundations and talked about philanthropy's role in relieving the taxpayer, of "the burdens of government." Supporters of the tax constructed the issue on the basis of equity—every sector of society should contribute to funding the government, they said. These terms of

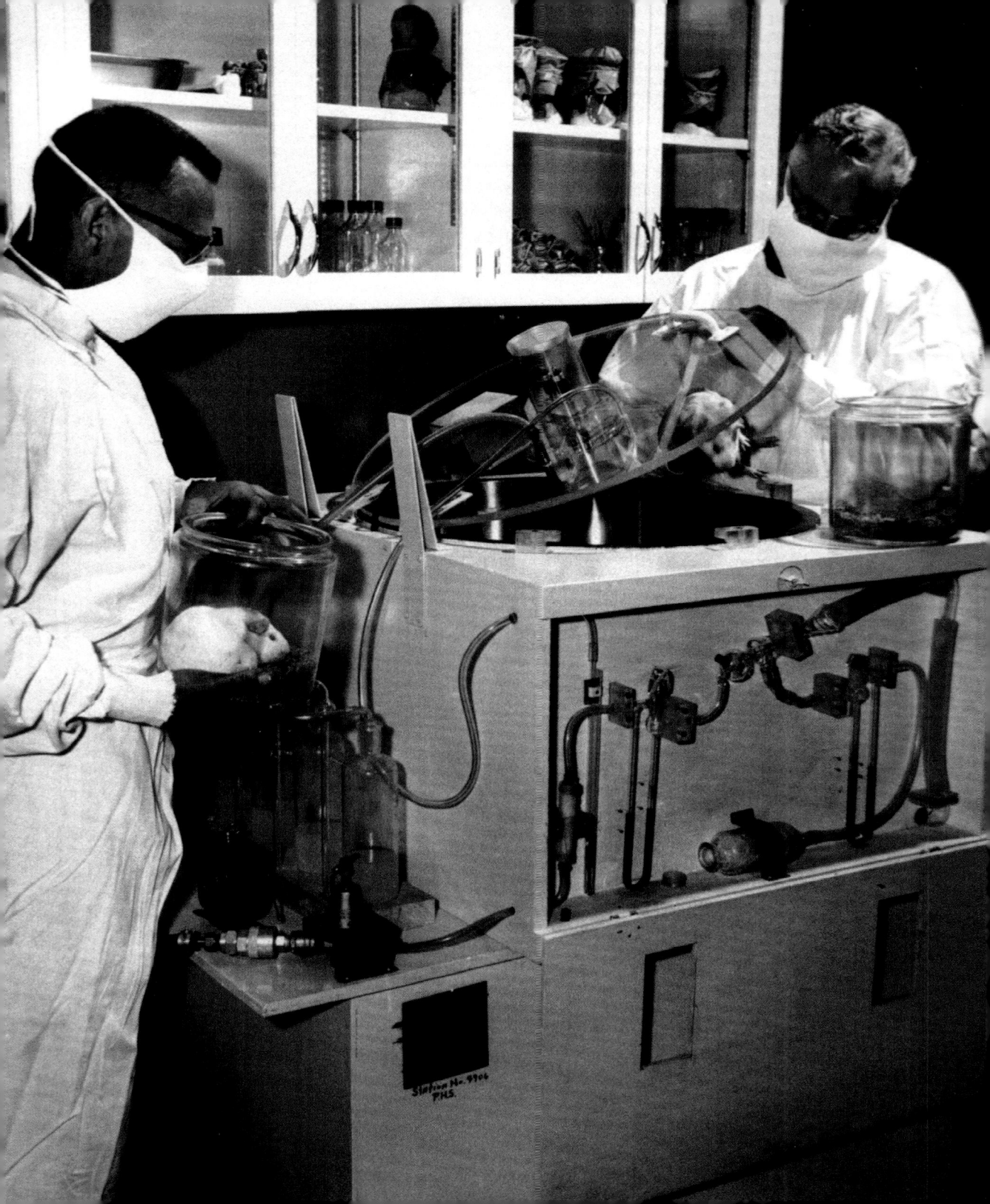

debate shifted the traditional arguments against taxation, which focused more on the work that charitable institutions did to create a better society—not simply by easing the burdens of government, but by cultivating morals (churches and schools) and civil society.

The foundations acknowledged that government did operate in many of the arenas occupied by philanthropy, but, according to the Council on Foundations, "We submit that this co-existence vitalizes and strengthens the democratic process." As David Freeman, the president of the Council on Foundations, noted: "When the people, speaking through Congress or at other levels of government, vote to carry forward foundation-sponsored initiatives, as in the case of the Salk vaccine or the Head Start program, the public has exercised ultimate judgment over foundation programs."

By the fall, the issue was moving forward with more speed. Freeman, Harrar, and Alan Pifer, head of the Carnegie Corporation, testified together before the Senate Finance Committee in September. In their statements, the witnesses raised the stakes. The philanthropic leaders expressed their strong opposition to the proposed seven-and-a-half-percent tax on foundation income, suggesting that Congress's decision on the matter would go to "the very nature of the American system" and set a terrible precedent for the tax-exempt status of nonprofit organizations. As they pointed out, tax exemption was "part of a centuries old tradition under which charitable organizations have been granted special privileges by the state because they relieve it of responsibilities it would otherwise have to meet with public funds." With regard to the income tax, this exemption went back to the creation of the tax in 1913.

Rockefeller, Carnegie, and the Council on Foundations suggested that the proposed tax on foundation income would lead to taxes on other charitable organizations by the federal government, as well as by agencies of state and local government. For this reason, they asserted, "It is pluralism that is really at stake in the decision on the tax and we believe it should be debated on these terms." Furthermore, they claimed, "the House bill signals the beginning of the end of private philanthropy." From their point of view, the bill represented "a highly dangerous first step on the road toward the total disappearance from our national life of the traditional income tax exemption enjoyed by charitable organizations. Such an eventuality would of course greatly weaken the private non-profit sector and diminish the role it plays in our society in favor of further accretion of the power of government."

The foundations insisted that with government moving increasingly into the field of social welfare, the work of private foundations became more necessary rather than less. Foundations could work more rapidly and operate more flexibly than government, while foundation-sponsored demonstrations of the need for and feasibility of undertakings in the public interest offered a logical precursor to the allocation of substantial government funds for new programs.

The foundations also asserted that they were clearly more efficient than government. If the Carnegie Corporation had been subject to a seven-and-a-half-percent tax on income, for example, "some $40 million of private support would by now have been denied to a host of worthy institutions and talented individuals." Ignoring the idea that government might have provided valuable services with that $40 million, the foundation leaders asserted: "The nation at large would have been the ultimate loser." For its part, the Rockefeller Foundation estimated that going forward with the tax would diminish its grantmaking by more than $3 million a year.

The foundations dismissed the idea that asking private foundations to pay taxes on their income was an equalization of the burden of taxation across all sectors of society. The proposed tax would not apply to all tax-exempt organizations—only private foundations—and the potential revenue was trivial in terms of the overall federal budget. According to the witnesses, "The tax is a punitive measure—not tax reform." The foundations were not insensitive, however, to the call for greater oversight or the need to find revenues to cover the cost of regulation. They recommended a "supervisory fee" to pay for monitoring private foundations.

Harrar and his associates also explained the role of private foundations within the pluralistic nonprofit sector. In 1968, personal charitable contributions in the United States totaled an estimated $16 billion. Private foundations accounted for only nine percent of this total. Because they were "organized and professionally staffed . . . flexible and can supply continuity of effort, and because they can provide critical masses of money when problems require them, foundations are the advance scouts of philanthropy."

As the end of 1969 approached, it became clear that Congress would act and that the Ways and Means Committee bill would provide the basic framework for legislation. Foundation leaders expressed frustration. At a New York City Bar Association forum, McGeorge Bundy, the head of the Ford Foundation, appeared on a panel focused on private foundations. He blamed the foundation community for failing to take the initiative in 1965—after the Treasury Department had submitted its original proposals—and for generally doing a poor job of reporting and explaining their activities.

Bundy had caused quite a stir, however, when he appeared before the Ways and Means Committee. Ford Foundation grants to former members of Robert Kennedy's staff had fueled the Committee's desire to curtail grants to individuals. A Ford grant to the Congress of Racial Equality for voter registration in African-American neighborhoods in Cleveland would prompt language that restricted grants for voter registration activities. In his defense of these grants, Bundy had been less than conciliatory. Moreover, by the fall of 1969, the weight of evidence indicating examples of foundation abuse, along with the massive publicity generated by Wright Patman's years of investigations and reports, suggested that Congress would have to act.

The Rockefeller and Ford Foundations and the Carnegie Corporation came together in November to make one last effort to shape the final bill. In the end, there were two key provisions that they hoped to change: the 40-year limit on the life of a private foundation (introduced by Senator Albert Gore Sr. of Tennessee) and the amount of the tax on investment income. Meeting at the Carnegie Corporation on November 6, they were confident that the 40-year limit would be killed when the bill was debated on the Senate floor. But they were nervous that if the issue came to a roll call vote and they lost, the issue could not be salvaged in the conference committee between the Senate and the House. In the middle of the meeting, Bundy learned that Wilbur Mills was against the 40-year limit and would kill the plan in the conference committee as long as the foundations didn't shoot themselves in the foot by forcing a roll call vote, which might go against them, in the Senate.

Minnesota Senator Walter Mondale played a key role in defeating a proposed amendment to the Tax Reform Act that would have limited the life of a private foundation to 40 years. (Warren K. Leffler. Library of Congress.)

When the bill came to the floor of the Senate, Walter Mondale, a Democrat from Minnesota, spoke on behalf of the foundations. The debate was broad and lively, but in the end Gore's proposal was defeated. Other provisions that had concerned the foundations were also not included in the final bill. The so-called "audit fee" was reduced to four percent. The required annual payout was set at six percent (later reduced). The law also barred foundations from owning more than 20 percent of the stock of a single business. Nevertheless, as attorney Thomas Troyer has written, "Even at the high-water mark of Congressional displeasure with foundations, Congress decided that private foundations should remain a functioning part of American society, without a federally mandated restriction on the duration of their lives or their fundamental tax benefits."

Legacies

The Rockefeller Foundation, like most of the other major private foundations in the country, was disappointed with the Tax Reform Act of 1969. Writing in the Foundation's annual report, J. George Harrar noted, "The new law does essentially nothing to help foundations perform their function better." He pointed out that "It certainly makes the work of private philanthropy—which has been of such enormous value to so many people for so many years—a more difficult task, and subjects private foundations to discriminatory taxation." Nevertheless, he expressed his hope that the new law "may help to prevent the kind of abuses of the tax-exemption privilege which have occasionally been identified."

If it did nothing else, the Tax Reform Act of 1969 helped to restore Congressional confidence that the great private wealth held by private foundations would indeed be used for charitable purposes. It also brought to the forefront the debate over the role of philanthropy in a new era in the nation's history, an era in which the federal government played a large part in the day-to-day business of the nation. As John Knowles, Harrar's successor as president of the Rockefeller Foundation in the 1970s, pointed out, the expansion of what he called "liberal ideology" suggested a major role for a "beneficent State" in social arenas ranging from education to health, welfare, civil rights, housing, transportation, urban renewal, the environment, population control, and economic development, as well as the arts and humanities. With this expansion, philanthropy had to redefine or at least reassess its role and function in society. It had to be more accountable to the public. Knowles's successor, Richard W. Lyman, writing in 1987, reaffirmed the Foundation's commitment to winning and keeping the public's trust. "We have a duty to provide the information that makes it possible for citizens to judge how well we have fulfilled the mandate that entitles us to tax exemption."

In the decades that followed the Tax Reform Act of 1969, the Rockefeller Foundation sought to continue the relationship with government that George Harrar had described to the Ways and Means Committee, a relationship that cast the Foundation in the role of innovator and social entrepreneur, testing ideas and programs to find solutions for the country's abiding challenges. And at this time in the nation's history, few problems seemed more enduring or more troubling to the American dream than the problem of race and the lack of equal opportunity.

CASE STUDIES IN INNOVATION

Southern Regional Council

In 1960, only three out of ten African-American adults in the South were registered to vote. Discriminatory laws, poll taxes, and violent threats kept many from exercising this basic right. For years the National Association for the Advancement of Colored People (NAACP) had fought to overturn discriminatory laws and uphold the right of African-American citizens to vote. Gradually, black registrations had increased from 3 percent in 1940 to nearly 30 percent in 1960. But as the civil rights movement gained momentum in the late 1950s, leaders in the black community, officials in the Kennedy administration, and a handful of private foundations sought to do more.

For all of these would-be champions of the black vote in 1960, there were enormous political and personal risks. The Kennedy administration worried about alienating white Democratic voters in the South if federal authority was used to force state and local officials to accept black registrations. Meanwhile, volunteers engaged in voter-registration

After the Rockefeller Foundation committed general support to the Southern Regional Council in 1961, the Council was able to launch a massive Voter Education Project in the American South. John Lewis served as one of the directors of the project. (Boyd Lewis. Kenan Research Center. Atlanta History Center.)

campaigns were frequently harassed, arrested, jailed, beaten, and even murdered. For private foundations, the risks were less grave, but they were existential.

Federal law barred tax-exempt organizations from engaging in political activity on behalf of individual candidates, and the Rockefeller Foundation's experience with the Cox and Reece hearings in the House of Representatives made it clear that Congress was watching.

With project support from a handful of private foundations, the Southern Regional Council provided grants to various organizations to launch voter registration drives, including the National Urban League, the Southern Christian Leadership Conference, the Student Nonviolent Coordinating Committee, the NAACP and CORE. (Boyd Lewis. Kenan Research Center. Atlanta History Center.)

Providing funding to non-partisan, non-profit voter registration initiatives was clearly allowed, but in the highly charged political environment of the South in the civil rights era, it would be seen by many, especially those who opposed integration, as political activity.

The Atlanta-based Southern Regional Council (SRC), which had been created in 1944 to promote interracial dialogue and a gradual transition to full equality for African Americans, had developed a number of voter-education programs aimed at black voters. As part of a major fundraising initiative to expand the council's program, the SRC's executive director, Harold Fleming, went to New York in 1960 to ask the Rockefeller Foundation for support. Fleming and Foundation President Dean Rusk had much in common. Both had spent much of their childhood in rural Georgia. During World War Two, each had been affected by the dissonance between the abiding racist attitudes that permeated their nation and the democratic ideals espoused by the United States and its allies. Rusk had been an Army senior staff official in Asia; Fleming was a captain, a white officer leading an all-African-American company of soldiers. Rusk felt that segregation and discrimination undermined American credibility abroad. Fleming believed that it profoundly retarded the social and economic development of the South and perpetuated an unjust society.

CASE STUDIES IN INNOVATION

In 1960 the Rockefeller Foundation did not have a program that would encompass civil rights. Rusk had asked the Division of Social Sciences to explore options that would allow the Foundation to make a difference in the "race relations questions currently tormenting the South, embarrassing the nation, and agitating world relations." But when Harold Fleming and the SRC submitted a formal grant request later that year, the Foundation hesitated. As Leland DeVinney wrote, the grant, if made, "would involve a substantial departure from present program in The Rockefeller Foundation. Nevertheless, in view of the importance of the problems with which the Council is concerned, the officers are disposed to give careful consideration to the possibility of a special recommendation to our Trustees."

Meanwhile, the SRC sent President-elect John F. Kennedy a report entitled "The Federal Executive and Civil Rights." It outlined an activist

The Voter Education Project became an independent nonprofit in 1972. By 1978, the black electorate in the South had grown from 1.5 million registered voters to nearly 4 million. At the same time, the number of African-American elected officials had risen from 50 to 2,100. (Boyd Lewis. Kenan Research Center. Atlanta History Center.)

role for the federal government in the emerging battle over integration, particularly with regard to the Justice Department's authority to defend voting rights. Kennedy's brother Robert—who would become Attorney General—was interested in the report and hoped to forge an alliance with civil rights groups in support of voter registration as an alternative to the movement's increasingly confrontational tactics related to segregation.

As the Foundation staff did its homework on the SRC, Leland DeVinney traveled to Atlanta to meet with newspaper editors, civic leaders, and academics. He was cautioned that integration would have to evolve gradually and that any institution associated with accelerating the process would face a backlash from segregationists at a time when tensions were rising in the South.

Despite the advice from these more cautious voices, the Rockefeller Foundation's trustees awarded the SRC a five-year grant of $250,000 to support its efforts to promote racial integration. The grant provided a crucial financial base for the SRC at a critical moment in the history of the civil rights movement. A month later, as Freedom Riders testing the enforcement of the Supreme Court's ban on segregated seating in interstate bus travel were beaten and jailed, tensions in the South were heightened and conflicts over strategy increased between various civil rights groups.

In the midst of these events, the Southern Regional Council, with the Rockefeller Foundation's base support as well as funding from the Taconic and Field Foundations, organized the Voter Education Project to empower African-American citizens at the ballot box. Launched in 1962, the project involved nearly all of the major civil rights organizations in the South. Over the next two years, it registered more than 325,000 black voters, contributing to an overall increase of nearly 1,750,000 black voters in the South. To support the project, the SRC was able to raise $890,000 from foundations and private donors. According to a later report by the Ford Foundation, the result was achieved economically and without incident. Throughout the campaign "the name of the Southern Regional Council never even appeared in the newspapers."

The impact of these new registrations in the South was significant. In the fall of 1966, the black vote played a key role in one Senate race, one or two gubernatorial contests, and at least two House races. Twenty African Americans were elected to state legislatures in the South, increasing the total by nine. Just as important, African Americans were elected to county-level posts in Georgia, Louisiana, Alabama, and Mississippi.

REYNOLDS COTTAGE   MacVICAR HOSPITAL   ROCKEFELLER HALL

SPELMAN SEMINARY
FOU

ATLANTA. GEORGIA
1881

CHAPTER VI

EQUAL OPPORTUNITY FOR ALL

In the spring of 1901, John D. Rockefeller Jr. and 50 other northern philanthropists boarded a train in New York for a tour of the American South. The trip had been organized by Philadelphia merchant Robert C. Ogden. "For years Ogden had dreamed of the possibility of building up the educational facilities of the Negroes in the southern states," Raymond Fosdick explained in his biography of Rockefeller Jr. The travelers were particularly interested in the condition of black higher education and its precarious accommodation with the rigid laws of southern segregation.

The Great Migration of African Americans to the cities of the North had barely begun, and the businessmen on Ogden's train shared a belief that the South, home to eight million African Americans, had been left behind by America's industrialization and economic development. The legacies of slavery and institutional segregation had strangled southern economic development in its infancy, creating a permanent underclass of blacks and poor whites.

Southern reporters disparaged the train as the "Millionaire's Special," loaded with wealthy, paternalistic northern whites who did not understand southern culture, and whose own attitudes of racial superiority were only thinly veiled. But even at the age of 27, Rockefeller Jr. brought an understanding of the complex problems facing the South that set him apart. "The younger Rockefeller shared with his father and mother, as well as with his Spelman grandparents, a deep and abiding interest in the education and welfare of the Negro race," Fosdick wrote. "Although he was born nine years after Lincoln's

The founders of Spelman Seminary (renamed Spelman College in 1924) rejected advice that they should prepare African-American women for menial jobs in the southern economy. Their goal was to build the best liberal arts college in the South, with classes in the natural sciences, political economy, literature, Latin, and moral philosophy as well as home economics, nursing, and teacher-training. (Rockefeller Archive Center.)

death, the younger Rockefeller was reared in an atmosphere that still reverberated to the song of 'John Brown's Body.' No influence in his life was more pervasive or lasting."

At centers for African-American education, Rockefeller re-engaged his family's history. He visited Hampton Normal and Agricultural Institute in Virginia, Spelman College (then called Spelman Seminary) at Atlanta University, and Tuskegee Normal and Industrial Institute in the heart of the Black Belt of Alabama. These were the bright lights of African-American higher education, and the Rockefeller family had a long history with each of them.

The family commitment to racial justice traced its roots to the Spelman home in Ohio, where runaway slaves found refuge on the Underground Railroad before the Civil War. It was deepened by the family's Baptist faith. Unafraid of breaching the color bar, John D. Rockefeller Sr. loved attending small African-American churches during his business trips to the South, and found inspiration in gospel hymns.

In 1882, Rockefeller Sr. began investing in a Baptist seminary for African-American women in Atlanta that operated out of a leaky basement with barely enough money to survive week to week. By 1900 the family had expanded the campus land base and built half a dozen new buildings,

Democracy & Philanthropy

including a new hospital, two dormitories, a power plant, dining hall, and kitchen. Rockefeller Sr. had also contributed to Morehouse College (then known as Atlanta Baptist Seminary) in Atlanta in 1886, and through the Baptist Home Mission Society he channeled numerous other contributions to leading institutions of black education. Following the end of Reconstruction in the South, as segregationists consolidated their control of government, these institutions represented what historian Eric Foner has called "the seeds of educational progress," which could not be entirely uprooted by the collapse of Reconstruction.

Junior had his own personal experiences that tied him to family traditions. With his parents' encouragement, he had corresponded with a pen pal at Hampton Institute—a student whose scholarship had been paid for by the family. In 1884, when he was ten, his parents took him by train to Atlanta to celebrate the third anniversary of the Atlanta Baptist Female Seminary. During the ceremonies, the school was named Spelman Seminary in honor of his mother's family (it would be renamed Spelman College in 1924). Returning to

Eight million African Americans lived in the South at the turn of the century, where they remained the backbone of the agricultural economy. Most were poor and landless, with no formal education. When many of them joined the Great Migration to industrial jobs in the North, reformers looked for ways to create more opportunity for African Americans in the South. (William Henry Jackson. Library of Congress.)

Spelman during his 1901 train tour, Junior spoke to the students and, like his father before him, enjoyed the gospel music of the college chorus. The entire tour was a key moment in Junior's professional development. He described the tour as "the most instructive experience of my life."

Though still in his 20s, Junior was already a close counselor to his father, and he was poised to play an increasing role in the family's philanthropic endeavors. His generation would inherit the responsibility of unraveling the nation's most complicated problems of race and development. "For several years the question of colored education has been much in our minds and in our thoughts." Rockefeller told Ogden, the Philadelphia merchant. "We have endeavored to arrive at some plan which might help in working out this great question."

The status of primary and secondary education in the South was far behind that in the North, especially for African Americans. Only 4.6 percent of the American population was illiterate, but in the South, 12 percent of whites and 50 percent of blacks couldn't read. Everywhere the philanthropists looked, education, public health, and economic development were exponentially worse in African-American neighborhoods than in even the poorest white communities. For almost 40 years, since the end of slavery, African-American leaders had aspired to create systems of independent, self-sustaining secondary education for black communities, only to have their efforts suppressed by local white governments and business leaders.

On the trip back to New York, the conversation among the philanthropists was galvanized by the idea of establishing an organization to coordinate and fund African-American education in the South. Even before the trip, Rockefeller Jr. had been thinking about the creation of a Negro education board. But in Virginia, after Henry St. George Tucker, the president of Washington and Lee University, boarded the train, he turned the conversation on its head: "If it is your idea to educate the Negro you must have the white of the South with you. If the poor white sees the son of a Negro neighbor enjoying through your munificence benefits denied to his boy, it raises in him a feeling that will render futile all your work. You must lift up the 'poor white' and the Negro together if you would ever approach success."

No one recorded Rockefeller's reaction to Tucker's comments, but according to a reporter for the *New York World*, the applause from the other men in the group "drowned even the noise of the train." A subtle threshold had been crossed. The view that slavery, the black codes, and the enforced segregation of the Jim Crow South had created a special circumstance requiring special attention to the educational, economic, social, and legal condition of America's African-American population was replaced by the view, widely held among southern leaders, that philanthropic efforts should benefit

BOOKER WASHINGTON AND SOME OF HIS DISTINGUISHED GUESTS.
From left to right, George T. McAneny, Robert C. Ogden, J. G. Phelps Stokes, Booker T. Washington, Dr. Lyman Abbott, President H. B. Frissell of Hampton Institute, and President Charles W Eliot of Harvard.

(From Stereograph, Copyright, 1906, by Underwood & Underwood, New York.)

both whites and blacks, who were segregated by law and custom, and that northern philanthropists should coordinate their work through the public institutions that enforced southern segregation.

In the year that followed the "Millionaire's Special," John D. Rockefeller Jr. and his father struggled to find the right balance between the desire to assist the education of African Americans in the South, rooted in their own family history, and the practical limits of working within segregated communities.

Rockefeller Sr. committed $1 million to the new project, to be known as the General Education Board (GEB). The first of the great Rockefeller philanthropies, the GEB received a federal charter in January 1903. Its charter, echoing themes of American pluralism that would play a critical

Booker T. Washington (center) had tremendous influence on the northern philanthropists. He encouraged philanthropists to help create economic opportunities in African-American communities in the South and to invest in education. (Library of Congress.)

role in the history of the Rockefeller Foundation, was the "promotion of education within the United States without distinction of race, sex or creed."

The GEB built high schools, funded the endowments of African-American colleges, and organized farm demonstration programs to increase the productivity of small southern farms. Meanwhile, the GEB's sister organization, the Rockefeller Sanitary Commission for the Eradication of Hookworm Disease (later absorbed by the Rockefeller Foundation), organized public health initiatives like the hookworm campaign in the South. In all of these efforts, the GEB's leaders sought to address the well-being of the most impoverished and disenfranchised people in the region, especially African Americans. But because their efforts were constrained by the segregationist policies that permeated the South, funds flowed overwhelmingly to white communities. Foundation President Raymond Fosdick later offered a painful assessment of the GEB's experience. "And so, for the first decade of its existence, the philanthropy which originally was to have been called the Negro Education Board did relatively little for the children to whom nature had given darker skins."

In their effort to avoid a confrontation with southern leaders that might make it impossible to work in the South at all, the leaders of the General Education Board accommodated laws that denied equal opportunities to African Americans and opposed black demands for the vote and for civil rights. Under the auspices of the GEB, black higher education focused on literacy, Christian morals, and vocational education. As progressive as the Rockefeller family had been in its own history, the philanthropic institutions that Rockefeller's agents built at the turn of the twentieth century were no match for the deep roots of segregation and white supremacy.

The General Education Board continued its work for half a century. After the creation of the Rockefeller Foundation in 1913, several trustees of the GEB served on the Foundation's board as well. The two entities shared offices and administrative staff. Grantmaking, especially to educational institutions, was often coordinated. During these years, the GEB served as the principal Rockefeller philanthropy dealing with race and equal opportunity.

The frustrating experience with segregation, however, diminished the Foundation's efforts to solve a seemingly intractable social problem. This frustration was compounded by disappointments in other social arenas, such as labor and municipal government. There were occasional efforts to return to the problem. In December 1927, for example, the Rockefeller Foundation and the Laura Spelman Rockefeller Memorial organized a conference on black and white relations at Yale. Attendees included Will Alexander of the Atlanta-based Commission on Interracial Cooperation;

Charles S. Johnson of the National Urban League; the directors of both the National Urban League and the National Association for the Advancement of Colored People (NAACP); and the presidents of four historically black colleges. Several church organizations were also represented, as well as business, labor, medicine, and the YMCA. But increasingly in the 1920s and 1930s, the Foundation turned away from volatile social issues to focus on public health, medicine, and basic research.

Despite Fosdick's disappointment in the GEB experience with race, the philanthropic investments in this era did produce a social return. Through the 1920s and 1930s, against overwhelming odds, African Americans organized to assert their rights to equal opportunity and social justice. Leaders of the NAACP, founded in 1909, challenged the constitutionality of segregationist laws, fought for integration in the armed forces, and promoted expanded opportunities for African Americans. Many of the leaders in the burgeoning civil rights movement were associated as students or teachers with the African-American colleges that had been supported by the GEB. Martin Luther King Jr.'s parents, for example, met at Spelman College in 1920, and King himself graduated from Morehouse College in 1948. Also trained at these schools were leaders from the Southern Christian Leadership Conference, including Ralph Abernathy, Wyatt Tee Walker, and Julian Bond. These graduates of all-black colleges would help bring the nation and the Rockefeller Foundation back to the issue of equal opportunity after World War Two.

African Americans did not escape segregation when they migrated north, even within New Deal programs. The Works Progress Administration (WPA) built hundreds of community swimming pools and invited children of all ages to "Learn to Swim." Many of these pools were segregated. (John Wagner. Library of Congress.)

The Revival of Equal Opportunity

Dean Rusk was a poor Georgia farm boy, a child of the segregated South. But a liberal education, a career in the State Department, and world travel had broadened his social views. By the time he was appointed president of the Rockefeller Foundation in 1952, Rusk was a social liberal and internationalist with an interest in the emerging nationalism of the old colonial world of Africa and Asia.

Rusk had a habit of prodding Leland DeVinney, a program officer in the Foundation's Division of Social Sciences, about developing a program that addressed the subject of American racism. "Rusk was hearing worrisome reports from former associates in the State Department about the treatment to which African diplomats were being subjected in segregated Washington: nasty incidents in restaurants, theaters, and clubs," DeVinney told Elizabeth Romney, who wrote a history of the Foundation's equal opportunity

programs. As DeVinney described it, "The United States…was becoming thought of as backward on the race question in the eyes of the rest of the world."

Rusk was pushing the Foundation to engage the world as it was, to engage problems in the real world, but DeVinney was a product of the Foundation's culture of basic scientific research and scholarship. DeVinney explained to Romney that he could not see how the Foundation might engage "so large, untenable, and unmanageable" a problem. He agreed with Rusk that "the situation was 'a blatant violation of everything we stood for' as a nation, yet in terms of advanced research in the social sciences, I could not think what to do about it." A decade later DeVinney would have to confront this challenge when he was named director of the Foundation's new Equal Opportunity program.

Leland C. DeVinney was a surprising choice to lead the Equal Opportunity program. Trained in sociology at the University of Chicago, he had joined the Social Science Division of the Foundation in 1948 with a deep commitment to scientific method and advanced scholarship, rather than advocacy. But he became a strong advocate for the new initiative. (Rockefeller Archive Center.)

For several years after the U.S. Supreme Court's landmark 1954 decision in *Brown v. Board of Education*, it was unclear how Rusk intended to take the initiative on race relations. In 1960 he proposed that the Foundation give a grant to the politically active Southern Regional Council (SRC). It was a bold recommendation. The SRC reflected a revival of the network of inter-racial committees that had grown up in the South in the two decades before World War Two to promote racial cooperation. The GEB, whose operations were now being funded to a large extent by the Rockefeller Foundation, had supported the SRC between 1942 and 1949 with a small $51,000 grant. Rusk was recommending that the Foundation double down.

The reputation of the Southern Regional Council was controversial in the South. It was made up of black civil rights activists, white liberals, academics, and southern business leaders who recognized that the South's economic development continued to lag far behind the rest of the nation. But the southern establishment viewed the Council as a threat to segregation.

Before Rusk could take his proposal to the trustees, John F. Kennedy was elected President, and Rusk was nominated to be the new Secretary of State. J. George Harrar succeeded Rusk as president of the Rockefeller Foundation. Having spent most of the 1950s in Mexico, launching the Foundation's agricultural program, Harrar was, by temperament and organizational style, a man of action. He was a scientist who advocated scientific research, but he was also an activist who promoted direct engagement with the world's problems.

Harrar pushed Rusk's proposal onto the trustees' agenda, and began a rapid, dramatic pivot away from the constraints that the GEB had toiled under for so long. Harrar was "well aware," Elizabeth Romney asserted, "that with this proposed grant the Foundation was stepping out of its normal role of supporting research and education, and getting into the much more complicated business of support to action programs." Indeed, Harrar's support for the Southern Regional Council challenged a core principle of the Foundation's first generation—to avoid political activism or advocacy, and to work with, not against, local government authorities. But it also reflected a core value that championed pluralism in the United States.

Presenting the application to the trustees in April 1961, the Foundation's officers noted the special circumstances surrounding the grant and the break in precedent that it reflected: "The Foundation does not as a matter of policy undertake support for an organization devoted to promoting social reform. The officers are convinced that this is a wise rule. The question is raised, however, whether the unique

For most of its history the Southern Regional Council (SRC) avoided a direct confrontation with segregation laws. After the Council publicly announced its opposition to segregation in 1949, most of the organization's white Southern moderates withdrew. With Rockefeller Foundation support, the SRC focused on educating and registering African-American voters in the early 1960s. (Dorothea Lange. Library of Congress)

Democracy & Philanthropy

character and special urgency of problems in race relations in the United States, in their bearing on world relations, are not sufficient to justify an exception to policy in this instance."

The trustees agreed. In approving the grant they specifically noted that race relations in the South remained a "unique" and "special" circumstance, and that the Foundation was adopting an innovative strategy that embraced a greater degree of activism. To be sure, they remained cautious. Rather than offer a single grant, they divided the funding into more modest annual grants of $50,000 over five years, with the stipulation that the funding could be revoked if the programs of the Southern Regional Council became too controversial. In fact, efforts by the SRC and the Kennedy administration to steer the civil rights movement into the arenas of voter education and voting rights were soon overwhelmed by the increasingly confrontational strategies of the leaders of the movement who favored sit-ins and direct action as a way to draw the nation's attention to the injustices of segregation. Shadowed by Congress's investigations of foundation activities that had been deemed political, the Rockefeller Foundation and other major private foundations moved cautiously.

George Harrar, however, agreed with the leaders of the civil rights movement that African Americans could realize their full potential only if they had "full civil rights, equal educational opportunities, and the chance to utilize their abilities." Indeed, after 50 years in existence the Foundation crossed back over the threshold in 1963, determined to engage the American problem of race relations and civil rights. That year, with plans in motion to end grantmaking by the General Education Board, the trustees established a new programmatic focus on Equal Opportunity, one of five new areas of concentration.

Despite Harrar's idealism, the trustees were by no means confident in their first steps. The intransigence of the South and the struggles and compromises of the GEB had had a deep impact. By this time, John D. Rockefeller Jr. had passed away. His son, John D. Rockefeller 3rd, who had become chairman of the Rockefeller Foundation in 1952, was among those who were cautious about committing the Foundation to a seemingly intractable social problem.

Education and the Path to Opportunity

Under Harrar's leadership, the first initiative of the Equal Opportunity program was to focus on what the Foundation did best. "Because so much of its long experience lies in education," Harrar wrote in his 1963 President's Review, "The Foundation ... has chosen to help stimulate greater educational opportunity for the disadvantaged citizens of this country." The program rested on a three-legged stool. First, it created a scholarship program for talented young African-American students specifically designed to assist the desegregation of four private universities in the South. Second, the Foundation offered grants to three prestigious white colleges to host summer enrichment programs to prepare talented black high school graduates for college life. And third, the Foundation provided continuing support for America's black colleges. From the start, there was a recognition that the lack of opportunity in the United States took many forms. "The position of the Negro, however, is not and has never been the same as that of others," Harrar wrote in 1963. That reality imposed immediate complications with deep historical roots.

The four universities selected to participate in the scholarship program were Emory in Atlanta, Georgia; Tulane in New Orleans, Louisiana; Duke in Durham, North Carolina; and Vanderbilt in Nashville, Tennessee. The Foundation refused to support public southern universities, whose governance remained in the hands of pro-segregation state legislatures.

The director of the new program, Leland DeVinney, quickly discovered that the administrators at several of the chosen colleges were hostile to a scholarship program that focused exclusively on black students. Their concerns echoed the concerns of southern leaders 60 years earlier, when John D. Rockefeller founded the GEB. Both President Herbert Longenecker at Tulane and Chancellor Alexander Heard at Vanderbilt argued that a program exclusively focused on blacks betrayed the spirit of the Supreme Court's decision in *Brown v. Board of Education*, to move away from racial segregation and promote integration.

As DeVinney recorded in his officer's diary on November 20, 1963: "[Longenecker] spoke very emphatically against foundations or others supporting any programs exclusively for Negroes. He says he feels this simply perpetuates the race problem and the principle of segregation." Thus, by the end of 1963, Romney writes, "the original intention of the scholarship grant—to provide monies for Negroes exclusively—had been changed to 'Negroes primarily.'"

In exchanges between Foundation staff and university administrators, the emphasis on black scholarships was crossed out and replaced with language that reflected an emphasis on diversity—"graduates from increasingly broad and diverse economic and social sectors of the population" or "greater opportunity for culturally deprived individuals." An informal compromise was reached between the Foundation and the universities. Seventy percent of the scholarships would be offered to qualified African-American students, and 30 percent to qualified, economically disadvantaged whites.

DeVinney believed that once the walls of segregation were breached, the universities would find plenty of bright, capable black high school graduates eager to attend elite colleges. The problem had been the suppression of opportunity, DeVinney argued, not a lack of ability. The universities simply needed to do a better job of recruiting qualified high school students. If they could not find qualified students, it meant that they weren't recruiting hard enough, not that the students weren't there. "The taproot of American discrimination against the Negro was the widespread belief in his inherent intellectual inferiority," DeVinney wrote in a report on the Equal Opportunity program. He was determined to overturn stereotypes.

The Foundation quickly discovered, however, that the problem of long-term, systemic discrimination in education could not be addressed so easily. Given the poorly funded system of education for African-American students, qualified black high school graduates were not available in the numbers that DeVinney anticipated. "The vast majority of southern Negro high school seniors were under-prepared to the point of being out of the running" for Rockefeller Foundation scholarships, Elizabeth Romney reported.

At Tulane, the director of admissions stumbled on a remedial strategy. He discovered that the best tutoring program on campus was in the athletic department. As students on Rockefeller Foundation scholarships struggled through their first years at Tulane, he routed them to the athletic department. Within a year, athletic department tutors were assisting all Foundation students at the university. Despite the pressure of developing a scholarship program in the heat of the moment, a very high percentage of the students made their way through college.

The second leg of the Equal Opportunity program was designed to address the lack of preparation among black high school students. The Foundation allocated $2 million to develop summer programs for talented African-American students at Princeton University, Dartmouth College, and Oberlin College. At Princeton, the summer program was designed to intervene with students after their sophomore year in high school. The university also provided follow-up academic counseling and assistance with college applications during the regular academic year. Dartmouth took a more aggressive approach, and promised to place students in elite prep schools after they completed the summer program, as a stepping-stone to college. At Oberlin, the summer program focused on middle-school students.

These summer programs opened the door to many African-American students. To be sure, they attracted middle-class black families who had made education a family priority. The Princeton program, however, became a model for the federal Upward Bound initiative, which was created after passage of the Economic Opportunity Act in 1964. Dartmouth, meanwhile, was so successful that the college eventually began to place its summer school graduates in successful suburban public high schools in addition to private prep schools.

Success drew other resources to these efforts. As the federal government launched its War on Poverty, which included programs like Upward Bound for African-American high school students, the Foundation turned to an even greater challenge. Students in poorer communities, who had complicated family and social problems, also wanted to go to college. But programs designed for these students suffered lower rates of completion, and placement declined.

The third leg of the Equal Opportunity program thus paralleled the Foundation's interest in university development in countries newly liberated from colonialism. Under Harrar's stewardship, the Foundation had launched a University Development Program (UDP) in Asia, Africa, and Latin America, which provided visiting faculty and faculty training fellowships to raise the quality of teaching. As the Equal Opportunity program explored the possibility of investing more deeply in historically black colleges in the South, many of the programmatic strategies developed for the UDP, particularly the assignment of visiting faculty, were applied to the southern black colleges.

This third element of the Equal Opportunity program, however, was controversial within the Foundation. Trustees and staff in the 1960s were deeply ambivalent about the future of black colleges. The civil rights movement had been born in these schools, but as the movement for desegregation won greater acceptance, white universities opened their doors and public schools in the North and West increased their enrollment of the best black students. Among the trustees, concern developed that the Foundation should not perpetuate segregated education, even if the intention was to support black colleges that had been

During the first year of the summer enrichment program at Dartmouth College, project organizers worried that prep schools would refuse to accept African-American students who had successfully completed the course. But after three years, 600 minority students had passed through the program, and all but seven had been placed in 100 residential prep schools. (Dartmouth College Library.)

As the civil rights movement divided the nation in June 1963, President Kennedy suggested, "The heart of the question is whether all Americans are to be afforded equal rights and equal opportunities." Rockefeller Foundation trustees created the Equal Opportunity program in September to address what Kennedy called this great moral issue. (Abbie Rowe. John F. Kennedy Presidential Library & Museum.)

built in a very different time, under very different circumstances. The internal debate was intense, and a consensus emerged among staff and trustees that requests for support from the United Negro College Fund (UNCF) should be declined. The debate turned, however, when the board received a letter from President Kennedy on May 21, 1963, encouraging the Foundation to make a $5 million grant to the UNCF.

Kennedy was insistent. "I know of course of the long time interest of the Rockefeller family in the cause of higher education for the Negro," he wrote. "Had it not been for the generosity of the General Education Board over the decades, many of these institutions might well have ceased to exist." Kennedy reminded the trustees that the Ford Foundation had already agreed to a $15 million grant. And he ended his letter by writing that the stability of the black colleges was of the "utmost importance to the Nation." It was a forceful appeal. Nevertheless, at the Foundation's Executive Board meeting of June 21, a month after Kennedy's letter arrived, the trustees voted to decline the grant. Harrar reported that prior to the vote, during the staff's docket conference, there had been "extensive discussion… with very negative reaction to giving further support to segregated institutions."

Harrar pocketed the decision, and never informed the presidents of the black colleges. Over the following months, with the support of John D. Rockefeller 3rd, he deftly lobbied the trustees. He argued that the Foundation's historical relationship should not be abandoned. He suggested that the black colleges remained essential for training black teachers. Moreover, the Foundation simply could not turn its back on the President of the United States.

"It is clear that now and for some years to come many Negroes in the South will find in the predominantly Negro colleges their only realistic opportunity for higher education," George Harrar wrote in his 1964 President's Review. "Perhaps even more important is the fact that the teachers of most Negro children in the South will continue for an indefinite period to come from these colleges, and that any improvement in their training will help to improve the quality of primary and secondary schooling."

In the end Harrar prevailed. The trustees granted $2.5 million to the United Negro College Fund, plus $405,000 to support scholarships for black undergraduates through the Woodrow Wilson Fellowship Program. Additional funding went directly to colleges. In 1965 Fisk University received a grant of $110,000, Hampton Institute $300,000, Lincoln University $15,000, and Tuskegee $300,000, all for academic reinforcement and enrichment of entering students. The Foundation also awarded $280,000 to Education Services, Inc. to create summer institutes for teachers from black colleges.

Altogether, the Rockefeller Foundation's three-pronged strategy—with its focus on higher education and the development of black leaders—represented a series of incremental efforts designed to increase the opportunities available to rising members of the black middle class. But the pace of change was quickening. In the year following the assassination of President Kennedy, the ascendance of Lyndon Johnson, and Martin Luther King Jr.'s "I Have a Dream" speech, delivered from the Lincoln Memorial in Washington, D.C., to more than a quarter million civil rights supporters, there was no clear path to an America where individuals would "not be judged by the color of their skin, but by the content of their character." In the African-American neighborhoods of America's biggest cities, people were increasingly impatient.

Beyond the Black Middle Class—Confronting the Ghetto

The Equal Opportunity program's focus on higher education was designed to provide opportunity for the brightest black students who might become the foundation of a black middle class, rising within government, universities, and corporate leadership. But the numbers were small, and the broad social impact paled in comparison to the expectations

created by the Civil Rights Act of 1964 and the beginnings of Lyndon Johnson's War on Poverty. Most importantly, the Equal Opportunity program was focused so intently on the "special circumstances" of race relations in the South that the Foundation did not recognize the effects of the Great Migration of African Americans, who had fled the segregation and poverty of the region for the promise of jobs and personal freedom in northern cities during the first half of the 20th century.

By the millions, these African-American families had been forced to settle primarily in segregated neighborhoods in the inner cities of the North and West. Even after the Supreme Court barred the enforcement of discriminatory housing codes and covenants in the late 1940s, de facto segregation continued. The "ghettos" described in press reports reflected racial discrimination, economic stagnation, poverty, and social confinement. These neighborhoods often lacked the capital to stimulate economic development, and local governments devoted little attention to the communities where many African Americans worked to raise families, put food on the table, and assert their own influence on the cultural life of the nation.

By 1965 the contours of the civil rights movement had shifted from non-violent civil disobedience in the South to rage, riot, and confrontation in America's inner cities. Speaking in the aftermath of the Watts Riots in Los Angeles in August 1965, United Nations Under-Secretary-General and Rockefeller Foundation Trustee Ralph Bunche warned that "the ominous message of Watts, I fear, for all America, is that it has produced, raw and ugly, the bitterest fruit of the black ghetto." He exhorted city, state, and federal authorities to eliminate "every black ghetto in this land."

Bunche knew what he was talking about. He had been born in Detroit but raised in Watts. He had graduated from UCLA and received his Ph.D. in political science from Harvard. The Rockefeller Foundation supported his research in Africa as a graduate student, and his close friend, Dean Rusk, invited him to join the Foundation board in 1955. A world-renowned diplomat, Bunche had already won the Nobel Peace Prize in 1950 for his arbitration of the Palestinian-Israeli conflict. He had been head of the United Nations delegation to the Congo during the terror-filled days after independence was granted in 1960. He had been at Martin Luther King Jr.'s side during the March on Washington in 1963, and again two years later for the march from Selma to Montgomery. More than any single individual, Ralph Bunche provided Foundation leaders with a deep understanding of the demands and evolution of the civil rights movement.

When 200,000 people gathered at the Lincoln Memorial on August 28, 1963, for the March on Washington, progressives recognized that the explosion of grassroots activism had forced the issues of civil rights and economic justice far beyond the go-slow approach of both the Kennedy administration and the nation's most influential foundations. (Warren K. Leffler. Library of Congress)

By the time another summer of riots erupted in 1967 in Newark, Detroit, and Milwaukee, Bunche had been a member of the board for more than a decade. He did not have fingerprints on any of the Foundation's primary programs, and he was only a year away from mandatory retirement, but in December of that year he challenged the Foundation to steer the Equal Opportunity program in an entirely new direction. He rose during a trustees' meeting to address the problem of ghettos, proposing that the Foundation invest heavily in an effort to understand the basic dynamics of how ghettos formed, and how they could be eliminated.

Minutes of internal trustee discussions are not published, but several trustees later described Bunche's presentation as an intellectual and emotional tour de force. Dr. Frank Stanton, president of Columbia Broadcasting System (CBS), called it "the high water mark of all the board discussions that I knew.… The man was so eloquent, and so sweeping that a hush fell over the meeting. Ralph leaned back almost as though he had decided to make a passing comment—the group was so interested that he may have gone beyond what he intended. He was so good that he stopped the meeting." Another trustee observed that there was a feeling on the part of the trustees that "We were whistling Dixie while the country was burning."

Lyndon Johnson's signatures on the Civil Rights Act of 1964 and the Voting Rights Act of 1965 marked major milestones in U.S. civil rights history. Facing continuing discrimination and a lack of economic opportunity, some African-American activists grew more militant. The movement also expanded from the rural South to the cities of the North. (Cecil Stoughton. LBJ Library.)

The core of Bunche's thinking was his belief that ghettos represent a form of forced confinement, a re-segregation of America, and could not be reformed. Only a month before the trustee meeting Bunche had outlined his ideas for a convention of high school students from North and South Carolina. He asserted that it wasn't going to help too much to simply increase employment or improve schools or housing. Building on the ideas that anchored NAACP attorney Thurgood Marshall's arguments in *Brown v. Board of Education*, Bunche argued that segregation itself was the root of the problem. "With ghetto confinement goes ghetto psychology," he said. "The only solution in my view is to eliminate ghettos."

The consensus of the trustees at the December meeting was that a joint trustee-staff subcommittee be formed then and there to study ways in which the Foundation could change direction. Trustee Thomas J. Watson, president of IBM, agreed to be its chairman. According to records of the first meeting on December 28, Watson "pointed out that the Foundation's efforts in education have concentrated on the most able young Negroes, and that the threat to the country today is not that group but the least able, most disturbed, and least employable. He thinks we should look for ways of reducing tension and minimizing the risk of violence." Watson's use of words like "threat to the country" and his description of people in the pathological language of "most disturbed" suggest the intensity of the moment and the sense of urgency that surrounded the Foundation's search for new programs.

Bunche played an active role in the subcommittee's deliberations. Referring to the reconstruction of Europe after World War Two, he seemed to be suggesting a black Marshall Plan for American cities. George Harrar remembered Bunche saying, over and over, "We must eliminate the ghetto; we must eliminate the ghetto." The officers and trustees struggled to translate Bunche's passion into specific programs, but they did not understand the internal dynamics of ghetto life. Except for Bunche, none had grown up in an inner city neighborhood of color.

Nobel Laureate Ralph Bunche brought tremendous authority on matters of race to the Rockefeller Foundation's Board of Trustees. His plea for the Foundation to confront the structural problems of urban ghettos shifted the focus of the Equal Opportunity program to the most marginalized Americans: the permanently unemployed, the poorest of the poor, the least educated, and single mothers. (Rowland Scherman. National Archives and Records Administration.)

Democracy & Philanthropy

Bunche suggested that researchers should focus on a single ghetto and drill down to keep from being overwhelmed by broad generalities. Meetings were contentious and difficult, and Bunche was sometimes demanding and strident, but slowly the subcommittee came to a consensus that could be presented to the trustees. In 1968 the Foundation implemented another three-faceted strategy for the Equal Opportunity program that combined research with action.

In the wake of Martin Luther King Jr.'s assassination in 1968, more than a hundred American cities experienced the rage and despair of their American-American communities. In Washington, D.C., 1,200 buildings were burned and looted. The destruction seemed to confirm Ralph Bunche's view that urban ghettos had to be replaced. (Warren K. Leffler. Library of Congress.)

On the research side, a grant of $625,000 was given to Dr. Kenneth Clark at the Metropolitan Applied Research Center in New York for "an intensive study of urban ghettos—their characteristics and causes, and possible remedies for their ills." Clark, a renowned psychologist, had already published a study of ghetto life in 1965, *Dark Ghetto: Dilemmas of Social Power*. For Bunche and Clark, this new investigation held the promise of re-visiting many of the themes explored by Gunnar Myrdal in *An American Dilemma*, his ground-breaking study of American race relations in the 1920s and 30s. Bunche had been a member of Myrdal's staff, and had written an extensive study, *The Political Status of the Negro in the Age of FDR*, as part of the scholarship that accompanied Myrdal's investigation.

Clark toiled on the ghetto study for several years. His staff interviewed hundreds of experts and community leaders. The Foundation also funded a team from the University of Chicago to study "the causes and effects of poverty as revealed in the characteristics and behavior of individuals and social groups in Chicago's slum areas."

Meanwhile, two other facets of the Foundation's initiative were of a more practical nature and devoted to the development of urban leadership. Departing from past practice, the Foundation looked outside of universities to the inner cities themselves to recruit community leaders for training. Secondly, in St. Louis, Los Angeles, Cleveland, Minneapolis, Philadelphia, and Gary, Indiana, the Foundation supported experimental programs to transform public secondary schools into centers of community activism. "In all these efforts, the public school serves as a hub of neighborhood solidarity and of the community's participation in the education of its children and young people," Harrar reported in 1969.

In microcosm, these initiatives were successful. They influenced individual lives. But the scale and complexity of the ghetto problem dwarfed the Foundation's resources at a time when the Foundation was also deeply invested in international programming, food and agriculture, and international population stabilization. In frustration, George Harrar wrote in 1971, the last year of his presidency: "The Sixties were violent, angry, revolutionary—and exuberant. As the decade wore on, foundation staff learned what the nation learned to its sorrow: there are no easy answers."

Equal Opportunity and the Crisis of American Confidence

In the 1970s, the Foundation, like much of the country, lost confidence in its ability to create lasting change. Victories were incremental and slow to take effect, at a time when the Vietnam War and the Watergate scandal were shaking the nation's faith in the institutions of government. "While significant gains were made during the last decade in granting legal or administrative rights, in many instances these rights still have to be put into practice," John Knowles, Harrar's successor, wrote in his first Rockefeller Foundation President's Review in 1972. "It is one thing to decree an end to segregated schools; quite another to implement school integration programs effectively."

Knowles captured the great national malaise. Massive federal programs initiated as part of President Lyndon Johnson's Great Society reforms of the 1960s had accomplished much good, but the electorate seemed reluctant to vote for their continuance, as problems with poverty in the inner cities continued and taxes kept rising. As Knowles wrote, "Our traditional belief in inevitable progress through science and technology is fading rapidly as we confront mounting pollution, urban decay, crime, and persistent inequality."

The mixed results of the Foundation's University Development Program abroad, along with the increasingly high cost of operational programs that required large staffs and top-down strategies in the new nations of the world, added to the sense of discouragement among the Foundation's trustees. Nevertheless, Knowles advocated a sustained Foundation commitment to equal opportunity. "There are indications that many individuals and groups which were active in the civil rights field during the past few years have wearied of the battle and shifted their attention to

RF ILLUSTRATED

VOL. 1, NO. 1, OCTOBER, 1972

THE ROCKEFELLER FOUNDATION, 111 WEST 50TH STREET, NEW YORK, NEW YORK 10020

THE WELLBEING OF MANKIND THROUGHOUT THE WORLD

CONTENTS

Good Guys 2
Should Science Have a Conscience? 4
Bradfield's Little Acres 6
Saul Alinsky: A Memoir 3
RF Board of Trustees 3
Grants & Programs 8

THE 29: NEW GROUP AIDS AGRISEARCH

The future of hundreds of millions of the world's poor has been brightened by a recent, little publicized event: the organization of the International Consultative Group for Agricultural Research.

The Consultative Group is a unique consortium of international banks, assistance agencies, governments and private foundations. This year alone it has raised over $15 million for the 1972 operations of four international agricultural research and training centers that were originally established by the Ford and Rockefeller Foundations. For 1973 it hopes to marshal some $23 million for expanded activities of these four institutes and for the creation of two new ones. The major objective of the Consultative Group, and of the international centers it finances, is to assist the poorer nations to rapidly increase output of basic food crops both to meet the food needs of growing populations and to speed the economic development that is needed if the living standards of both rural and urban people are to be improved.

Among the centers being supported are:

The International Rice Research Institute (IRRI) founded in 1960 in the Philippines by the Ford and Rockefeller Foundations in cooperation with the government of the Philippines. This institute over the past decade has produced the widely heralded "miracle" rice varieties and their related technology. It has trained hundreds of Asian scientists and technicians and has provided direct technical assistance to national research and development organizations in most of the rice-growing nations of tropical Asia.

The International Maize and Wheat Improvement Center (CIMMYT, from its name in Spanish) established by the Rockefeller Foundation and the Government of Mexico in 1966. From CIMMYT, and from the earlier Rockefeller Foundation-Mexico cooperative agricultural program, have come the high-yielding dwarf wheats now in worldwide usage. CIMMYT also has significant work underway internationally in corn improvement. The center's work in wheat is directed by the Rockefeller Foundation's Dr. Norman E. Borlaug, the recipient of the 1970 Nobel Peace Prize.

The International Institute of Tropical Agriculture (IITA) in Nigeria, established in 1967 by the Ford and Rockefeller Foundations in cooperation with the government of that country. It serves particularly the low, humid areas of Africa, concentrating its work on cowpeas and other legumes, the long-neglected root crops, corn, rice and tropical cropping systems.

World Bank's McNamara RF's Wortman

The International Center for Tropical Agriculture (CIAT, from its name in Spanish) near Cali, Colombia. Established in 1967 by the Ford and Rockefeller Foundations and the government of Colombia, CIAT is attempting to speed the agricultural development of the humid tropics, especially in the Americas, for human benefit. It concentrates particularly on beef-production systems and on improved production of cassava, field beans and other important crops.

The International Crops Research Institute for the Semi-Arid Tropics (ICRISAT) at Hyderabad, India. This new institute will be concerned with the improvement of four crops especially important to farmers in the low-rainfall areas of Asia—sorghum, millets, chick-peas and pigeon peas. It was established in mid-1972 by the World Bank and UNDP in cooperation with the government of India. It was organized for the Consultative Group by the Ford Foundation and is based on an original design by the Rockefeller Foundation's Dr. Clarence Gray.

The International Potato Center (CIP) in Peru. Organized initially by USAID and the North Carolina State University in cooperation with the government of Peru, this center seeks to intensify production of the white potato, a staple food of people in high elevations in the Andes and in many other regions of the world.

The Consultative Group membership comprises the three sponsors (World Bank, UNDP, FAO) the Inter-American Development Bank, the Asian Development Bank, the African Development Bank, the European Fund for Economic Development (FED), and the governments of 13 nations: Australia, Belgium, Canada, Denmark, Federal Republic of Germany, France, Japan, Netherlands, Norway, Sweden, Switzerland, United Kingdom and the United States. Also members are the International Development Research Center of Canada, the Kellogg Foundation, the Ford Foundation and the Rockefeller Foundation. Representatives of each of five developing regions of the world participate in Group meetings. It is hoped that additional nations, agencies and foundations will choose to join the worldwide effort.

According to Dr. Sterling Wortman of the Rockefeller Foundation, the creation of this network of activities may be the greatest single advance in international cooperation in agriculture of this century, and certainly it is the most significant recent one. It will bring to bear, if successful, the speedy application of scientific advances wherever they occur on problems of farming, whatever and wherever they may be. Dr. Wortman gives particular credit to Dr. J. George Harrar, former president of the Rockefeller Foundation and to Dr. F. F. Hill of the Ford Foundation for the concept of the institutes, and to the World Bank and its president, Robert McNamara, for having had the vision to find the way, in cooperation with other sponsors, to marshal the funds so urgently needed for international research.

RF PROGRAM REVIEWS UNDERWAY

During the past six months, under the leadership of a new president, John H. Knowles, M.D., officers and staff have searched for answers to two deceptively simple questions:

- What are the great needs of our times, toward whose solutions private initiative could make a decisive contribution?
- Given an inflationary trend, how could the RF compound its influence above and beyond its grant-making capacity?

As a first step, Dr. Knowles has organized the staff into 17 Ad Hoc Committees. Their mandates range from examining the position of women and young people in America to arriving at an "integrated approach to defined populations" in the less-developed countries—from analyzing the potential value of war and peace studies, to structuring a means for evaluating the effectiveness of RF grants and programs. Similar groups are examining the RF's current programs, concerned about possibly redefining their broad goals, and also about the relationships between potential benefits and inherent costs.

In their deliberations, the Committees have been assisted by distinguished men and women from outside the RF. Humanists such as Hannah Arendt, Paul Freund and Hans Morgenthau, men with great experience in public administration such as McGeorge Bundy, Don Price and Francis Fisher have met with the Committees. For the environmental sciences, Dr. Philip Johnson, Division Director at the National Science Foundation, Dr. Norton Nelson, Director of the Institute of Environmental Medi-

(continued to page five)

A New President: John H. Knowles, M.D.

During the six months that John Knowles has presided over the RF he has raised more questions than he has provided answers. (See left.) But from his first day he has set a style that is likely to characterize his administration—and very possibly the influence of the RF on changing times. A restless, probing, passionate intensity, a compulsive appetite for work, a constructive dissatisfaction with life as it is compared with life as it could be—all this leavened by a self-mocking sense of humor—appear to be the characteristics of the eighth president of The Rockefeller Foundation.

Dr. Knowles came to the RF from the Massachusetts General Hospital, where in ten years he had risen from intern to General Director—at 35 the youngest in the institution's 150-year history. During the following decade he made what was already one of the world's best teaching and patient-care hospitals even better, and increased annual donations sixteenfold by turning the hospital into one of Boston's most visible institutions. In the process, he captured the imagination of people everywhere.

"Often controversial, never wishy-washy and certainly never dull, he has fought for his ideas and ideals with a ferocity and fearlessness that has sometimes angered opponents," MGH News editorialized on his departure for the RF. "His very intensity and determined refusal to back off from what he considers a just cause have often won the war after losing the battle."

John Knowles was born in Chicago, but his roots are in New England. At school and college (Belmont Hill and Harvard '47) he exercised his self-assertiveness through competitive sports (baseball, hockey, squash) and his sociability by playing the piano at the old Imperial Hotel in Boston's seedy Scollay Square. The result of that much high spirits and low life was that Knowles was accepted by only one of the 12 medical schools to which he applied. But he had learned his lesson: he graduated from Washington University Medical School at the top of his class and was selected as one of the few "outsiders" to intern at the Massachusetts General Hospital.

What brought Dr. Knowles from Boston to the RF is his evangelical belief in voluntarism. "One of the great disjunctions of the times we live in," says Knowles, "is how we are going to keep the idea in the heads of individuals that they, individually, are going to make a difference in an increasingly complex and interdependent world. As the press toward equalization occurs with the steady expansion of the beneficent state, how can we, as individuals, make a difference?" Dr. Knowles's record, for instance in his battles with the AMA, prove him to be a strong advocate of a far more equitable distribution of all essential services. But, warns Knowles, "We hand over the sole resolution of social problems to government at our peril. We can end up with a beneficent welfare state, but also with the hazards of its inevitable expansion—a supine citizenry, an overweening bureaucracy, an erosion of individual initiative."

What is RF Illustrated?

The decade of the 1960's saw the values and moral commitment of essentially all American institutions and establishments challenged. American philanthropy and its institutional form, the foundation, was not spared its full share of criticism, which culminated in the Tax Reform Act of 1969. The most startling revelation during the Congressional inquiry was the widespread lack of public knowledge and understanding of the unique role that American foundations have played in the resolution of scientific and social problems and the significant contributions they have made to social melioration.

With this first issue of a new publication, we of The Rockefeller Foundation are seeking to explain what we do, and why we do it. We sincerely hope that you, the American people, will respond with constructive criticism as to how we can do better. We exist because you, through your elected representatives and their formulation of our tax laws, have in essence said that private philanthropy, voluntarism, and the foundations are unique instruments for the social good—and perform important functions which Government alone cannot accomplish. We know we can do better and we count on you to help us. This first issue is being sent to over 100,000 Americans in all walks of life; in addition, RF Illustrated will be distributed abroad, in both the less developed and the highly developed countries. Subsequent issues will be published quarterly. By modifying our routine publications, we shall reduce our costs even as we hope to gain more knowledge of and enthusiasm for our activities.

Last year alone, our support went to individuals and groups in 44 states and to 36 developing nations in Latin America, Africa and Asia. Domestic and international activities are both important, for there will be a single future for the world—or none at all.

Please write and send us your questions and suggestions. Every letter will be answered.

J.H.K.

1

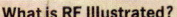

other concerns," he wrote. Given these developments, it was important for the Foundation to stay the course.

Knowles followed up by increasing the budget for the key initiatives of the Equal Opportunity program. In his era, the program focused on leadership development and training, career development and professional training, and experimental programs in community education. Among the Foundation's core programs in 1973, the Equal Opportunity program ranked fourth in its level of funding. The Conquest of Hunger Program was first, with almost 20 percent ($8.6 million) of the Foundation's appropriations that year, while Equal Opportunity received only 8.6 percent ($3.8 million). By 1976, however, with Knowles's support, the projected budget reduced the Conquest of Hunger appropriations to 15.4 percent ($6.9 million) and raised the Equal Opportunity appropriations to 14.3 percent ($6.4 million). With the additional resources, Equal Opportunity grants were extended to include the Latino community, Native Americans, and a regional emphasis on poverty in the South.

As the nation's understanding of racial issues shifted from the question of relations between blacks and whites to a greater recognition of cultural and racial diversity that included Hispanic, Asian, Indian, and other minorities, the Foundation broadened its approach. In 1976 it recognized a need to defend and expand the legal gains of the 1960s. Major grants were given to the Mexican American Legal Defense and Educational Fund ($300,000) and the American Indian Lawyer Training Project ($200,000). In 1977 "securing and protecting basic rights" became a focus of the program for the first time. The Foundation made a $500,000 grant to the NAACP Special Contribution Fund to help fight segregation in cities as well as employment discrimination based on race throughout the country.

All of these efforts, however, took place during a period of existential crisis for the Foundation. A dramatic increase in inflation, causing a decline in the purchasing power of the endowment, forced the trustees to wrestle with the question of whether the Foundation itself should continue or the assets should be spent down. In his remarkably candid President's Review in the 1977 annual report, Knowles's successor, Richard Lyman, presented the arguments for and against continuing as they related to each of the Foundation's programs. Writing about Equal Opportunity, he offered compelling reasons for ending the program: substantial progress had been made during the previous ten years, represented particularly by new laws; public funds were now available to address the

Physician John Knowles became president of the Rockefeller Foundation in 1972. With inflation rising and the value of the endowment declining, he launched a fundamental review of the Foundation's programs. After the review was complete, Knowles reaffirmed the Foundation's commitment to equal opportunity and increased the budget for grantmaking in that area. (Rockefeller Archive Center.)

issue; several of the Foundation's major objectives had been accomplished; and finally, the Foundation's role was "miniscule compared with the magnitude of the problem."

But there were equally compelling reasons for persistence. Lyman noted the Foundation's historic commitment to the issue and the need to build on what the Foundation had learned and achieved. Moreover, the field needed money for small-scale experiments designed to combat racial discrimination, to support the development of leaders, and "to strengthen institutions devoted to resolving the plight of minorities."

The trustees decided to continue the Foundation's work despite the challenges of the economy, and Lyman implemented a major restructuring of the Foundation's programs to lower overhead. The board remained committed to Equal Opportunity, one of four core programs in the Foundation's redesigned strategy. But once again, changes in the larger society and in the ongoing experiment in democracy would soon reshape the landscape for philanthropy and race in America.

The Politics of a Changing Era

The election of Ronald Reagan as President of the United States in 1980 turned the Foundation's approach to problem-solving upside down. For 67 years the trustees and staff had built the programs of the Foundation on the fundamental Progressive Era premise that the expertise of scientists could be mobilized in the public interest and implemented by government. This was the partnership that Starr Murphy and Jerome Greene had promised to Congress during the time of the charter debate. It was the authority and resources of government that could leverage the insights of experts into broad social effect, and democracy demanded the vote of the people's representatives to legitimize the social reforms pioneered by innovative philanthropists. In the New Frontier of the Kennedy administration and the Great Society of the Johnson administration, the Foundation had found partners committed to equal opportunity and social change.

Reagan's election signaled the ascendance of other voices in the nation that challenged the existing relationship between the philanthropic community and the government. Historian Lee Edwards summarized the conservative critique of liberalism and its deep connections between mainline philanthropy and government in *The Power of Ideas*, his book on the Heritage Foundation: "Time and again, a liberal professor would write an article suggesting the creation of a new federal program. The article would be quoted approvingly in the pages of the *New York Times* or the *Washington Post*.

President Ronald Reagan introduced a new conservative perspective in government that compelled many in the foundation community to look for more ways to collaborate with and enlist the support of the private sector in efforts to address inner-city problems. (Carol M. Highsmith. Library of Congress.)

Studies of the suggested program would be underwritten by the Ford or Rockefeller Foundation. Scholars at Brookings would meet with members of Congress and their staffs to discuss how the program might be legislatively framed. Special interest groups would endorse the proposed legislation and contact their congressmen and senators. And, finally, a broad-based coalition would emerge—seemingly out of nowhere—backing the bill. The rest would roll smoothly into place: The liberal idea would become law, a new government agency would be created, a new social experiment would begin, and taxes would be raised."

From the Reagan White House and conservatives in Congress came a legislative strategy to cut the very programs in job training, urban development, social welfare, and education that the Rockefeller Foundation and others had worked to model with their various philanthropic initiatives. President Reagan promoted voluntarism and private philanthropy, not as a way to stimulate government programs but as a replacement for government programs. The President's vision ignited a new debate about the role of philanthropy and its relationship to government in the United States. To respond to this debate, the Rockefeller Foundation helped fund a major study by the Urban Institute of the role of philanthropy and the nonprofit sector, to understand the capacity of the philanthropic community for filling the gap created by cuts in government spending.

As the public engaged this conversation, the Rockefeller Foundation forged ahead with its Equal Opportunity program, delving deeper and deeper into the intractable problems of race and poverty. The Foundation provided major funding for the Jobs for America's Graduates program—designed to improve the employability of high school seniors "most likely to enter the unemployment rolls after graduation"—in Boston, St. Louis, Kansas City, Memphis, and several communities in Arizona. Building on research that suggested a strong correlation between poverty in African-

American communities and families headed by single women, the Foundation provided grants to community organizations to increase the employability of single mothers. The Foundation invested $1.75 million in the new initiative, with the hope of helping 10,000 women over five years. But without a partner in government, the scale of the investment paled next to the scale of the problem.

Georgetown University law professor Eleanor Holmes Norton became a trustee in 1981. The former chair of the U.S. Equal Opportunity Commission, she was a leading defender of the rights of women and racial minorities. She went on to serve as Washington, D.C.'s non-voting delegate to the U.S. House of Representatives. (Suzie Fitzhugh. Rockefeller Archive Center.)

There were signs of progress by 1984, Foundation President Richard Lyman noted, but a long road yet to travel. "Once-segregated America has been de-segregated dramatically with respect to public—and most private—facilities. At the same time, for large numbers of minority people, there has been no change, or change for the worse.... The problems of intractable poverty, family disintegration, the drug and crime culture, teen-age pregnancy, and widespread illiteracy, remain untouched and apparently untouchable by the legal and other mechanisms that have helped others to rise into the middle class."

Lyman organized a trustee committee to investigate how the Foundation might advance its Equal Opportunity program in the face of a dramatically changing political landscape in Washington. The recommendation was to redouble the Foundation's efforts among the poorest of the poor. "The conclusion we have reached," Lyman reported in 1984, "is to focus even more sharply upon the problems surrounding hard core poverty, the problems of those left behind by the civil rights revolution."

The Foundation's deepening commitment to equal opportunity overlapped with the election of civil rights activist Eleanor Holmes Norton to the Board of Trustees in 1981. Norton had served as the first woman chair of the U.S. Equal Employment Opportunity Commission from 1977 to 1981, under President Jimmy Carter. Her expertise in civil rights law, urban affairs, employment and poverty, and the women's movement made Norton a powerful voice for the Equal Opportunity program in the 1980s.

By 1987 appropriations to the Equal Opportunity program were second only to those for the global agriculture program, but the scale of the issue kept increasing. As the Foundation reported, "Although the number of people in poverty grew by 18 percent from 28 million in 1967 to 33 million in 1985, the number of poor people living in concentrated poverty areas (census tracts with a poverty rate of 40 percent or more) has grown rapidly, by roughly 50 percent between 1970 and 1980—from 3.5 million persons to 5.6 million persons." Over the same period the underclass grew by roughly 234 percent—from 750,000 to 2.5 million. This American underclass, Lyman noted, "is characterized by a growing separation from the rest of society, its norms, and especially its resources."

In the 1990s, long after Ralph Bunche first encouraged the Foundation to invest in the elimination of urban ghettos, the trustees returned to the theme: "In view of the enormity of this problem, the Equal Opportunity division is moving away from its focus on general problems of opportunity for minorities to wrestle with the most difficult hard-core poverty facing American cities." Ralph Bunche had been criticized for being vague about how to deal with ghetto poverty and for advocating the elimination of ghettos. The Foundation's programs of the late 1980s had taken a different approach. They sought to reform the inner cities, not eliminate them.

School Reform

At the center of the equal opportunity strategy was a renewed commitment to school reform, which fit well with the emerging technology sector of the American economy and its dependence on advanced education. It also reflected the Foundation's historical belief that education smoothed the road to opportunity.

To help with this initiative, the Foundation formed a partnership with Dr. James Comer, a child development psychologist at the Yale University School of Medicine who had been working successfully in the poorest, most racially segregated and failing schools in New Haven, Connecticut. Comer's School Development Program put child development at the center of public education. He stressed the importance of a child's psychological preparation for school and the role of parents and faculty in the development of the whole child, not just the academic child. Comer emphasized developing a child's social skills as well as ethical foundation, while transforming schools into community centers.

Foundation grants supported a variety of programs aimed at determining whether Comer's work in New Haven could be systematized and extended across the country. Some grants, for example, helped teachers expand the cultural perspectives of their students. Other grants went to summer leadership

Dr. James Comer's research tied education reform to the psychological and social development of children. It was a natural fit for the Rockefeller Foundation's traditional interest in science-driven public policy. Comer's success at two inner-city schools in New Haven, Connecticut, led the Foundation to invest heavily in school districts that implemented his program. (Peter Casolino. New Haven Register.)

academies to train principals and teachers to work with highly at-risk students. Community groups were funded to promote parental and community involvement in schools. And grants were made to explore "new ways to test alternative methods of assessing talent and intelligence in young people."

By 1991 the combined programs of Equal Opportunity and School Reform, with an appropriation of $20 million, constituted the largest commitment of the Rockefeller Foundation, followed by Agricultural Sciences at $17.8 million. But the problem of race in America and its relationship to economic security remained elusive. In 1995, in the wake of the O.J. Simpson murder trial, President Peter Goldmark, who succeeded Lyman in 1988, argued, "We urgently need to have a national conversation about race. We need to talk with candor about the implications of personal and institutional racism in order to overcome it."

From Goldmark's perspective, the heart of the problem remained the withdrawal of government from the field of equal opportunity and racial equality. Goldmark insisted in his 1996 President's Review, "Just as the community-renewal effort is growing and succeeding, legislatures in Washington and in state capitals are cutting funds on which these communities rely. Neither the Rockefeller Foundation nor partnerships between the Foundation and other philanthropies could hope to compensate for the decline in public commitment to racial justice and economic opportunity."

A New Approach

In April 1998 the Rockefeller Foundation had a president who, for the first time, was not an American. Born in the United Kingdom, Gordon Conway had earned degrees in the U.K., Trinidad, and the United States on the way to becoming a leading voice in ecology and agriculture. As president of the Rockefeller Foundation he took a decidedly global view, and the program changes that followed his arrival reflected this new perspective. "We have long had separate international and domestic sections," Conway wrote in the 1999 annual report, "but the processes of globalization mean it is sensible and timely for the Foundation to drop these distinctions and to seek a more integrated global approach to our grantmaking."

In the process of restructuring the Foundation's work to focus on "Creativity & Culture, Food Security, Health Equity and Working Communities," the program on Equal Opportunity came to an end. A final set of grants were made to long-standing initiatives aimed at increasing employment opportunities; building stronger communities; strengthening organizations and constituencies working to promote change in inner-city neighborhoods; improving urban schools; promoting citizen engagement and strengthening democracy in low-income areas; and advancing basic rights. All of these initiatives carried forward basic values that had been embedded in John D. Rockefeller's personal philanthropy and in the work of the Rockefeller Foundation. They sought to strengthen the ability of marginalized populations to participate more fully in society, empowering them to shape their destiny through the instruments of representative democracy.

To help provide relevant curriculum to teachers of students of color, the Rockefeller Foundation funded Collaboratives for Humanities and Arts Teaching (CHART) in the 1980s. This early school reform initiative developed 17 projects in urban school districts across the country. (John T. Miller. Rockefeller Archive Center.)

Over the course of a century, the Rockefeller Foundation had changed many lives as a consequence of its grantmaking to black colleges, civil rights organizations, African-American students, inner-city schools, single mothers, community development organizations, and a host of other individuals and institutions. To be sure, the problems of racial discrimination—against Hispanics, Asians, Indians, and other groups of color, as well as African Americans—had not been solved. Going forward, the Foundation would view this challenge as part of a broader set of issues surrounding poverty, both in the United States and globally. The rich imagery of the Rockefeller Foundation's annual report in 1999, rendered in black and white, highlighted the diversity of cultures in the United States and in other countries where the Foundation was working. In reality, for more than three decades, the Foundation's efforts to address equal opportunity had increasingly focused not just on color barriers—as they had in the nineteenth century when John D. Rockefeller began contributing to schools for African Americans—but on the totality of factors that tended to marginalize and isolate the poor in an affluent society. In this sense the Foundation was moving to the same framework it had embraced in its international initiatives, which focused on health, agriculture, and economic development regardless of color or ethnicity. Under Conway and his successor, Judith Rodin, the poor and vulnerable in the United States and throughout the world would become the Foundation's primary focus. As new weather patterns emerged, driven by climate change, it was the poor in cities like New Orleans who would be most vulnerable to storm-driven disasters.

CASE STUDIES IN INNOVATION

MINORITY SUPERINTENDENTS PROGRAM

Nearly 15 years after the U.S. Supreme Court's landmark desegregation decision in *Brown v. Board of Education* in 1954, inner-city schools were in fact still segregated. And according to a study by the U.S. Commission on Civil Rights, segregation was growing, and with it came an increasing gap in student achievement. Test scores were dramatically lower in the inner cities than in suburban schools, and African-American students in metropolitan areas of the North and West were three times more likely than white students to drop out of high school. As the National Advisory Commission on Civil Disorders reported in 1968, inner-city schools were failing to provide the educational experiences that would equip students to realize their potential and to participate fully in American life. This failure was "one of the persistent sources of grievance and resentment within the Negro community."

Minority residents in historically segregated neighborhoods could see that many of the older schools in their communities were falling apart and that the teachers were less experienced. Moreover, these teachers rarely lived in the inner-city neighborhoods where they worked. Even in predominately black or Hispanic schools, most of the staff members, including senior administrators, were white. To build new trust and shared commitment to the process of education in inner-city communities, the National Advisory Commission recommended that "new links must be built between the schools and the communities they serve."

The Rockefeller Foundation recognized that to build this trust, a new generation of school administrators would have to be drawn from urban communities of color. Prejudice and institutional inertia, however, prevented many potential candidates from rising to senior leadership in the nation's school districts. In the South, African-American educators who had long years of experience running segregated black schools were denied opportunities to lead integrated schools. Meanwhile, in urban districts of the North and West, there were fewer teachers of color from which to draw a new cadre of administrators.

Under the aegis of its Equal Opportunity program, the Foundation created a fellowship program in 1970 to train African-American, Hispanic, and Asian educators to become senior administrators in their own communities and to overcome structural prejudices that prevented them from rising to leadership positions in urban districts.

DEMOCRACY & PHILANTHROPY

The Superintendents' Training Program focused largely on the concept of mentorship. Qualified and experienced minority-group administrators were given opportunities to serve as interns with senior leaders in other school districts. The fellows rotated through a variety of experiences in several settings, allowing them to see how upper-level school administration functioned in different communities. The process was designed to "familiarize the candidates with the problems of inner-city schools and to provide them with experiences that would normally take many years to acquire on the job." The grant program also provided consultants who worked for and with the fellows to respond to their needs on-site. The immediate goal was to prepare experienced administrators for high-level duties in the nation's school systems, while the long-term aim was to "help structure demonstrably improved environments" in America's public schools.

In the year leading up to the establishment of the Superintendents' Training Program, the Foundation had already funded similar initiatives. It gave money to Baltimore and Detroit to launch internship programs for school principals, and Philadelphia initiated a similar program for educational planners. The Foundation also appropriated secondary grants in 1970 to the Baltimore City Public School System to appoint additional trainees, as the first group was promoted to administrative posts following their year of internship.

African-American and white children rode the bus to an inner city school in Charlotte, North Carolina, in 1973 as part of a desegregation effort. The Rockefeller Foundation's Superintendents' Training Program sought to integrate the leadership of large, urban school districts. (Warren K. Leffler. Library of Congress.)

CASE STUDIES IN INNOVATION

Expanding on these efforts, in 1970 the Superintendents' Training Program funded the first seven fellows to serve in the school superintendent's office in two cities, for one semester each. The superintendents of schools in Cleveland, Minneapolis, Detroit, Rochester, San Diego, Gary, Philadelphia, and Baltimore participated. Fellows worked on such issues as decentralization, bond referendums, court litigations, and curriculum, all common to a superintendent's office.

Three years into the program, the Rockefeller Foundation sought to assess its impact. By 1973, 29 administrators had participated as fellows, including ten men and two women who were interns in the 1972-73 academic year. After completing the program, many of the fellows stepped into positions of increased leadership and responsibility in their own communities, serving as school superintendents; deputy, associate, or assistant superintendents; and as educational program directors, area assistants, or regional superintendents. Moreover, former fellows were increasingly in positions where they served as mentors to other rising administrators of color.

As the program blossomed in the early 1970s, the Equal

School administrator Dr. Philip del Campo (right) receives a certificate from the president of the school board (left) and the mayor (center) upon the completion of his internship in Rochester, New York, in 1971. Del Campo was Dean of Student Affairs at San Diego City College when he was selected for the Rockefeller Foundation's Superintendents' Training Program. He also interned in Gary, Indiana. (Rockefeller Archive Center.)

DEMOCRACY & PHILANTHROPY

Opportunity program also began to fund efforts to train administrators for suburban public schools as well as community colleges, state universities, and other post-secondary educational institutions.

Long after the program had ended, its impact continued to be felt in urban school districts, community colleges, and universities across the country. Philip del Campo, a former Marine who fought in Korea and later worked as an elementary school teacher in San Diego, participated in the program in 1971. He later became dean of students at San Diego City College and director of Adult and Continuing Education. Laval Wilson trained in Philadelphia and Detroit from 1970 to 1971 as part of the Superintendents' Training Program. Over the course of a long career, he served as superintendent in school districts in Boston, Rochester, Berkeley, Poughkeepsie, and East Orange and Paterson. Charles Townsel became superintendent in the Del Paso Heights district of Sacramento, California, shortly after finishing the Foundation program. In 1973, at the first annual conference of the National Alliance of Black School Educators, Townsel was elected to be the organization's president. Paul L. Vance, who came to the program from Philadelphia, where he had been a teacher, principal, and administrator, served as an intern superintendent in the District of Columbia. After leaving the program, he became deputy superintendent of the Baltimore City Public Schools and, later, superintendent in Montgomery County, Maryland, and the District of Columbia.

Wayman W. Smith was Federal Programs Administrator for the Cleveland Public Schools when he was invited to join the Superintendents' Training Program. Smith interned in Rochester and Minneapolis before returning to Cleveland, where he became a senior administrator. (Rockefeller Archive Center.)

The career paths of these educators reflected, on one level, the success of the Rockefeller Foundation's program. But by the mid-1990s it was increasingly clear—as Gary Orfield and Susan Eaton wrote in their book *Dismantling Desegregation*—that "the race of the superintendent, school board, or administrators did not alter the systemic problems in the city." Inner-city schools suffered from the continuing loss of middle-class families of all colors, as well as disinvestment by corporate America as businesses moved jobs to suburban communities. In this context, by the 1980s it became increasingly clear to leaders in education and at the Rockefeller Foundation that systemic school reform was needed.

DEMOCRACY AND DESIGN IN AMERICA'S CITIES

As a young woman and long before she wrote her classic book *The Death and Life of Great American Cities*, writer Jane Jacobs often fantasized conversations with famous people from history. She imagined herself explaining the modern world to people long dead, for whom the modern age might seem bewildering. According to her biographer, she began this practice with President Thomas Jefferson, who had died 90 years before she was born. She then moved on to colloquies with Benjamin Franklin, who shared her fascination for the everyday aspects of American life.

Unlike Jacobs, Jefferson did not like cities, and Franklin believed they were inimical to democracy. Cities in the eighteenth century bred disease and corruption. During an epidemic of yellow fever in Baltimore, Jefferson confessed to his friend Dr. Benjamin Rush that he viewed great cities "as pestilential to the morals, the health and the liberties of man." His friend and neighbor James Madison, the principal author of the Constitution and fourth President of the United States, shared Jefferson's concerns.

As these Founders of the American republic looked to Europe, and especially England, during the Revolutionary era, they believed that the wealth of great cities was based on the manufacture and trade of luxury exports. This kind of economy bred enormous inequality and fostered political corruption, with leaders and citizens primarily concerned for their own self interest rather than the common good. In English cities, Madison suggested, the masses of urban residents owned no property, were poorly educated, and had little ability to shape their own destiny. In the United States, he and other leaders of the era hoped to cultivate a society where public virtue would be characterized by an "austere and unselfish devotion to the common good," and private virtue, including "frugality, temperance, and rigorous self-control," would be reflected in the behavior of ordinary citizens.

Jefferson, especially, idealized the independent farmer as the paragon of republican virtue and the key to the success of American democracy. Yeoman farmers who owned their own land, he suggested, would not be unduly influenced by a landlord. Producing their own food, building their own homes, and making their own household necessities, these farmers on the western frontier would not be pressured by an employer or creditor. They would, therefore, be able to vote their own conscience.

Thomas Jefferson believed that the success of the American experiment depended on independent and "virtuous" citizens who would not be influenced by employers or landlords when they cast their ballot. In Jefferson's mind, rural communities, and not cities, offered the best hope for the country's future. (Rembrandt Peale. National Archives and Records Administration.)

Jefferson believed so strongly in the importance of the independent farmer to the success of the American experiment that he accelerated the purchase of the Louisiana territory from France in 1803, despite his personal conviction that such a move required a Constitutional amendment. He was willing to compromise his convictions because he believed that this enormous land deal would postpone for generations the urbanization of the country and the inevitable corruption of American democracy that would follow.

Madison believed that this future was not so far off. During the Constitutional Convention of 1787 he had predicted that eventually "a great majority of the people" would be without land or property. They would be forced into cities to work in manufacturing for wages that would only afford them the bare necessities of life. With the Louisiana Purchase, Madison suggested in 1829, the United States had postponed the inevitable by a hundred years or maybe a little more. After that, the country would have to confront the challenge of promoting democracy within the context of an increasingly urban society.

For Jane Jacobs, this challenge hardly seemed insurmountable. In 1958, when she received a grant from the Rockefeller Foundation to help support her work on *The Death and Life of Great American Cities*, she was already convinced that cities could be and were an inspiration to democratic society. But this small grant marked a turning point for the Rockefeller Foundation.

Jane Jacobs in New York City

By the time Jane Jacobs arrived in New York in 1934 to begin a career as a writer and editor, the Rockefeller Foundation and its sister organizations had already devoted more than two decades to improving governance and the quality of life in American cities. In the early decades of the twentieth century, cities drew attention because they housed people in great number, including densely concentrated pockets of immigrants, ethnic minorities, the poor, and unskilled workers. In this era, the Foundation was concerned with ameliorating the attendant social problems, including crime, corruption, juvenile delinquency, prostitution, contagious disease, and

In 1803, when France offered the United States the huge and unexplored territory of Louisiana, Thomas Jefferson seized the opportunity. With this land, Jefferson hoped that many new generations could become independent farmers, postponing the inevitable growth of urban America. (Emanuel Bowen. Library of Congress.)

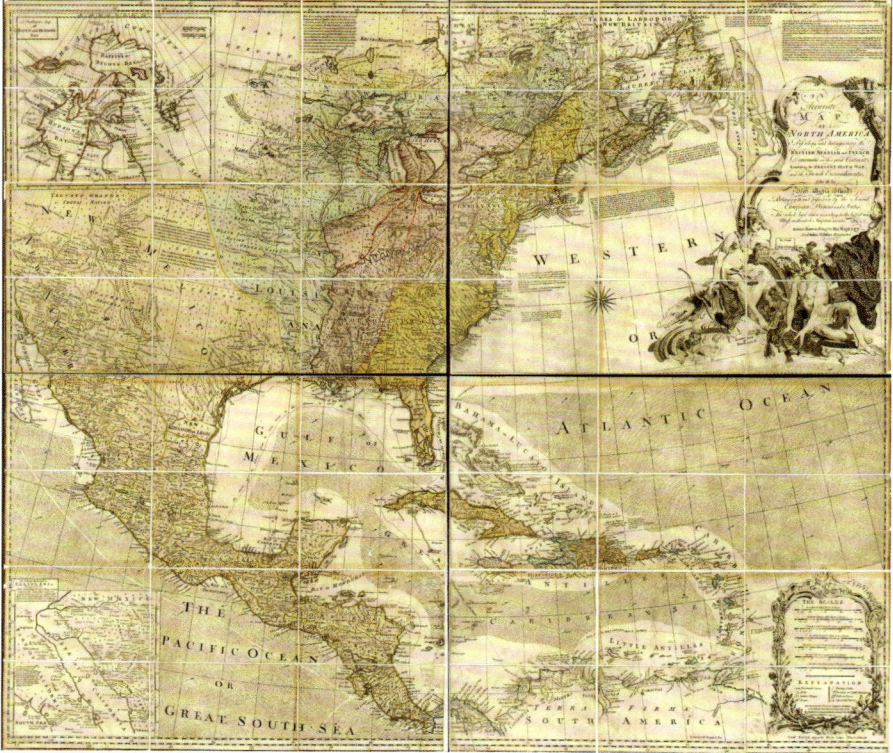

general "vice," rather than effecting change to the physical cityscape or research on urban planning.

Both John D. Rockefeller Jr. and Rockefeller Foundation general counsel Starr J. Murphy were founding board members of the Bureau of Social Hygiene, a private, nongovernmental and nonpartisan organization launched in 1911 to address what Rockefeller called "social evil." The Foundation issued several grants to the Bureau, for studies relating to human sexuality; a diagnostic laboratory at the New York Department of Health; and its general New York City work. Other support went to the Association for Improving the Conditions of the Poor, for aid to dependent widows and the promotion of "mental hygiene"; the New York Milk Committee; and New York City and the Brooklyn Bureau of Charities, for preventive measures and after-care during the infantile paralysis (polio) epidemic. Another early grant went to the Charity Organization Society in 1914 as a "special contribution in view of the unusual amount of distress in the city, due to the war and industrial depression."

Immigrants contributed to the dramatic growth of American cities at the end of the nineteenth century. The Laura Spelman Rockefeller Memorial, an affiliate of the Rockefeller Foundation, provided funding for programs to help these newcomers learn English and adjust to life in the United States. (Rockefeller Archive Center.)

Throughout the 1920s, the Foundation continued funding aimed at improving the safety and the quality of life in cities. It also began to focus increasingly on better governance as a means to curtail corruption and to manage urban populations more efficiently, effectively, and productively. This interest was enacted primarily through social science organizations, especially the Bureau of Municipal Research, and professional associations such as the International City Managers' Association and the Municipal Finance Officers' Association. These and similar Foundation-sponsored endeavors—like the Public Administration Clearinghouse in Chicago, the University of California's Institute of Public Administration, and Syracuse University's Maxwell School of Citizenship and Public Affairs—helped build the new field of public administration, which prepared students specifically to become government officials and municipal managers.

The governmental reform efforts the Foundation helped promote were a response to the heavy in-migration to cities between approximately 1870 and 1920, when workers poured in from abroad and from American farms and small towns, seeking industrial jobs. Often termed "good government," these Progressive reforms valued "businesslike" government by experts and technicians, as opposed to the often-corrupt, machine-dominated "political" governments predicated on favors, bribes, and coercion. The new movement aimed to make government more democratic and less boss-dominated, but other effects included an increased centralization of decision-making and the removal of more governmental functions from electoral control. In 1922, for example, Progressive reformers helped promote a landmark moment in urban planning with the creation of the Committee on a Regional Plan for New York and its Environs. Funded by John D. Rockefeller Jr., the plan outlined the framework for the region's continued growth.

These good-government efforts were sometimes criticized, however, by those whose influence on government had been diminished. Progressive reforms, for example, led to a decrease in the number of lower-income and working-class citizens elected to city councils. Thus the culture of the expert planner and public administrator stood always, to some degree, in tension with democratic values. The profusion of New Deal federal programs during the Depression pushed the field of public administration forward even further, creating a demand for more trained administrators and managers.

For a shockingly broad swath of Americans during the Great Depression of the 1930s, the need for employment and housing became paramount. These problems took on massive and potentially explosive proportions in American cities. In 1934 the Foundation's trustees set up a special committee to respond to the national emergency with a fund of $1.5 million. Not surprisingly, its major grants targeted urban issues, including support for the Slum Clearance Committee of New York, the National Association of Housing Officials, and the American Municipal Association, which used its grant to dispatch field agents to 6,000 American cities. New Deal legislation, meanwhile, laid the groundwork for what would become a seismic shift in the American landscape after World War Two, including mortgage assistance and incentives to stem the tide of foreclosures on family homes, as well as the establishment of the Federal Housing Administration (FHA), which offered low-interest, long-term loans to public agencies for slum clearance and redevelopment.

Myriad changes in the American landscape, economy, and population distribution after World War Two shaped new directions for the Foundation's interest in cities. The GI Bill, often dubbed the "magic carpet to the middle class," provided low-interest, no-money-down loans to returning veterans for home purchases, along with mortgage

With the creation of the Federal Housing Administration during the Depression, the federal government supported the expansion of homeownership by offering mortgage guarantees to lenders. Rockefeller Foundation grants helped planners and local officials work with this and other New Deal programs. (Library of Congress.)

insurance that minimized risks for builders, bankers, and insurance companies. Such mortgages, however, were restricted to single-family, detached homes, and thus the bill helped fuel an unprecedented boom in suburban growth.

Many American cities shrank as white, middle-class residents moved to the suburbs, but some, like New York, simply traded one population for another. "White flight" left New York with a disproportionately impoverished central city comprised of ethnic minorities, including African Americans leaving the South and Puerto Ricans fleeing the poverty of their homeland, among others. At the same time, federal policy promoted automobile usage through subsidies for road-building while inner-city public transportation deteriorated. Urban landlords received no incentives to maintain or renovate aging structures; thus, residents who remained in cities faced an actual shortage of safe, affordable housing.

The growing crisis in American cities, however, was tempered by a rising confidence in the emerging field of urban planning. "Given the burgeoning administrative capacities of modern systems (public and private)," historian Christopher Klemek has written, "government could become the organizing master of the hitherto unmanageable cities." In this new realm, private philanthropy would play a critical role in developing the social science needed to shape government's plans. In 1948, for example, Rockefeller Foundation funding and leadership enabled Columbia University to establish the Institute for Urban Land Use and Housing Studies, for the purpose of conducting a "many-sided attack" on the housing problem. The Institute's scholars were drawn from economics, law, sociology, business, architecture, and public health. They compiled surveys, collected and analyzed data, and aimed to increase understanding of the complicated network of factors driving the housing crisis. Like many of the research institutes the Foundation had supported in the past, for

As the nation confronted a housing shortage after World War Two, the Social Science Research Council organized experts to study the dynamics of the industry and help shape public policy. The Rockefeller Foundation provided a three-year grant to support this work. (Jules Schick. Rockefeller Archive Center.)

Chapter Seven: Democracy and Design in America's Cities

New York City writer and activist Jane Jacobs fought efforts to build expressways through existing neighborhoods, as well as a plan to have her West Village community demolished for urban renewal. In 1961, when her book The Death and Life of Great American Cities was published, she was chair of the Committee to Save the West Village. (Phil Stanziola. Library of Congress.)

example Brookings and the National Bureau of Economic Research, the Columbia Institute served in a consulting capacity to government planning agencies, city planning commissions, housing projects, and other universities. The use of empirical methods and the collection of reliable data, in short the realization of a "science of urban form and structure," was its ultimate aim. "At bottom," a bulletin to the trustees explained, "the urban housing problem is a question of the scientific use of land in cities."

The scientific impulse in urban planning was not original to the postwar era, but technological innovations and an economy of prosperity made large-scale redevelopment more feasible than ever before. In the 1930s, New York's first federally subsidized public housing projects had been low-rises. But beginning in 1941, when the first high-rise project was constructed in East Harlem, city officials realized that housing people in towers was cost-efficient. Furthermore, high-rises were considered not only economically but aesthetically superior. Compared to dark tenement houses, they had light and ventilation, and they were built in clusters interspersed with green spaces that offered, at least theoretically, play

In the late 1950s, New York City's Robert Moses (left) was one of the most influential urban planners in the United States. He managed the construction of new automobile expressways and bridges and the development of tens of thousands of apartments on land cleared by urban renewal. (Walter Albertin. Library of Congress.)

spaces for children similar to those in the suburbs.

Unfortunately, these clustered high-rises also removed their residents from a more traditional, mixed-use urban scene, a phenomenon Jane Jacobs would take to task in *The Death and Life of Great American Cities*, which was published in 1961. The warehousing aspect of high-rise projects separated low-income residents from a true diversity of neighbors, and their living spaces from street-level commerce and interaction. Although metropolitan in appearance, high-rises actually employed a suburban organizational plan of residential, retail, and industrial zones segregated into separate spheres.

Jacobs found the high-rise projects monotonous, sterile, and vulgar, not to mention paternalistic and authoritarian. "The trouble with paternalists," Jacobs asserted, "is that they want to make impossibly profound changes, and they choose impossibly superficial means for doing so." Mid-century urban renewal projects may have looked tidier than the slums they replaced, but in Jacobs's view they were as much of a ghetto, if not more so.

Death and Life was written with support from the Rockefeller Foundation from approximately 1958 to 1960. These funds enabled Jacobs, an editor at the renowned journal *Architectural Forum*, to take a leave and support herself while researching and writing what turned out to be a path-breaking volume in urban planning and criticism. The *New York Times* described the book as "perhaps the single most influential work in the history of town planning."

Jacobs swam against the tide of her times, arguing that the last thing cities needed was more top-down, technocratic science. As she put it, "The pseudoscience of planning seems almost neurotic in its determination to imitate empiric failure and ignore empiric success." Amateur, untrained citizens would make the best rules for themselves, Jacobs believed, and professional planners should get out of their way. In keeping with that quintessentially democratic proposition, Jacobs actually observed and analyzed how city streets and sidewalks worked or didn't work, rather than rely on theory.

Where Jefferson and other Founders had reviled cities as inherently anti-democratic, dangerous, and corrupting, Jacobs viewed them as quite the opposite. To her mind, cities encouraged "an intricate network of voluntary controls and standards among the people themselves." Counterintuitively, cities provided better safety because residents, merchants, and passers-by all kept their eyes on the street. People were more likely to help each other because they had regular opportunities to interact. Children who were engaged in rough play, flirtation, or loitering could be seen and taken to task by older residents of the community. Jacobs's work strongly suggests that small-scale, high-density neighborhoods, even shabby ones, were the seat of democratic values and the democratic process. Only a grassroots, piecemeal, organic, and slightly disordered environment—as real cities left to their own devices tended to be—would foster such values.

While the rush for the suburbs seemed to confirm Americans' desire for more privacy, Jacobs claimed that traditional cities in fact offered greater privacy by keeping public and private spaces separate. Rather than having to invite an acquaintance into the home, for example, visiting could occur on the stoop or street corner. Jacobs argued that organic cities were ultimately a place of freedom, whereas planned suburbs (and housing projects) were "very nice towns if you were docile and had no plans of your own and did not mind spending your life with others with no plans of their own. As in all Utopias, the right to have plans of any significance belonged only to the planner in charge."

Death and Life was lauded immediately by all the major figures of the day in urban thinking, from Lewis Mumford to William H. Whyte. Almost as if to prove its significance, the book was also excoriated by government officials and developers, including Jacobs's longtime nemesis, Robert Moses, New York's powerful Parks Commissioner and head of the slum clearance program. Jacobs and her Greenwich Village neighborhood association had successfully defeated Moses's proposed multi-lane highway through Washington Square Park only a few years earlier. To Humanities Division officer Chadbourne Gilpatric, her main contact at the Foundation, Jacobs joked: "As an antidote to the praise, I am getting a spate of furiously angry and denunciatory letters from planners and housers who seem to have me tabbed as an irresponsible, if not vicious, demagogue!"

Jacobs's frank, epigrammatic writing style and the power of her ideas and insights won many fans to her stance on cities. Her book has also had staying power, influencing countless architects, planners, and urbanists ever since.

It seemed to express a new point of view that community activists longed to hear in the early 1960s. By the time of its 1961 publication, New York and similar cities had experienced more than a decade of relentless slum clearance and modernist urban plans emphasizing super-blocks and high-rise towers, not to mention alarm over alleged urban decline despite countless renewal projects. Yet as historian Samuel Zipp points out, while Jacobs "seemed to materialize from the streets, storefronts and cafes of Greenwich Village like an urban Rachel Carson ... it would be a mistake to imagine that the ideas Jacobs championed arose solely out of the mind of one *Architectural Forum* editor concerned to preserve the quaint bonhomie of Greenwich Village." In reality, Zipp explains, *Death and Life* reflected an intellectual culmination of a wide array of ideas that grew out of resistance to urban renewal in the 1950s. But Jacobs was well known among a small circle of influential writers and urbanists, and it was this pedigree that prompted Gilpatric's willingness to invest Foundation funds in her work.

The Debate Over Lincoln Center and Urban Renewal

Jacobs's compelling and authoritative voice fit well within a larger Rockefeller Foundation initiative responding to urban crises created by the postwar housing shortage and urban renewal projects of the 1950s and 1960s. One prong of the program supported the data-driven housing research at Columbia's Institute for Urban Land Use and Housing Studies, while the other, sponsored by the Humanities Division, supported scholars and writers who investigated the broader cultural, aesthetic, and socioeconomic dimensions of urban design. Between 1955 and 1965, the Foundation funded work by Kevin Lynch, Grady Clay, E.A. Gutkind, Ian McHarg, Christopher Alexander, and half a dozen others, much of which has been formative to the field and continues to be influential in city planning today. Architectural historian Peter Laurence argues that the Rockefeller Foundation's early recognition that aesthetic design issues were equally as important as technical issues put it in the postwar avant-garde of architectural and urban theory.

In 1958 the Foundation sponsored a Conference on Urban Design Criticism at the University of Pennsylvania, a turning point in the field that was attended by leaders including J.B. Jackson, Louis Kahn, Louis Mumford, Catherine Bauer, and I.M. Pei, as well as Jacobs and other major figures whom the Foundation directly supported. The conference helped foster a network of graduate programs in architectural history, criticism, and theory that emerged throughout the 1960s. Perhaps most important to the Foundation, however, and to Gilpatric in particular, were the participants' contributions to public discourse about cities through a surge in articles published in popular magazines such as *Fortune*, *Holiday*, *The New Yorker*, and *The Saturday Evening Post*.

Ironically, even as it encouraged public engagement with urban design by supporting writers who criticized top-down, technocratic modernist redevelopment, the Foundation was a lead funder for one of the biggest projects of the kind: the Lincoln Center for the Performing Arts in New York City. This project would force the Foundation to reconcile its faith in experts and urban planning with its efforts to promote a more democratic society.

Initiated in 1956 and opened in phases from 1962 to 1966, Lincoln Center included buildings designed by leading architects of the time, including Max Abramovitz, Eero Saarinen, Wallace Harrison, Gordon Bunshaft, and Philip Johnson. The plan envisioned the Center as the high-culture cornerstone of the Lincoln Square Renewal Project, masterminded by Jane Jacobs's adversary Robert Moses.

But clearing the site for Lincoln Square would require designating (and demolishing) 19 city blocks as "slums," replacing a community that reflected precisely the kind of urban fabric that Jane Jacobs celebrated. The neighborhood was

Planners in New York and other cities sought to eliminate areas deemed to be blighted. Jane Jacobs argued that these planners ignored the informal ways in which residents, including youth, appropriated spaces to meet community needs. (Al Ravenna. Library of Congress.)

full of three- to six-story residential buildings, including apartments, rooming houses, and small businesses. It was densely populated and diverse. Although the area was perceived as being in decline, most residents had lived there for over 10 years. They held working and lower-middle class jobs, with median incomes matching the median for Manhattan incomes overall. The streetscape was dotted with luncheonettes, shoe stores, clothing stores, bars, grocers, barbers, beauty parlors, toy stores, tailors, radio and television repair shops, auto parts stores, hardware stores, a funeral parlor, and newsstands.

In the end, it was the neighborhood's physical condition that led to its designation as a slum. There had been no new construction in the area for years, and banks avoided loaning money for new mortgages or improvements there. In this era of postwar prosperity, the absence of growth came to indicate decline rather than stability. While over half of the units had complete bathrooms, running water, and central heat, Moses and the Committee on Slum Clearance focused on the percentage that did not. Tenants and businesspeople took their objections to the highest levels of city government, to no avail. Yet the case they made cut right to the heart of core questions about democratic values in a free society. Protesters questioned the privileging and subsidizing of elite culture over ordinary, self-supporting human culture as expressed in neighborhood life and commerce. As one housing activist put it, "If we are going to talk about progress, we have to talk about human progress first.... I say no matter how impressive any cultural institution may be, or educational institution, there is nothing more important in a democracy than the human beings involved."

Neighborhood groups mounted a vigorous opposition to the Lincoln Center Project. These protests gained the attention of a citywide audience and began to articulate some of the problems endemic to urban renewal. Critics noted that substandard housing was not being replaced with better housing, but rather by real estate deals serving tax-exempt organizations that would further drain the city's coffers while doing little to solve the housing shortage.

In 1956, residents of the Lincoln Square area protested the proposed demolition of their community, forcing planners to recognize that neighborhoods represent informal systems of social connections that play a key role in community development. (Phil Stanziola. Library of Congress.)

In addition, the scattering of ethnic communities was destructive, and relocating ethnic groups to targeted public housing projects far from the city center exacerbated racial segregation. This kind of bureaucratic planning, according to Jacobs and others, was dehumanizing, even if it did result in new housing. Furthermore, although the city was required to provide relocation services to residents, there was no such provision for the area's 600 businesses, which caused devastating economic losses to a healthy commercial community.

The Foundation, represented on the Lincoln Center Project by board chairman John D. Rockefeller 3rd and Humanities program officer Charles Fahs, brought to the table its signature scientific and statistical thoroughness. Fahs took care to keep Foundation officers abreast of transportation surveys, audience questionnaires, and other studies, all of which provided reassurance that the Center would strive to reach the broadest possible public. Interestingly, however, one of its studies, of other Manhattan theaters, showed that "in the present economy, the cheaper seats are the most difficult to sell," further underscoring the question of whose interests the Center would truly serve.

Ultimately, the Lincoln Center Project forced the Foundation to begin to try to reconcile its competing and sometimes contradictory ambitions in the urban environment. While it sought to promote high standards in the arts and humanities and in urban design, the Foundation also had a long history of promoting a democratic approach to culture and community. One of the most lasting effects of the Lincoln Center controversy would be a renewed effort on the part of the Foundation to promote critical voices in urban design, and to shift toward collaborative community development initiatives rather than the technocratic prescriptions of experts as a means of addressing urban problems from the mid-1960s forward.

Strengthening Institutions

If urban renewal proved increasingly disappointing in the 1960s, it did not reflect any less concern for cities on the part of policymakers. Many shared the view articulated by President Lyndon Johnson: "Our society will never be great until our cities are great. Today the frontier of imagination and innovation lies inside those cities and not beyond their boundaries." Johnson bolstered his pledge with resources when he elevated urban issues to cabinet-level priority by creating the Department of Housing and Urban Development in 1965.

But by 1969, shortly after Johnson was succeeded by President Richard Nixon and as the United States celebrated the technological triumph of landing a man on the moon, many policymakers were frustrated by their inability to improve life in America's largest cities. The disappointing results of urban renewal had shown that changing the built environment was not enough. Policymakers were "traumatized by the realization that everything relates to everything," quipped Daniel Patrick Moynihan, President Nixon's advisor for urban affairs.

Many private foundations in the United States, concerned about the explosive character of inner-city problems as evidenced by urban riots, were slow to tackle these complex issues. But some, including the Rockefeller Foundation, were leaders. The Mott Foundation in Michigan, for example, had pioneered a special partnership with the Board of Education in Flint to develop the "community school concept" to expand the role of the neighborhood school beyond classroom education to serve as a resource for the entire community, providing consumer and health education for adults and recreation and social activities for senior citizens. In this way, they sought to strengthen social capital in low-income neighborhoods. The Ford Foundation also began to focus on urban issues beginning in the early 1960s. Its Great Cities educational grants supported a wide-ranging series of innovative projects designed to make big-city schools more responsive to their communities. Its Gray Areas programs emphasized "investment in people, not just property," and became a model for elements of President Lyndon Johnson's Great Society programs.

Meanwhile, the Rockefeller Foundation focused its urban initiatives in the 1960s and 1970s on the systemic problems that seemed to lie at the heart of urban America. These efforts, as described in Chapter Six, aimed to support equal opportunity for African Americans and other minorities in the nation's largest cities. Like Mott and Ford, the Rockefeller Foundation aimed particularly at strengthening the inner-city school's role as a cohesive force in neighborhoods. Demonstration projects were launched in Los Angeles, St. Louis, Minneapolis, and Chicago that included innovative efforts to incorporate the community in school planning, develop community counseling and career

Daniel Patrick Moynihan served as an urban affairs advisor to Presidents Johnson and Nixon. Although he contributed to the development of Johnson's Great Society programs, he became a leading critic of federal urban renewal programs and a proponent of giving local governments wider authority to direct federal funding for community development. (Thomas J. O'Halloran. Library of Congress.)

planning services, and generally help schools find new ways of developing meaningful community relationships.

Recognizing that strong institutions depended on strong leadership, the Foundation also launched an initiative in 1969 to accelerate the training and development of minority superintendents and principals in inner-city school districts. The Foundation provided funding to administrator internship programs in Baltimore, Philadelphia, and Detroit in 1970. The Foundation also supported the Portal School Program, launched by Temple University in Philadelphia, to increase the involvement of community residents and parents in school activities and to bring more community paraprofessionals into the classroom.

As the Foundation reported, its efforts to address the issues in America's largest cities increasingly sought to ensure that city dwellers had "an authentic voice in decisions affecting their own affairs." In a very real way, this effort picked up the challenge laid down by James Madison in 1829 to reform the political economy of the nation's cities in ways that would strengthen democracy. The Foundation's grants were focused less on issues related to the built environment or urban systems and more on existing institutional systems—like schools.

The Foundation's focus on human capacity reflected, in part, the fact that the federal government's role in shaping the built environment and infrastructure of urban America in the 1970s was changing. President Nixon pushed to decentralize funding for urban projects by giving more authority to local governments. The Housing and Community Development Act of 1974, for example, created the Community Development Block Grant (CDBG) program, which consolidated earlier urban renewal, urban parks, and Model Cities grant programs to provide significant resources for housing and infrastructure development, as well as services to low-income communities. Under President Jimmy Carter, Congress created in 1977 the federal Urban Development Action Grant program, which provided additional resources for land acquisition, site clearance, and infrastructure development. CDBG grants also provided a major funding source for the growth of new nonprofit, grassroots organizations.

But in the 1980s, the political, economic, and philanthropic landscape in the United States began to change dramatically. A growing fiscal crisis, reflected in runaway inflation and rising unemployment, combined with a change in the political mood of the nation that led to Ronald Reagan's election as president, threatened dramatic reductions in federal support for cities and an abrupt end to many of the grassroots organizations that seemed to hold out the greatest promise for urban community revitalization.

A Grand Partnership for American Communities

As American presidents called for a smaller role for government in the 1980s and 1990s, philanthropic institutions and community organizations had to rethink their approach to the inner cities. Given the scale of the problems, no private foundation had the resources to go it alone. Collaboration would be critical. In the 1990s, the Rockefeller Foundation joined long-time partners at the Ford Foundation and other philanthropies to launch a large-scale, cooperative initiative with hopes for a nationwide impact.

The Community Development Corporation (CDC) model had been "one of the few real success stories in the uneven history of attempts to better conditions in America's central cities." The model relied on neighborhood-based groups with local roots and constituencies to sponsor physical rebuilding projects that would also lead to social revitalization. But Rockefeller Foundation President Peter Goldmark asked in 1990 whether the movement could become big enough to make a sustained, widespread impact on America's central cities?

In a bold effort to try to take the concept to a much larger scale, Goldmark met with Mitchell Sviridoff, a former assembly plant worker and labor organizer who rose to become president of the A.F.L.-C.I.O. in Connecticut. In the early 1960s he had been the first executive director of Community Progress Inc., an antipoverty program in New Haven supported by a grant from the Ford Foundation. In its first 30 months, according to the *New York Times*, the project helped 1,500 people find jobs and became a national model. After a brief tenure working for the City of New York, Sviridoff joined the Ford Foundation as vice president for national affairs. In 1979 Ford produced a discussion paper entitled *Communities and Neighborhoods: A Possible Private Sector Initiative for the 1980s*. The report called for the creation of a new organization to support self-help community organizations in declining cities as critical players in the process of revitalization. Sviridoff left Ford to found the Local Initiatives Support Corporation (LISC) with Ford funding. Through the 1980s, even after Sviridoff retired, LISC played a key role in supporting a growing community development movement.

Goldmark and Sviridoff teamed up in 1991, and the Rockefeller Foundation convened 15 foundations and corporations to talk about how to increase the impact of the community development movement. This rich conversation led to the establishment of the National Community Development Initiative (NCDI).

Rockefeller Foundation trustees John R. Evans, Arthur Levitt Jr., Alice Stone Ilchman and others toured the Bronx in 1989 to understand the work of community development corporations. The tour helped build board support for major grants to the National Community Development Initiative. (Richard Hughes. Rockefeller Archive Center.)

NCDI had three broad goals: to accelerate the growth of the community development movement, to enlist additional funders and lenders from the public and private sectors in fostering collaboration across sectors, and to put in place a framework that would channel patient, private-sector capital into inner-city neighborhoods.

At the grassroots, NCDI built on a long tradition of community organizing for neighborhood improvement. On a national scale, however, it represented an innovative partnership that included private foundations, intermediary financial organizations, private-sector lenders, and government-sponsored enterprises, including the Federal Home Loan Mortgage Corporation (Freddie Mac), a government-sponsored entity providing a secondary market for home loans. Goldmark recognized that a partnership on this scale was risky, but he also noted that "our resources in the foundation world are small." Innovative institutional relationships offered a path to greater effectiveness.

Leveraging private capital to address the needs of inner-city neighborhoods represented an important part of the overall strategy for NCDI. Program-Related Investments constituted a critical component of this strategy. Authorized by the Tax Reform Act of 1969, this still-nascent concept allowed foundations to invest or make loans to further their tax-exempt purposes, even when these investments might not appeal to a so-called "prudent" investor. With these tools, the project hoped to bring to bear $500 million in capital, in addition to the $62 million in grants pledged by the project's major

Rockefeller Foundation President Peter Goldmark and Sharon Pratt Dixon, the mayor of Washington, D.C., listened as Leland Brendsel, CEO of the Federal Home Loan Mortgage Corporation, spoke at a press conference to launch the National Community Development Initiative on February 27, 1991. Brendsel announced that as part of the project "Freddie Mac" would buy $100 million in low-income rental housing mortgages to help spark local housing development. (Rockefeller Archive Center.)

funders. Prudential provided valuable leadership in adding the "largest social investment it ever made in America's low-income urban areas." Freddie Mac, meanwhile, would contribute fixed-rate mortgage money for local projects.

NCDI began operations in 1991, funneling money through its intermediary agencies to community development projects in 20 U.S. cities. The immediate goal was to "grow in scope and competence" and to increase the productivity and impact of housing and other capital projects under development by community development corporations. Unlike the urban renewal projects of the 1960s, these local initiatives were run by people living and working in the inner city who were investing in housing and business properties. The Rockefeller Foundation hoped to build leadership, capital, and power in these neighborhoods through the community development process. Early NCDI loans were made to multi- and single-family housing projects, as well as for training and technical assistance in Philadelphia, St. Paul, Newark, Portland, and Kansas City.

The Rockefeller Foundation contributed funding to NCDI through its Equal Opportunity program. From the Foundation's point of view, this work was connected to a distinctly American past and anchored in the ideas of mutualism and self-help that Tocqueville had admired in the 1830s. Goldmark advocated a "long, concerted national effort to reverse the complex set of social and economic factors that exacerbate chronic urban poverty." Noting the Equal Opportunity program's "historic commitment to the plight of the urban poor," he said in 1993, that the Foundation would "increasingly focus on strengthening the intersection of work and community in blighted urban neighborhoods."

Goldmark and others at the Rockefeller Foundation hoped that the community development corporations funded by NCDI would influence the American conversation on urban poverty measures. By the time the project was five years old, he suggested that the number and strength of community development corporations could mark the beginning of a "national alliance of serious, seasoned and professional community organizations that can bring a concerted voice to bear on shaping the urban agenda."

Though the Foundation's initial commitment was for only three years, it renewed funding for the period from 1994 to 1997. The community development corporations had "proven to be singularly effective in enabling inner-city residents to develop local leadership and bring in new investment in tangible capital assets."

The willingness of other funders to come to the table proved critical to the consortium's early success. Five new donors joined the effort in 1994, including foundations, as well as additional banks and the United States Department of Housing and Urban Development. In 1996 the Rockefeller Foundation appropriated another $9 million for a third round of assistance, and continued to provide core support for the two funding intermediaries.

In 1999, following Gordon Conway's assumption of the Rockefeller Foundation's presidential post, the goals of the Equal Opportunity program were transitioned into a new effort called Working Communities, which continued to make ongoing grants to NCDI and its funding intermediaries.

By the time NCDI entered its second decade, the program had become an independent nonprofit organization and was renamed "Living Cities: National Community Development Initiative." In 2002 the Foundation pledged $4 million to support the second 10-year phase of work. The funding partnership now included eight foundations, seven financial institutions, and two U.S. government agencies.

Persistent problems still remained in America's inner cities, including poverty, income inequality, and public schooling inadequacies, all of which affected racial minorities and non-English speakers disproportionately. The continuing promise

The National Community Development Initiative was created after the Rockefeller Foundation brought 15 foundations and corporations together to explore ways to increase the scale and impact of local community development corporations. NCDI was later renamed Living Cities, Inc. (Rockefeller Archive Center.)

of the partnership, however, was evident in the growth of available resources. Living Cities pledged $500 million over ten years to continue to promote urban revitalization. The new investment aimed to build upon past experience, supporting 300 community organizations and spurring billions of dollars in added funding for affordable housing and commercial business development.

In 2007 stimulated in part by the Rockefeller Foundation's increasing focus on systems approaches led by its new president, Judith Rodin, Living Cities shifted its core focus from community development to a multidisciplinary approach to neighborhood and system transformation." Leadership also engineered a fundamental shift in the nature of the organization. Living Cities became a member-driven partnership, with members organized into working groups to steer the collaboration's agenda. Moving away from a focus on individual neighborhoods or a single urban system, the new approach looked at whole cities as products of multiple, integrated systems. Within this context, practitioners focused on four key strategies: bottom-up change led by neighborhood or local nonprofits; top-down or public-sector-led integrative systems change; the alignment of philanthropy to broad, integrated goals; and the strategic engagement of the private sector.

Characteristically, the Rockefeller Foundation provided more than direct funding for the strategic objectives of Living Cities. As part of its ongoing efforts to take a more systems-focused approach to addressing urban issues in the United States, the Foundation tackled associated systems issues. For example, it launched its Promoting Equitable, Sustainable Transportation Initiative in 2008 to promote affordable, environmentally responsible transit solutions as part of a broad-based effort to develop, at local and national levels, a new transportation policy for the United States. The Foundation also explored green job creation through its Sustainable Employment in a Green U.S. Economy Initiative, to ensure that low- and moderate-income workers in cities would benefit from efforts to expand environmentally friendly industries.

As Living Cities marked the beginning of its third decade in 2011, the scale and complexity of the enterprise—its most innovative feature—also made evaluation challenging. One level of success was apparent in the numbers. More than 150,000 homes, stores, schools, and community facilities had been completed in America's inner cities. But program participants tended to emphasize the catalytic power of the model. Clearly, NCDI/Living Cities had provided a profound alternative to the government-driven urban renewal concept of the 1960s. It created a new model for public- and private-sector collaboration anchored in self-help and rejuvenation in the nation's most hard-pressed neighborhoods.

Living Cities' work was assisted by other Rockefeller Foundation funding initiatives. Grants to the Project on Municipal Innovation, for example, aided mayors with policy and program development assistance. Another Foundation grantee, Green for All, worked with Living Cities to create the Energy Efficiency Opportunity Fund, which invested in large-scale building and energy retrofits that provided jobs, helped improve the quality of the local built environment, reduced the burden of energy costs, and supported broader environmental goals. The Rockefeller Foundation also provided funding to PolicyLink, an Oakland, California-based nonprofit working to help federal agencies involved with housing, transportation, and urban infrastructure make economic and social equity a critical factor in their planning and funding initiatives. PolicyLink has also helped employers and civic leaders understand how changing demographics are affecting the transportation needs of an increasingly diverse workforce.

American Cities: Seen Through a New Lens

Seemingly in crisis for decades, many of America's largest cities experienced a renaissance of sorts in the twenty-first century. For decades the image of the inner city had been associated with crumbling infrastructure, crime, economic abandonment, fiscal crisis, and more. A wave of downtown development focused on high-quality living quarters close to jobs transformed cities like New York, San Francisco, and Chicago. Urban experts like Richard Florida highlighted the increasingly important role of the "creative class" in driving American prosperity, then pointed out that the creative class prefers vibrant, diverse, and tolerant urban communities in which to live and work. Thus the health of cities was critical to American prosperity.

At the Rockefeller Foundation, a new president seemed to symbolize the promise of this new era of urban revitalization. Judith Rodin had been provost of Yale, the president of the University of Pennsylvania, and the first woman to lead an Ivy League institution. She had spent a great deal of time working to revitalize cities like Philadelphia and New Haven, and had written a seminal book, *The University and Urban Revival*, about the special role and responsibility of urban universities in inner-city neighborhoods. She came to the Foundation with hands-on experience in urban development. At the University of Pennsylvania, she spearheaded an effective community development effort in neighborhoods surrounding the university, which led to significant economic advancement and opportunity for community residents. Her efforts were seen as a model for other communities seeking to use "anchor institutions" like universities and hospitals to improve the health of urban neighborhoods, especially in the wake of the out-migration of many traditional downtown employers in financial and corporate services. She also comprehended the growing importance of knowledge workers and the skills gap both in the American economy and around the globe.

Rodin understood that American metropolitan regions were undergoing enormous change. As the 2010 Census revealed, poverty was growing in the suburbs of the United States. Nearly two-thirds of the nation's population lived in the 100 most populous metropolitan regions (all of them with more than 500,000 inhabitants). Despite the long crisis, these regions had slightly increased their share of population since 1970 (from 63 to 65 percent). Their share of poverty, however, had grown considerably (from 50 percent of the nation's poor to 61 percent). Between 2000 and 2010, as the nation's poor population increased dramatically, the number of people in poverty in suburbs grew by 53 percent, compared to 23 percent in cities. For the first time in the nation's history, a greater percentage of the poor lived in suburbs than in cities.

In keeping with its tradition of investing in new knowledge as well as applying that knowledge in the fields and the streets, the Rockefeller Foundation partnered with the Brookings Institution in an effort to understand what was happening. With support from the Rockefeller Foundation, Brookings drew attention to these changes and highlighted important implications not only for American prosperity, but also global climate change. The suburbs tended to be poorly served by public transportation. With increasing gas prices, transportation had become the second-largest expense for most American households, exceeded only by the cost of shelter. Most of this money was spent on automobiles with emissions that contributed to the problem of global warming.

In concert with Brookings, the Rockefeller Foundation made it clear that access to affordable and sustainable transportation was key not only to economic prosperity, but also to democracy. As Rodin told leaders in New York, "It's a conduit to the American dream." With funding from the Foundation, Brookings launched its Blueprint for American Prosperity program, which sought to "unleash the potential of a metropolitan nation." A 2008 Brookings report, entitled "A Bridge to Somewhere: Rethinking American Transportation for the 21st Century," highlighted the nation's need to invest its transportation resources more strategically. This study was complemented in 2010 by "Driven Apart," a Rockefeller Foundation study that emphasized the consequences of increasing urban sprawl on commute times. Also in 2010, the Rockefeller Foundation entered into a $10-million-dollar partnership with Brookings to provide expert help and guidance to major U.S. metropolitan regions for developing new plans for job growth in the post-recession economy. And in 2013 the Foundation announced $1.2 million in grants to support plans for high-quality bus rapid transit in American cities. Consistent with the Foundation's deeper efforts to empower urban residents in the spirit of Jane Jacobs, these grants would support research, communications, and community outreach to engage and educate local stakeholders in the development of these transportation systems.

Many of the Rockefeller Foundation's urban initiatives in the last several decades have been inspired by Jacobs. After she died in 2007, the Foundation established the Jane Jacobs Medal Program to honor two individuals each year whose ongoing work and accomplishments represent her principles and practices in action in New York City. Speaking to the honorees in 2009, Judith Rodin reminded the audience that Jacobs had once written that "in order for a society to flourish, there must be a flourishing city at its core." Rodin elaborated by highlighting an idea that was implicit in Jacobs's work: "In order for a city to flourish, there must be active and engaged citizens at its core, dreamers and doers who embrace the notion that citizenship is only given meaning by the measure of our actions." Jefferson, Madison, Franklin, and other founding fathers would have understood this sentiment. In the context of an increasingly urban America, threatened by economic shocks and storms driven by global climate change, engaged urban citizens are essential to the resilience of the American experiment.

Encouraging planners and public officials to take a systems approach to urban infrastructure, the Rockefeller Foundation helped sponsor research and community initiatives to reduce inequities in access to public transportation and to encourage environmentally sustainable development. (Jonas Bendiksen. Rockefeller Foundation.)

CASE STUDIES IN INNOVATION

Quality of the Environment

On April 22, 1970, 20 million Americans mobilized for a national "teach-in" on the environment. This first Earth Day reflected a growing concern that water and air pollution were degrading the nation's quality of life and posing long-term hazards to the planet.

For leaders at the Rockefeller Foundation, many of the themes addressed in classrooms, community centers, public parks, and civic forums on Earth Day were all too familiar. For decades the Foundation had promoted family planning initiatives to ease the burden of population explosion on the planet's resources. Public health initiatives had worked to ensure clean water and sanitation. As part of a major realignment of its programs in 1963, the Foundation had adopted five major goals, including support for "efforts toward the improvement of the quality of the environment in this country." But by the late 1960s, the Foundation and environmental activists realized that more was needed.

Four months before the first Earth Day—on December 7, 1969—the Foundation had announced that it was establishing a new program entitled Quality of the Environment to support scientists and scholars working on problems related to pollution and the physical environment in the United States. As in the past, this first initiative represented a positive effort to contribute to the development of environmental policies in the United States and a way for the Foundation to learn more about the issues and how it could make a difference.

In announcing the program, the Foundation cited widespread environmental concerns. The new program's initial goal was to "concentrate resources on a few selected aspects of the many needs in this field." These included analyzing the causes of environmental blight and prospects for its reversal, along with a review of existing public and private programs to address the problem.

Air pollution in New York, Los Angeles, and other large American cities became a chronic problem in the 1950s. When conditions were particularly bad in New York, for example, they contributed to the deaths of 25 to 30 people a day. Scientists helped identify the sources of air pollution, and these discoveries led to a series of laws passed in the 1960s to protect the public. (Walter Albertin. Library of Congress.)

To this end, it selected several general areas for initial support. In 1970, the focus areas included funding university programs, researching the management of residuals and components of the ecosystem, monitoring pollutant levels, reducing pollution, training technicians, and studying societal action.

As the program developed, the goals became more specific: to "help develop an improved understanding of and solutions to important environmental problems and, in so doing, to assist in the creation of institutional capabilities to deal with them and to build a better base for public understanding of environmental issues." The program was thus heavily anchored in the Foundation's historic relationships with universities and basic research. It also sought to explore alternative models of environmental analysis and management, the management of pollutants and natural resources, international collaboration, and the study of public perceptions of environmental problems.

Volunteers helped to clean up parks and highways across the United States on Earth Day in 1970. On the Potomac River near Washington, D.C., they worked from canoes to gather trash and debris. (Thomas J. O'Halloran. Library of Congress.)

While the scientific aspects of environmentalism were key, the Foundation saw the problem as requiring an interdisciplinary approach from the beginning. It tied these initiatives to its agriculture work in the developing world, advocating for a new approach to the production and protection of food crops without resorting to the use of persistent, toxic chemicals. It funded social science initiatives to address the "interlocking problems of overpopulation, economic development, and environmental quality." The Foundation wanted to blend skills from a variety of disciplines, including the physical and natural sciences, public health, social psychology, economics, engineering, and population studies. The Foundation also played a key role as convener of academics and policymakers of different backgrounds to discuss environmental issues. In 1975, for example, Foundation staff from the Conflict in International Relations, Quality of the Environment, and Conquest of Hunger programs collaborated to organize an international conference on "Climate Change, Food Production, and Interstate Conflict."

CASE STUDIES IN INNOVATION

The students participating in this outdoor class in the Hopkins Memorial Forest at Williams College in Massachusetts were associated with the Center for Environmental Studies. One of the first programs of its kind in the United States, the center was launched in 1967 with a $75,000 grant from the Rockefeller Foundation. An additional $200,000 planning grant in 1969 allowed the college to create a program in environmental studies for undergraduates. (Rockefeller Archive Center.)

Another key to the Foundation's interdisciplinary approach was providing support for professional development to address the "critical shortages of scientists, managers, technicians, and other trained personnel," with the hope that "men with broad, multidisciplinary competence and understanding" could "staff existing public and private institutions and agencies," working at both the "managerial and scientific level." With Foundation grants, universities provided opportunities for training, research, and the development of interdisciplinary centers for study and action. The Foundation also funded an Environmental Affairs fellowship program, started in 1974 as part of a ramp-up of domestic fellowships.

All of these measures worked to influence institutions in the United States at the structural level. They helped educate a "whole new generation of students in the importance of taking an ecological view, whatever their individual fields of interest." The Foundation hoped that these efforts would indirectly guide politicians and decision makers as well as "private citizens." "Everyone is endangered by foul air, impure water, and toxic chemicals in food," the Foundation noted in its 1971 annual report. In attacking these collective problems with collective action, "citizen involvement, especially of the young, is indispensable." Indeed, John Knowles, who became president of the Rockefeller Foundation in 1972, hoped that the American people would "provide a model of ethical and intellectual suasion for an interdependent world of nation states, based on self-restraint and emphasizing the quality, as contrasted with the quantity, of life." Knowles suggested this development would require marked changes in the "life styles, traditions and beliefs of all Americans" to cultivate a new ethic in which less is more.

DEMOCRACY & PHILANTHROPY

No one had anticipated the scale of the public reaction on that first Earth Day in 1970, nor the reaction of policymakers. Within a short time, Congress passed and President Nixon signed landmark legislation, including the Clean Air Act, and established the Environmental Protection Agency. In the private sector, millions of philanthropic dollars were directed toward environmental issues.

The Foundation ended the Quality of the Environment program in June 1978 and gradually phased out its existing grants. Among the program's major achievements the Foundation counted improvement of water-quality management, especially in the Midwest and the Northeastern United States; the development of new approaches to wastewater management implemented in Florida; the expansion of regional environmental planning in the Hudson River Basin and with the Rocky Mountain Institute; and research into alternatives to highly toxic pesticides.

Lessons learned in the Quality of the Environment program would continue to shape the Foundation's philanthropy in the United States and around the world. In 1979 the Conquest of Hunger program—a part of the Green Revolution launched by the Rockefeller Foundation, which aimed to increase food production in the developing world—adopted a new focus for what would later be termed sustainable agriculture in regions with environmentally sensitive or marginal lands. The Foundation also expanded its investment in water and land-use management as well as the search for alternatives to highly toxic pesticides. In its work in International Relations, the Foundation promoted the development of alternative energy policies. Thus, over the next several decades, the seeds planted in the Quality of the Environment program would grow to fruition as an abiding value in the Rockefeller Foundation's work, reflected in an ongoing commitment to sustainable ecosystems and environmentally friendly development.

In the 1970s, the Rockefeller Foundation added an emphasis on environmental sustainability to its ongoing research in agriculture. At the University of Arizona's Environmental Research Laboratory, with the support of the Foundation, scientists worked on developing a high-yield, zero-pollution agricultural system for producing tomatoes and other crops in controlled environments. (Rockefeller Archive Center.)

Refugees from Hurricane Katrina were victimized by the storm and the failure of levees and other public systems. The

CONCLUSION

Resilience and the American Spirit

While the deadly winds of Hurricane Katrina gathered force over the Gulf of Mexico on August 28, 2005, thousands of people crowded into cars and headed north. Newscasters warned that the storm was ferocious, a Category 5 hurricane as it churned over the Gulf, moving toward the southeast coast of Louisiana. But tens of thousands of residents of New Orleans were unable to flee. They included the homebound elderly, patients in hospitals and nursing homes, and low-income families, primarily African-American, without sufficient transportation—in short, the most vulnerable populations in the region.

When the storm struck the following morning as a Category 3 hurricane, it ripped through communities all along the Gulf Coast. Levees failed in New Orleans, allowing floodwaters to inundate neighborhoods. Altogether, at least 1,833 people lost their lives. Causing nearly $81 billion in damage, Katrina was the costliest storm-driven disaster in American history. In its wake, public officials at the local, state, and federal levels were criticized for actions taken years before the storm (in the design and maintenance of the levees, for example) as well as for their response during the emergency. Thus Katrina not only posed a great challenge for the people who suffered from its destruction, but also raised questions for all Americans about whether the mechanics of American democracy were truly serving all its citizens.

CONCLUSION

Facing Forward

This was not the first disastrous storm to hit the United States during the century of the Rockefeller Foundation's existence, but it was a harbinger of things to come for low-lying coastal cities in the hurricane belt in an era of climate change. With a warming climate, scientists expect sea levels to rise significantly and hurricanes and other storms to intensify. Thus, as the Rockefeller Foundation responded to the disaster in New Orleans and other communities in Katrina's path, it did so with an eye to helping these communities prepare for the future.

In post-Katrina New Orleans, especially, key questions needed to be answered. Once the floodwaters were pumped from the streets, would the most disadvantaged communities be able to recover? And how could they be strengthened to respond to the next crisis—whether it be environmental, economic, or social? Could something good come from the disaster? Would the recovery bring new resources to bear on the long-standing pattern of neglect and inequality in the most vulnerable neighborhoods? Or would the process of reconstruction continue to favor the wealthy over the poor?

To address these questions and focus on long-term planning, the Rockefeller Foundation provided grants to three organizations with deep roots in New Orleans: the Local Initiatives Support Corporation, the Enterprise Foundation, and Habitat for Humanity. These groups launched a series of innovative efforts to rebuild housing and kick-start new businesses, all aimed at strengthening the resilience of low-income communities in the area. These initiatives also prompted leaders at the Rockefeller Foundation to think more deeply about how other cities, both in the United States and around the world, would respond to similar and ever-growing risks associated with climate change.

DEMOCRACY & PHILANTHROPY

Judith Rodin, like other newly appointed leaders before her, began her tenure in a time of crisis. The first woman president of the Rockefeller Foundation, Dr. Rodin had been in office for only a matter of months when Katrina struck. Rodin was a leading researcher in psychology and was deeply familiar with the concept of resilience in the study of behavior and personality. She and others at the Rockefeller Foundation increasingly came to believe that borrowing the concept of resilience—not only from psychology but also from engineering and ecology—could provide a powerful framework for cities facing climate change and its attendant disasters.

Over the next eight years, the Foundation developed a series of initiatives designed to help communities around the world

Volunteers with Habitat for Humanity helped put siding on a new home in New Orleans. The outpouring of charitable contributions, philanthropic grants, and citizen volunteers to areas affected by the storm made it clear that Tocqueville's civil society was still alive and well in the United States in the twenty-first century. (Jonas Bendiksen. Rockefeller Foundation.)

CONCLUSION

After Judith Rodin became president in 2005, she focused the Rockefeller Foundation's work on systemic factors affecting the poor and vulnerable in a rapidly changing global economy. A renowned research psychologist and former president of the University of Pennsylvania, Rodin spurred the Foundation to explore ways to help communities become more resilient in the face of environmental and economic threats. (Rockefeller Foundation.)

and in the United States take steps to ensure that they would be able to survive and thrive whatever adversity, shock, or stress came their way. The first initiative was launched in ten cities in Asia, with a program titled the Asian Cities Climate Change Resilience Network (ACCCRN). The project focused on building the capacity to plan, finance, coordinate, and implement climate change resilience strategies at the city level. This work was supported by the development of a knowledge base as well as a network of experts to help train public officials and nonprofits and to facilitate collaboration.

After Hurricane Sandy hammered the mid-Atlantic and especially New York and New Jersey in 2012, the Foundation, already making grants focused on strengthening resilience in communities, expanded its U.S. work. At the invitation of New York Governor Andrew Cuomo, Judith Rodin served as co-chair of the New York State 2100 Commission, established to prepare the state for future storms and other crises. And on the occasion of its centennial, the Foundation launched the 100 Resilient Cities Centennial Challenge, a $100 million effort to build urban resilience in 100 cities across the United States and around the world.

Resilience and the American Spirit

The Foundation's work on resilience in the United States was timely. In 2007 Stephen Flynn, who was a senior fellow for National Security Studies at the Council on Foreign Relations, pointed out that responding to threats to the United States—from terrorism to natural disasters—has always required the broad engagement of its citizens. But in the political environment of the early twenty-first century, efforts to minimize these threats or, in the case of terrorism, keep information secret, has actually undermined the public's ability to constructively engage the problem. The Rockefeller Foundation's efforts, therefore, sought to increase citizen engagement by motivating local leaders to anticipate these threats and bring the public into a conversation about the public infrastructure needed to prepare for them.

In many ways, these initiatives were deeply rooted in American culture and reflected the history of the Rockefeller Foundation. Resilience in the face of adversity has often been celebrated as a core element of the American spirit. The first encounters between American Indians and Europeans tested both cultures in the context of a sometimes harsh environment. Frederick Jackson Turner, one of the most famous American

CONCLUSION

historians alive when the Rockefeller Foundation was established, suggested that these tests on the frontier profoundly shaped American identity. They also demonstrated that resilience does not guarantee fair and equitable outcomes. At the heart of the American experiment, as noted by Tocqueville as well as the authors of the Constitution of the United States, is the idea that a self-governing majority will accept limits on its own power in order to protect the individual rights of all. And in the moral equation, this majority will exercise power in the public and private sectors to promote equal opportunity for all, especially the poor and vulnerable in society.

In its work in the United States over the course of a century, the Rockefeller Foundation has been committed to balancing this moral equation and has worked tirelessly to build on the American

Six months after the hurricane, the Mardi Gras parade in New Orleans in 2006 celebrated with music and art the resilience and diversity of the community. (Carol M. Highsmith. Library of Congress.)

spirit of resilience. Early efforts to strengthen agriculture and education in the American South provided hope to African Americans struggling to overcome poverty and systemic racism. Investments in social science strengthened the capacity of government to respond to the economic crisis of the Great Depression. During World War Two, when the lights of free expression and scientific inquiry were threatened by the rise of totalitarian governments, the Rockefeller Foundation worked with many other individuals and institutions to protect the flame of knowledge. In the postwar era, when the Vietnam War sparked a cultural crisis of national identity, the Rockefeller Foundation helped support a broad-based effort to affirm that America's strength lay in the rich diversity of its people. The Foundation has continued to sponsor efforts to promote equal opportunity for all and, in the process, underscore the idea, embedded within the writings of Tocqueville and other thinkers, that the resilience of the American people lies in pluralism.

During the charter fight from 1910 to 1913, politicians and pundits worried that great private wealth concentrated in an organization like the Rockefeller Foundation would undermine the foundations of democracy. In reality, modern philanthropy—launched more than a century ago by the Foundation, the Carnegie Corporation, and other broadly purposed organizations—promotes the best work of a pluralistic society. Tens of thousands of grantees, in fields ranging from the arts and humanities to the natural and social sciences, have developed new ideas and initiatives to meet the needs of a changing society. Thus the Foundation and the entire philanthropic sector have played a critical role in promoting innovation and supporting the ongoing work of what Tocqueville called "the great experiment" of democracy.

ACKNOWLEDGMENTS

Democracy & Philanthropy is part of the Rockefeller Foundation's Centennial initiative. Members of the Rockefeller Foundation's staff were deeply involved with the development of this book. Dr. Judith Rodin helped to inspire the concept and provided critical insights, especially for the chapter on cities. Michael Myers, with the close and capable assistance of Charlanne Burke, shaped the manuscript and provided ongoing support and guidance. Nicholas Turner, who was a managing director at the Foundation and now heads the Vera Institute of Justice in New York City, offered important perspectives on the Foundation's urban initiatives. In the General Counsel's office, Shari Patrick and Erica Guyer provided legal guidance and feedback. Neill Coleman and Gary Toenniessen also read a draft manuscript and offered important suggestions for improving the text, as did Robert Bykofsky, the Foundation's director of Records Management. Bykofsky and Elizabeth Pena helped us identify and access current and historical materials that tell the story. In Communications, Kathy Gomez collected spectacular photographs highlighting the Foundation's recent work.

At the Rockefeller Archive Center (RAC) in Tarrytown, New York, President Jack Meyers and Vice President James Allen Smith encouraged this project and helped stimulate our thinking during various lunchtime conversations. Jim graciously read and commented on an early draft. Teresa Iacobelli generously shared her work from the RAC's own centennial project. Tom Rosenbaum, Amy Fitch, and the other archivists helped find materials and were infinitely patient with our tight deadlines. Michele Hiltzik, especially, interrupted her day on innumerable occasions to help us find and secure images at the last minute.

Members of the team from Teneo Strategy, the Foundation's strategic partner on the Centennial, have been deeply involved with this book. Andy Maas and Mike Coakley helped get us going and Max Dworin was the consummate communicator as he helped shepherd us all toward the finish line.

Researching and writing this book was a team effort. Each of the three authors drafted chapters on his or her own and then received help from the others as we refined the text. All along the way, Lois Facer was a fourth collaborator, reading and commenting on the text while relentlessly researching and managing images to illustrate this amazing story. Madeleine Adams helped shape several chapters as the project's developmental editor. Ernie Grafe copyedited the entire work with infinite patience and attention.

We are also grateful to Amanda Waterhouse, who found documents and journal articles, read chapters, and helped draft many of the case studies. Andrea Sheehan and Michael Ilardi provided research assistance. Jessica Boyd proofed the galleys. Craig Chapman and Vivian Jenkins compiled the index. Mindy Johnston and Leigh Armstrong tracked down photographers and copyright holders to make sure we recognized the creators of works that have been buried in the archives for many years.

At Pentagram, Michael Gericke, Matt McInerney, Janet Kim, and Kelly Sung turned all of this prose into a gorgeous book.

Everyone named above did his or her part to make this a better book. Any errors or omissions that remain should be attributed to us.

Eric John Abrahamson, Sam Hurst, and Barbara Shubinski

LIST OF ILLUSTRATIONS

2-3	People on capitol steps, Washington, D.C. (between 1913 and 1918).	Photo by Harris & Ewing. Source: Library of Congress.
4-5	Little Rock Central High School, Little Rock, AR (between 1980 and 2006).	Photo by Carol M. Highsmith. Source: Libraryof Congress.
6-7	Analysis by analog computer (1959).	Source: Rockefeller Archive Center.
8-9	Construction worker with shovel and American flags, New York, NY (2009).	Photo by Ruthie Abel. Source: The Rockefeller Foundation.
21	U.S. Constitution	Source: National Archives and Records Administration
22-23	Washington Monument (2006).	Photo by Carol M. Highsmith. Source: Libraryof Congress.
25	"Uncle John" Puck cover (1906).	Print by Frank A. Nankivell. Source: Libraryof Congress.
26	Alexis de Tocqueville (1850).	Painting by Théodore Chassériau. Source: Art Resource.
27	Dispensary scene, Dr. Caldwell in Alabama	Source: Rockefeller Archive Center.
28	Frederick Gates and Simon Flexner.	Source: Rockefeller Archive Center.
29	Spelman charity card (1882-1886).	Source: Rockefeller Archive Center.
30	John D. Rockefeller Senior and Junior (1918).	Photo by H.T. Koshiba. Source: Rockefeller Archive Center.
31	Starr J. Murphy (ca. 1897).	Source: Rockefeller Archive Center.
33	Standard Oil stock certificate (1870).	Source: Rockefeller Archive Center.
38	Weldon Heyburn (ca. 1910-1915).	Photo by Bain News Service. Source: Libraryof Congress.
40	George W. Wickersham (between 1905-1945).	Photo by Harris & Ewing. Source: Libraryof Congress.
43	Jerome Greene.	Source: Rockefeller Archive Center.
44-45	Rockefeller Foundation charter (1914).	Photo by: Source: Rockefeller Archive Center.
46-47	Woodrow Wilson inauguration (1913).	Photo by Bain News Service. Source: Library of Congress.
48-51	Scene about a cotton plantation.	Photo by William Henry Jackson. Source: Library of Congress.

48	Scene on a plantation (between 1880 and 1897).	Photo by William Henry Jackson. Source: Library of Congress.
49	Children at cotton mill, Laurel, MS (1911).	Photo by Lewis W. Hine. Source: Library of Congress.
50	Field in Saltillo, MS (1912).	Source: Rockefeller Archive Center.
51	Agents and boys in field.	Source: Rockefeller Archive Center.
53	Parade of unemployed (1909).	Photo by Bain News Service. Source: Library of Congress.
54	Laura Spelman Rockefeller.	Photo by Bain News Service. Source: Library of Congress.
55	Becky Edelson under arrest, Tarrytown, NY (1914).	Photo by Bain News Service. Source: Library of Congress.
56	Examining specimens, Cumberland County, VA	Source: Rockefeller Archive Center.
57	Johns Hopkins University School of Hygiene and Public Health.	Drawing by Archer and Allan Architects. Source: Rockefeller Archive Center.
59	George E. Vincent (1930).	Source: Rockefeller Archive Center.
61	Pouring liquor into sewer (ca. 1921).	Source: Library of Congress.
62	National Bureau of Economic Research (ca. 1947).	Source: Rockefeller Archive Center.
63	Bureau of the Census, Vital Statistics Section (between 1909 and 1940).	Source: Library of Congress.
64-65	Proposed plan for University of Chicago.	Image by Henry Ives Cobb. Source: Rockefeller Archive Center.
68	Food lineup, Arkansas (1937).	Photo by Walker Evans. Source: Library of Congress.
71	Knitting class at Henry Street Settlement house (1910).	Photo by Lewis Hine. Source: Library of Congress.
72	Herbert Hoover (ca. 1925).	Source: Library of Congress.
73	Edmund Day.	Source: Rockefeller Archive Center.
74	Works Progress Administration (between 1936 and 1941).	Drawing by Vera Bock. Source: Library of Congress.
76	Social Security Board Records Office (ca. 1937).	Photo by Harris & Ewing. Source: Library of Congress.

LIST OF ILLUSTRATIONS

79	Secretary of Treasury Andrew Mellon (1929).	Photo by Harris & Ewing. Source: Library of Congress.
84-87	A young Oglala girl in front of a tipi (1891).	Photo by John C.H. Grabill. Source: Library of Congress.
84	Girl students at St. Francis Mission, Rosebud Indian Reservation, SD [ca 1910-1920].	Source: Department of Special Collections and University Archives, Marquette University Libraries.
85	John Collier, with President Roosevelt and Pueblo Indians (1936).	Photo by Harris & Ewing. Source: Library of Congress.
86	Meeting with Navajo in Pinon, AZ (1934).	Photo by Winfrid Stauble. Source: Department of Special Collections and University Archives, Marquette University Libraries.
87	Pueblo Indian leaders in Washington, D.C. (1923).	Source: Library of Congress.
88-89	Sidewalk shoppers (2005).	Photo by Jonas Bendiksen. Source: The Rockefeller Foundation.
91	Raymond Fosdick.	Photo by Kaiden Keystone Photos. Source: Rockefeller Archive Center.
92	American Red Cross poster (1917).	Created by Hayden Hayden [Howard Crosby Renwick]. Source: Library of Congress.
95	Joseph Willits, director of Division of Social Sciences (1944).	Source: Rockefeller Archive Center.
96	President Franklin Delano Roosevelt fireside chat (1937).	Photo by Harris & Ewing. Source: Library of Congress.
97	U.S. Army language lesson (1944).	Photo by U.S. War Department. Source: Rockefeller Archive Center.
98	Draeger camera and microfilm reading machine (1938).	Photo by Science Services, Inc. Source: Rockefeller Archive Center.
99	American flight crew (1944).	Photo by Office of War Information. Source: Library of Congress.
100	American Library Association scholarly journals (1944).	Photo by Rockefeller Foundation. Source: Rockefeller Archive Center.
101	Ernest Lawrence at controls of cyclotron, UC Berkeley campus (1938).	Source: Lawrence Berkeley National Laboratory.

102	Cyclotron (1942).	Photo by Donald Cooksey. Lawrence Berkeley National Laboratory. Source: Rockefeller Archive Center.
105	Norman Hilberry and Leó Szilárd.	Source: U.S. Department of Energy.
106-109	Pyrethrum Farm. National Agricultural Research Bureau (1945).	Source: Rockefeller Archive Center.
107	Secretary of State Dean Rusk at a Cabinet Meeting, Washington, D.C. (1968).	Photo by Yoichi Okamoto. Source: LBJ Presidential Library.
108	Arabic studies seminar course, American University, Beirut, Lebanon (1949).	Source: Rockefeller Archive Center.
109	Dwight Eisenhower, Lyndon Johnson, John Foster Dulles, and other guests, Washington, D.C. (1955).	Photo by Thomas J. O'Halloran. Source: Library of Congress.
110-111	Subway mosaic (2009).	Photo by Ruthie Abel. Source: Rockefeller Foundation.
113	Leader [theater], Washington, D.C. (between 1920 and 1921).	Source: Library of Congress.
114	Agora Museum (1939).	Created by Rockefeller Foundation. Source: Rockefeller Archive Center.
115	Abraham Flexner.	Source: Rockefeller Archive Center.
116	David Stevens (1962).	Photo by Brenner. Source: Rockefeller Archive Center.
118	It Can't Happen Here poster (1936).	Created by Federal Theatre Project, WPA. Source: Library of Congress.
120	Carolina Playmakers program (1939-40).	Source: Rockefeller Archive Center.
121	Zora Neale Hurston, Rochelle French, Gabriel Brown (1935).	Photo by Alan Lomax. Source: Library of Congress.
122	"I am an American" sign, Oakland, CA (1942).	Photo by Dorothea Lange. Source: Library of Congress.
123	John Crow Ransom and other staff of the Kenyon Review (1952).	Photo by Rockefeller Foundation. Source: Rockefeller Archive Center.
126-127	Lincoln Center groundbreaking ceremony (1959).	Photo by Bob Serating. Source: Rockefeller Archive Center.
128	J. George Harrar.	Source: Rockefeller Archive Center.

LIST OF ILLUSTRATIONS

129	Folk musicians (1941).	Photo by Russell Lee. Source: Library of Congress.
131	Rockefeller Foundation Annual Report (1990).	Source: The Rockefeller Foundation.
133	Project Row House, Houston, TX (between 1980 and 2006).	Photo by Carol M. Highsmith. Source: Library of Congress.
135	Blackfoot chief phonographic record at Smithsonian (1916).	Photo by National Photo Company. Source: Library of Congress.
138-141	Orchestra during performance.	Photo by Lin Caufield Photographers, Inc. Courtesy of Photographic Archives. University of Louisville. Source: Rockefeller Archive Center.
138	Louisville Orchestra (1953).	Photo by James N. Keen. Source: Rockefeller Archive Center.
139	Mayor Charles Farnsley with Columbia Records engineer (1953).	Created by Columbia Records, Inc. Source: Rockefeller Archive Center.
141	Tenor Farold Stevens, with Robert Whitney, Lukas Foss, Howard Scott (1953).	Created by Columbia Records, Inc. Source: Rockefeller Archive Center.
142-143	U.S. Treasury Department building, Washington, D.C. (between 1980 and 2006).	Photo by Carol M. Highsmith. Source: Library of Congress.
145	Peking Union Medical College dedication (1921).	Source: Rockefeller Archive Center.
146-147	Cox Committee Questionnaire (1952).	Created by U.S. 82nd Congress, 1951-53. Source: Rockefeller Archive Center.
149	John D. Rockefeller 3rd and Dean Rusk (1952).	Source: Rockefeller Archive Center.
150	Editorial cartoon (1954).	Source: Rockefeller Archive Center.
157	Governor Nelson Rockefeller with Richard Nixon and his wife (1968).	Created by New York State. Source: New York State Archives.
158	President Lyndon B. Johnson meets with McGeorge Bundy (1967).	Photo by Yoichi Okamoto. Source: LBJ Presidential Library.
161	Immunologists at the National Institute of Health Rocky Mountain Laboratory	Source: U.S. National Library of Medicine.
164	Interview with Vice President Mondale (1977).	Photo by Warren K. Leffler. Source: Library of Congress.
166-169	Southern Regional Council logo.	Source: Rockefeller Archive Center.

DEMOCRACY & PHILANTHROPY

166	John Lewis, Voter Education Project, Atlanta, GA (c. 1973).	Photo by Boyd Lewis. Source: Kenan Research Center, Atlanta History Center.
167	Voter Registration, Atlanta, GA (1974).	Photo by Boyd Lewis. Source: Kenan Research Center, Atlanta History Center.
168	Shepherd's Restaurant (campaign posters), Atlanta, GA (1973).	Photo by Boyd Lewis. Source: Kenan Research Center, Atlanta History Center.
170-171	Silhouette and buildings (ca. 2005).	Photo by Jonas Bendiksen. Source: The Rockefeller Foundation.
172-173	Spelman Seminary panoramic.	Courtesy Spelman College Archives. Source: Rockefeller Archive Center.
175	Spelman Seminary graduates (1887).	Courtesy Spelman College Archives. Source: Rockefeller Archive Center.
176	African American farmers (between 1880 and 1897).	Photo by William Henry Jackson. Source: Library of Congress.
178	Booker T. Washington and guests (1906).	Photo by Underwood & Underwood. Source: Library of Congress.
181	"Learn to swim campaign" poster (between 1936 and 1940).	Poster by John Wagner. Source: Library of Congress.
182	Leland C. DeVinney.	Source: Rockefeller Archive Center.
183	"Rex Theatre for Colored People," Leland, MS. (1939).	Photo by Dorothea Lange. Source: Library of Congress.
187	Dartmouth College summer enrichment program (1964).	Source: Dartmouth College Library.
188	John F. Kennedy (1960).	Photo by Abbie Rowe. Source: John F. Kennedy Presidential Library & Museum.
190	March on Washington (1963).	Photo by Warren K. Leffler. Source: Library of Congress.
192	President Lyndon Johnson signs the Civil Rights Act (1964).	Photo by Cecil Stoughton. Source: LBJ Library.
193	Dr. Ralph Bunche at Civil Rights March on Washington, D.C. (1963).	Photo by Rowland Scherman. Source: National Archives and Records Administration.
194	Washington, D.C. riot aftermath (1968).	Photo by Warren K. Leffler. Source: Library of Congress.
196	John Knowles in "RF Illustrated" (1972).	Source: Rockefeller Archive Center.

LIST OF ILLUSTRATIONS

199	President Ronald Reagan with John McCain (1986).	Photo by Carol M. Highsmith. Source: Library of Congress.
200	Eleanor Holmes Norton.	Photo by Suzie Fitzhugh. Source: Rockefeller Archive Center.
202	Dr. James Comer (2011).	Photo by Peter Casolino. Source: New Haven Register.
205	Teaching class, Collaboratives for Humanities and Arts Teaching (CHART).	Photo by John T. Miller. Source: Rockefeller Archive Center.
206-209	Little Rock Central High School, Little Rock, AR (between 1980 and 2006).	Photo by Carol M. Highsmith. Source: Library of Congress.
207	Desegregated bus, Charlotte, NC (1973).	Photo by Warren K. Leffler. Source: Library of Congress.
208	Philip del Campo internship completion certificate (1971).	Source: Rockefeller Archive Center.
209	Wayman W. Smith (1972).	Source: Rockefeller Archive Center.
211	Thomas Jefferson (1800).	Portrait by Rembrandt Peale. Source: National Archives and Records Administration.
212	Louisiana Purchase map (1755).	Created by Emanuel Bowen. Source: Library of Congress.
213	Immigrant Class, Neighborhood Teacher's Association (1923).	Source: Rockefeller Archive Center.
215	New York City Housing Authority Poster: "Eliminate Crime" (1936).	Created by Federal Art Project. Source: Rockefeller Archive Center.
216	Social Science Research Council study (ca. 1947).	Photo by Jules Schick. Source: Rockefeller Archive Center.
217	Jane Jacobs (1961).	Photo by Phil Stanziola. Source: Library of Congress.
218	Robert Moses (l) in New York City with Mayor Robert Wagner (r), and Frank Meistrell (c) (1956).	Photo by Walter Albertin. Source: Library of Congress.
221	Boys playing in vacant lot (1954).	Photo by Al Ravenna (World Telegram & Sun). Source: Library of Congress.
222	Lincoln Square protest (1956).	Photo by Phil Stanziola. Source: Library of Congress.

224	Daniel Patrick Moynihan (1969).	Photo by Thomas J. O'Halloran. Source: Library of Congress.
227	RF trustees tour the Bronx (1989).	Photo by Richard Hughes. Source: Rockefeller Archive Center.
228	Leland Brendsel speaks at launch of NCDI (1991).	Source: Rockefeller Archive Center.
229	NCDI logo (1991).	Source: Rockefeller Archive Center.
233	Bus interior (2005).	Photo by Jonas Bendiksen. Source: The Rockefeller Foundation.
234-237	Stream pollution, Dubuque, IA (1940).	Photo by John Vachon. Source: Library of Congress.
234	Smog obscures view of Chrysler Building from Empire State Building, New York, NY (1953).	Photo by Walter Albertin. Source: Library of Congress.
235	Earth Day, Potomac River, Washington, D.C. (1970).	Photo by Thomas J. O'Halloran. Source: Library of Congress.
236	Williams College outdoor class, Hopkins Forest, Massachusetts.	Source: Rockefeller Archive Center.
237	University of Arizona Environmental Research Laboratory.	Source: Rockefeller Archive Center.
240	Survivor of Hurricane Katrina, New Orleans, LA (2005).	Photo by Michael Rieger/FEMA. Source: National Archives and Records Administration.
241	Men putting siding on a house, New Orleans, LA. (ca. 2005).	Photo by Jonas Bendiksen. Source: The Rockefeller Foundation.
242	Judith Rodin (2013).	Source: The Rockefeller Foundation.
244	Mardi Gras parade, New Orleans, Louis. (2006).	Photo by Carol M. Highsmith. Source: Library of Congress.

INDEX

Abernathy, Ralph, 180
Abramovitz, Max, 221
Agricultural Adjustment Administration, 83
Aldrich, Nelson (Senator), 24, 31-33, 41
Alexander, Christopher, 220
Alexander, Will, 179
Allison, Samuel, 104
American Baptist Education Society, 28. (*See also* University of Chicago)
American Council of Learned Societies (ACLS), 117; training of linguists, 98, 100, 107
"American Experiment," 15-17, 26, 52, 75, 97, 121, 124, 132, 134, 211, 233, 244
American Federation of Labor (AFL), 72; AFL-CIO, 226
American Film Center, 102
American Indian Lawyer Training Project, 197
American Library Association (ALA), 98, 100-01
American Municipal Association, 214
American Red Cross, 58, 93
American Studies, 106-09, 117, 119
American University, 82
American University of Beirut, 108
Amerika-Institut, 106
Andrews, F. Emerson, 148
Angell, James, 117
Applied psychology, 53
Archbold, John D., 35
Architectural Forum, 218, 220
Area Studies, 107-09
Army Specialized Training Program (ASTP), 107
Association for Improving the Conditions of the Poor, 213
Atomic bomb, 102-05, 145

Baptist Foreign Mission Society, 30
Baptist Home Mission Society, 176
Barnard, Chester, 148

Bauer, Catherine, 220
Boll weevil, 48-49
Bond, Julian, 180
Brilliant, Eleanor, 159
Broder, Nathan, 140
Brookings Institution, 73, 75, 83, 84, 198, 217, 232
Brooklyn Bureau of Charities, 213
Brown v. Board of Education, 182, 185, 193, 206
Buffalo Courier Express, 152
Bunche, Ralph, 191, 201; efforts to refocus Equal Opportunity Program, 192-94
Bundy, McGeorge, 158-59, 163-64
Bunshaft, Gordon, 221
Bureau of Municipal Research, 213
Bureau of Social Hygiene, 58, 213
Burgess, Ernest, 66
Burris-Meyer, Harold, 101
Buttrick, Wallace, 48

California Institute of Technology, 104
Cancer therapy, 104
Capitalism, 59, 69-70, 79-81
Carnegie, Andrew, 15, 24, 26, 30
Carnegie Corporation, 26, 44, 60, 108, 121, 158, 162-164, 245
Carnegie Endowment for International Peace, 40, 91, 145
Carnegie Foundation for the Advancement of Teaching, 26, 36
Carnegie Institution of Washington, 41
Carson, Rachel, 220
Carter, Jimmy, 201, 225
Central Bureau of Planning and Statistics, 67, 69
Charity Organization Society, 213
Chernow, Ron, 30, 39
Chicago Public Administration Clearinghouse, 82, 213
"Chicago School," 66
China, 93-94, 98, 106, 144-145

Civil Rights Act of 1964, 191-92
Clark, Kenneth, 194
Clay, Grady, 220
Clean Air Act, 237
Cohn, Edwin, 102
Cold War, 106, 122, 137, 144; effects on the Foundation, 108-09, 124, 128-129
Collaborative for Humanities and Arts Teaching (CHART), 204
Collier, John, 84-85, 87
Colorado Fuel and Iron Company, 54. (*See also* "Ludlow Massacre")
Colton, Joel, 120
Columbia University, 40, 63, 69, 151; Institute for Urban Land Use and Housing Studies, 216-217, 220; Russian Institute, 108
Comer, James, 202-03
Commission on Interracial Cooperation, 179
Committee on a Regional Plan for New York and its Environs, 214
Community Council of Philadelphia, 81
Community development corporations, 226-29
Community Progress, Inc., 226
Condon, Edward, 104
Conference on Climate Change, Food Production, and Interstate Conflict, 235-236
Conference on Urban Design Criticism, 220
Congress, U.S. See U.S. House of Representatives.
Constitutional Educational League, 145
Conway, Gordon, 137, 203-04, 229
Coolidge administration, 76
Copland, Aaron, 139
Council on Foreign Relations, 243
Council on Foundations, 162
Cox, Edward Eugene, 144-46, 149-150, 154
Cuomo, Andrew, 243
Cyclotron, 101-02, 104-05

Dartmouth College, 53, 117, 186-87
Day, Edmund E., 73, 75, 77-78
Department of Housing and Urban Development. *See* U.S. Department of Housing and Urban Development
Department of Justice. *See* U.S. Department of Justice.
Department of the Treasury. *See* U.S. Department of the Treasury.
Devine, Edward T., 38, 40
DeVinney, Leland, 168-69, 180, 182, 185-86
Dresden, Germany, 99
Duke University, 185
Dulles, Allen, 109
Dulles, John Foster, 108-109

Earth Day, 234-36
East Harlem, 217
Economic Opportunity Act, 186
Education Services, Inc., 189
Edwards, Lee, 198
Eisenhower, Dwight D., 109, 126, 151
Eliot, Charles W., 34, 40, 42, 112
Embree, Edwin, 114
Emory University, 185
Energy Efficiency Opportunity Fund, 231
Enterprise Foundation, 240
Environmental Protection Agency, 237
Ethnogeographic Board, 107

Fahs, Charles, 124, 223
Farnsley, Charles, 138-139
Fascism, 80
Federal Home Loan Mortgage Corporation (Freddie Mac), 227-28
Fermi, Enrico, 104-105
Field Foundation, 169
Fisk University, 189
Fleming, Harold, 167-168

Flexner, Abraham, 115
Flexner, Simon, 28
Florey, H.W., 102
Florida, Richard, 231
Flynn, Stephen, 243
Ford Foundation, 140, 158-59, 163-64, 169, 188, 198, 224, 226; *Communities and Neighborhoods: A Possible Private Sector Initiative for the 1980s* report, 226; Great Cities educational grants, 224; Gray Areas program, 224
Fosdick, Raymond, 28, 71, 75-77, 93-96, 99, 103-04, 116, 122, 134, 148, 174, 179-80; advocacy for the League of Nations, 90-91; faith in reason, 91, 95; *Newsweek* comments on, 90; on atomic research, 104-05
Foss, Lukas, 141
Foundation Library Center, 155
Frank, Lawrence K., 61-62
Franklin, Benjamin, 26, 210, 233
Freeman, David, 162
Friendship Baptist Church, 172. (*See also* Spelman College)

Gallinger, Jacob H., 31, 33, 35, 39, 40-42
Gates, Frederick T., 27-32, 34, 42, 48, 113, 123; advocacy of federal charter for Foundation, 31-32; early relationship with John D. Rockefeller, 27-29; mentorship to "Junior," 31; named to first Board of Trustees, 32; report to U.S. Secretary of Interior, 39; Southern agricultural education, 48, 50; steward of Rockefeller charitable giving, 28-30
Gay, Edwin, 69
General Education Board (GEB), 16, 26, 35-40, 48-51, 59, 73, 114-116, 152, 178-80, 182-85, 188
Germany, 93-94, 104
Ghettos, 191-94, 201
G.I. Bill, 124, 214
Gilpatric, Chadbourne, 219-20
Goldmark, Peter, 134, 203, 226-29

Gore, Albert, Sr., 164
Gould, Jay, 24
Great Depression, 75, 116, 214, 245; effects on applied science, 75
Great Migration, 174, 176, 191
Great Society, 195, 198, 224
Green, Paul, 119
Green for All, 231
Greene, Jerome, 42-44, 112-16, 123, 198
Greenwich Village, 219-20
Guggenheim Foundation, 123
Gutkind, E.A., 220

Hamilton, Alexander, 12, 14-15, 121
Hampton Institute, 176, 189
Hanover conferences, 67
Habitat for Humanity, 240-241
Harrar, J. George, 128, 130, 154, 165, 182-85, 187-89, 193, 195, 236; advocacy for Southern Regional Council funding, 183-84; advocacy for United Negro College Fund, 188-89; testimony before House Ways and Means Committee, 158-59; testimony before Senate Finance Committee, 162-63
Harrison, Wallace, 221
Harvard University, 40, 42, 56, 63, 75, 82, 102, 106, 112, 117, 191; School of Business, 69; School of Public Administration, 82
Havel, Vaclav, 136
Hawley, Ellis, 72
Hayes, Rutherford B., 26
Henry Street Settlement house, 71
Heard, Alexander, 185
Herring, Pendleton, 67-68
Heyburn, Weldon B., 38-39, 41
Hilberry, Norman, 105
Hiss, Alger, 145
Hitler, Adolf, 94-95, 116

Hitlerism, 103
Hookworm, 26-7, 37, 57, 179
Hoover administration, 76
Hoover, Herbert, 72, 79
Hopkins, Ernest, 117
House of Representatives. *See* U.S. House of Representatives.
Housing, 133, 165, 193, 214, 216-17, 219-220, 222-23, 225, 228, 230-31, 238, 240
Hurricane Katrina, 238-240, 244
Hurricane Sandy, 242

Indian Reorganization Act (IRA) of 1934, 84, 86-87
Industrial capitalism, 55, 72
Infantile paralysis (polio), 213
Institute of Economics, 73
Institute of Government Research (IGR), 73
International City Managers' Association, 213
International Education Board (IEB), 59, 93, 104, 114-15
International Workers of the World, 55

Jackson, J.B., 220
Jacobs, Jane, 210-12, 217-223, 233; *The Death and Life of Great American Cities*, 210-11, 217-20
Japanese-American relocation, 122
Jefferson, Thomas, 19, 121, 210-12, 219, 233
Johns Hopkins University, 40, 56-57; School of Hygiene and Public Health, 56-57
Johnson, Lyndon B., 156, 189, 191-92, 195, 223-24
Johnson, Philip, 221
July, Robert, 141

Kahn, Louis, 220
Keele, Harold M., 146
Kennedy, John F., 154, 158-59, 164, 168-69, 182, 188-89
Kennedy, Robert, 169
Kennedy administration, 166, 184, 191, 198

Kenyon Review, 123
Keynesian stimulus plan, 81
King, Martin Luther, Jr., 180, 189, 191, 194
Kinsey, Alfred, 151
Klemek, Christopher, 216
Knapp, Seaman, 48-51
Knowles, John, 165, 195-97, 236
Koch, Frederick, 120

Labor: laws, 53; organizers, 70-71; unions, 58
La Follette, Robert M., 31, 42
Laura Spelman Rockefeller Memorial (LSRM), 52, 54, 59-60, 62-63, 65-70, 73, 75-78, 82, 115, 179, 213; applied social sciences, 66; Progressive Era social work, 54, 60; social problems/issues, 59-60; establishment of, 54; developing university social science departments, 59, 62-63; establishment of independent research institutes, 66-68; Institute of Government Research (IGR), 73; relationship to Rockefeller Foundation, 59, 115
Laurence, Peter, 220
Lawrence, Ernest, 101-02, 104
League of Nations, 90-91
Leontief, Wassily, 107
Lewis, John, 166
Lewis, Sinclair, 119
Liberty League, 81
Lincoln Center for the Performing Arts, 126, 128-29, 137, 220-23
Lincoln Square Renewal Project, 221-22
Lincoln University, 189
Living Cities, 229-31. (See also National Community Development Initiative [NCDI])
Local Initiatives Support Corporation (LISC), 226, 240
Lomax, Alan, 120-21
London School of Economics, 63
London School of Tropical Medicine and Hygiene, 56

Longenecker, Herbert, 185
Louisiana Purchase, 211
Louisville Fund for the Arts, 139
Louisville Philharmonic Society, 125, 138-40
Louisville Symphony Orchestra, 138-39, 141
"Ludlow Massacre," 54-55, 58; Congressional investigation, 54; Industrial Relations study, 58
Luening, Otto, 139
Lyman, Richard W., 165, 197-98, 200-01, 203
Lynch, Kevin, 220

Madison, James, 19, 121, 210-11, 225, 233
Malone, Dumas, 121
Manchuria, invasion of, 93
Manhattan Project, 104
Mapplethorpe, Robert, 134
Marshall, John, 100-03, 116-17, 123, 140
Marshall, Thurgood, 193
Mason, Max, 116
Matthiessen, F. O., 107
McCarthy, Joseph, 145
McClaskey, Charles L., 155
McCormick, Harold, 32
McHarg, Ian, 220
Mead, Margaret, 107
Mellon, Andrew, 79
Meriam, Lewis, 84, 86-87
Merriam, Charles, 65-67; Social Science Research Council (SSRC), 67-69, 72-73, 75-76, 79, 81, 83, 107, 216
Metropolitan Opera, 101, 128,
Mexican American Legal Defense and Educational Fund, 197
Mitchell, Wesley, 69-70, 72
Monte Cassino, 99
"Millionaire's Special" (train), 174, 178
Mills, Wilbur D., 156, 164
Mondale, Walter, 164

Morehouse College, 176, 180
Morgan, J.P., 15, 24, 31
Morrill Act of 1862, 49
Moses, Robert, 218-19, 221-22
Mott Foundation, 224
Moynihan, Daniel Patrick, 224
Municipal Finance Officers' Association, 213
Mumford, Lewis, 219-20
Murphy, Starr J., 31-33, 36-44, 151, 198, 213
Myrdal, Gunnar, 194

Nankai University, 93
National Advisory Commission on Civil Disorders, 206
National Association for the Advancement of Colored People (NAACP), 166-67, 180, 193; Special Contribution Fund, 197
National Association of Foundations, 155
National Association of Housing Officials, 214
National Association of Manufacturers, 81
National Bureau of Economic Research (NBER), 62, 69-70, 72-73, 75, 82, 217
National Community Development Initiative (NCDI), 227-30. (*See also* Living Cities)
National Endowment for the Arts (NEA), 134
National Institute for Public Affairs (NIPA), 82, 85-87; internship program, 85-87
National Institutes of Health, 160
National Recovery Administration, 83
National Research Council, 104
National Security Studies, 243
National Urban Coalition, 158
National Urban League, 167, 180
Negro Education Board, 177, 179
New Deal, 80-83, 180, 214
New Frontier, 198
New Hampshire Foundation, 81
New Orleans, 132, 185, 204, 238-41, 244

New York Milk Committee, 213
New York City, 17, 32, 34, 126, 128, 137, 212-13, 218, 221, 233, 246
New York State 2100 Commission, 243
New York Times, 34, 36, 42, 116, 132, 198, 218, 226
Nixon, Richard, 156-57, 224-25, 237
Nixon administration, 160
Norton, Eleanor Holmes, 200-01

Oberlin College, 186
Ogden, Robert C., 174, 177
One Tenth of Our Nation (documentary), 103
Oppenheimer, Robert, 104

Park, Robert, 65-66
Patman, Wright, 154-56, 164
Pei, I.M., 220
Peking Union Medical College, 145
Peterson Commission, 156
Phillips-Fein, Kim, 81
Pifer, Alan, 162
Pillsbury, George, 28
PolicyLink, 231
Populist Democrats, 31, 154
Pound, Roscoe, 153
Program-related investments, 227
Princeton University, 97, 186
Progressive Era, 54, 60, 198; social work, 54; scientific surveys, 60
Progressive movement, 52
Prohibition, 61, 155
Project on Municipal Innovation, 231
Project Row Houses, 133, 136
Prudential, 228
Public administration fellowships, 82
Public Record Office of London, 99

Quantum physics, 104

Ransom, John Crowe, 123
Reagan, Ronald, 18, 198-99, 225
Reagan administration, 199; vision of philanthropy and role of government, 199
Reece, B. Carroll, 150-54, 167; Reece Committee, 150, 152-54
Regional Studies of American Life, 120
Republican Party, 31, 33, 41, 46, 146; Progressive Wing, 41-42
Revoldt, Daryl, 90, 103
Richardson, Malcolm, 120
Robber barons, 24
Rockefeller, Abby, 41
Rockefeller, John D., 15-17, 19-20, 24, 27-28, 30-34, 41-43, 48, 54, 62, 65, 91, 113, 149, 172, 175, 185, 204; contributions to African-American education, 175-76; initial funding of the Foundation, 32; origins of charitable giving, 27; richest man in the United States, 24; wealth of, 24
Rockefeller, John D. Jr. "Junior," 28, 30-31, 32, 34, 40-42, 44, 58-59, 91, 114, 174, 176-78, 184, 213-14; Bureau of Social Hygiene, 58, 213; Industrial Relations study, 58; named to first Board of Trustees, 32; response to Secretary Walcott, 41; retirement from Standard Oil, 34; role in creation of the Foundation, 31-32; secret lunch with President Taft, 41; reintroduction of federal charter bill, 42
Rockefeller, John D. 3rd, 109, 149, 156, 159, 184, 189, 223; speech on foundations, 156
Rockefeller Foundation; 100 Resilient Cities Centennial Challenge, 243; Agricultural Sciences Program, 203; Arts and Humanities Division, 135-36; Asian Cities Climate Change Resilience Network (ACCCRN), 242; Board of Trustees, 44, 116, 122, 153, 193, 201; China Medical Board, 59; Colorado Fuel and Iron

Company, 54; Conflict in International Relations, 235; Conquest of Hunger Program, 130, 197, 235, 237; creation of the Foundation, 15-17, 19, 24, 26; Division of Humanities, 98, 100, 115-16, 120; Division of Natural Sciences, 90, 103; Division of Social Sciences (DSS), 73, 75-78, 95, 106, 180; endowment, 25-27, 32; Equal Opportunity Program (Division), 182, 184, 186-89, 191-94, 197, 199, 201, 206, 208, 229; Environmental Affairs fellowship program, 236; federal charter, 24, 31-32, 40-41, 115, 149; Humanities Division and support for humanities, 101, 124, 135-136, 140-41, 219-20; Mission Statement, 115; Multicultural Arts Project initiative, 133; New York State charter approved, 44; Promoting Equitable, Sustainable Transportation Initiative, 230; Quality of the Environment, 234, 237; School Reform Program, 203; Superintendents' Training Program, 207-09; Sustainable Employment in a Green U.S. Economy Initiative, 230; Understanding Diversity in Changing Societies initiative, 136; University Development Program (UDP), 187, 195; use of scientific surveys and the scientific method, 54, 60, 78, 182

Rockefeller Institute for Medical Research, 26, 28, 37, 43

Rockefeller, Laura Spelman, 54

Rockefeller Sanitary Commission, 26-27, 37, 56, 179

Rocky Mountain Institute, 237

Rocky Mountain Laboratories, 160

Rodin, Judith, 14, 20, 137, 204, 230-33, 241-43, 246

Romney, Elizabeth, 180, 182-83, 185-86

Roosevelt, Franklin D., 80-81, 84-86, 96, 121

Roosevelt administration, 82-83, 86

Roosevelt, Theodore, 26, 32, 35, 39

Root, Elihu, 40

Ruml, Beardsley, 52-54, 59-61, 63, 66, 75

Rush, Benjamin, 210

Rusk, Dean, 106-09, 124-25, 128, 130, 134, 148-49, 152-54, 167, 180, 182-83, 191

Russell Sage Foundation, 27, 44, 60, 148

Saarinen, Eero, 221

Sage, Margaret Olivia Slocum, 26

Salzburg Seminar, 106

Saunders, E.W., 43

"Scientific philanthropy," 60, 71

School reform, 201, 204, 209

Scott, Howard, 141

Segregation, 167, 169, 174, 177-80, 182-85, 191, 193, 197, 206

Senate, U.S. See U.S. Senate.

Sherman Antitrust Act of 1890, 35, 38, 42

Shigekawa, Joan, 133

Sierra Club, 158

Slum Clearance Committee of New York, 214, 222

Smith, James Allen, 146, 150, 246

Smith-Lever Act, 51

Smithson, James, 42

Smithsonian Institution, 39, 41-42, 134

Smyth, Henry DeWolf, 104

Social sciences, 16, 20, 52-54, 56, 58-62, 65-67, 69, 71, 73, 75, 83, 182, 245; early lack of scientific method and Foundation avoidance of social issues, 58; movement into universities and independent research institutes, 59, 62, 66-67; research in the private sector, 61-62; as tools, 20; in World War One, 67; versus social work/social welfare, 66-67

Social Security Act of 1935, 69, 76, 78

Social Science Research Council (SSRC), 67-69, 72-73, 75-76, 79, 81, 83, 107, 216

Southern Christian Leadership Conference, 167, 180

Southern Regional Council (SRC), 166-69, 182-184; Voter Education Project, 166, 168-169

Soviet Union, 18, 93, 120, 135, 144

Spelman College (Seminary), 28, 172, 175-177, 180
Spooner, John, 32
Standard Oil Company, 24, 33, 38-39; antitrust lawsuit against, 26, 35, 38, 41; Supreme Court ruling against, 42
Stanton, Frank, 192
Stevens, David, 116-17
Stevens, Farrold, 141
Stevens Institute of Technology, 101
Stewart, Walter W., 122-23
Stivers, Camilla, 70
Stokes, Anson Phelps, 115-16
Student Nonviolent Coordinating Committee (SNCC), 167
Suburbs, 216, 218-19, 232; suburban poverty, 232
Sulzer, William, 44
Supreme Court, U.S. See U.S. Supreme Court.
Sviridoff, Mitchell, 226
Syracuse University, 35, 82; Maxwell School of Citizenship and Public Affairs, 213; ties with Standard Oil, 35
Szilárd, Leó, 104-05

Taconic Foundation, 169
Taft, Robert, 151
Taft, William Howard, 32, 38, 40-43
Tax Reform Act of 1969, 158, 160, 164-65; final provisions, 164; Nixon administration and, 160; testimony against, 160, 162-163
Teller, Edward, 104
Temple University, 225
Theiler, Max, 102
Tillman, Benjamin Ryan, 31
Tocqueville, Alexis de, 13-15, 17, 26, 44, 49, 113, 117, 119, 121, 137, 229, 241, 244-45
Tucker, Henry St. George, 177
Tulane University, 185-86

Turner, Frederick Jackson, 119, 244
Tuskegee Institute, 175, 189
Typhus, 102

Unemployment, 70, 78, 81, 199, 225,
United Negro College Fund (UNCF), 188-89
United States: Bureau of the Census, 2010 Census results, 232; Commission on Civil Rights, 206; Department of Agriculture, Cooperative Agricultural Extension System, 51; Department of Commerce, 72; Department of State, 106-09, 124, 144-45, 148, 180; Equal Employment Opportunity Commission, 201; federal budget in 1910, 26; Federal Housing Administration, 214; gross domestic product in 1910, 36; Housing and Community Development Act of 1974, 225; Department of Interior, Office of Indian Affairs (Bureau of Indian Affairs), 82, 84-87
U.S. Department of Housing and Urban Development, 223, 229, Community Development Block Grant (CDBG), 225, Model Cities, 225, Urban Development Action Grant, 225
U.S. Department of Justice, 35, 169, antitrust case against Standard Oil, 35, 41-42
U.S. Department of the Treasury, 155-56, 163, changes in tax law, 146, Internal Revenue Service, 152, 155, report on foundations, 155, tax reform studies and proposals, 156
U.S. House of Representatives, 42-43, 144, 148, 151, 154, 167, 200, Judiciary Committee approval of federal charter, 42, passage of charter bill, 43, Select Committee on Small Business, 154, House Reece Committee, 150, 152-54, final report, 152; House Ways and Means Committee, 155-56, 158-59, 163, 165, proposals for reform of foundations, 160; House Un-American Activities Committee, 145, 148; "Guide to Subversive Organizations and Publications," 148

INDEX

U.S. Senate, 31, 33, 36, 38-43, 46, 87, 90, 160, 162, 164, 169, Committee on the District of Columbia, 33, 36, investigation into bribery of public officials by Standard Oil, 43, Judiciary Committee approval of charter bill, 43, Senate Select Committee to Investigate Foundations and Other Organizations "Cox Committee," 146, 148-49, 151, final report of the Committee, 152-53, testimony by Foundation, 149, public reaction to Committee report, 151

U.S. Supreme Court, 18-19, 35, 38, 40, 42, 169, 182, 185, 191, *Citizens United v. Federal Election Commission*, 19, ruling against Standard Oil, 42

University of Arizona, Environmental Research Laboratory, 237

University of California at Berkeley, 82, 101, 105, 122; Institute of Public Administration, 213

University of Chicago, 29-30, 37, 40, 53, 63-65, 75, 105, 116, 182, 194

University of Göttingen, 93; anti-semitism and, 93

University of Pennsylvania, 137, 220, 231, 241-42

Upward Bound Initiative, 186-87

Uranium-235, 104

Urban Institute, 136, 199

Urban renewal, 165, 217-18, 220, 222-25, 228, 230

Urban sociology, 66

Vanderbilt, Cornelius, 24

Vanderbilt University, 185

Vietnam War, 156, 195, 245

Vincent, George E., 58-59, 114, 116

Walcott, Charles Doolittle, 39, 41

Walker, Wyatt Tee, 180

War Industries Board, 67, 69

War on Poverty, 187, 191

Washington Post, 33, 35, 198

Washington Square Park, 219

Watson, Thomas J., 193

Watts Riot, 191

Weaver, Warren, 55, 90, 103-04, 132

Welfare Council of New York City, 81

Whitney, Robert, 138, 141

Whyte, William H., 219

Wickersham, George W., 38, 40-42

Wilson administration, 69

Williams College, 236

Willits, Joseph, 95

Winthrop, John, 18-20, 26

Woodrow Wilson Fellowship Program, 189

Works Progress Administration (WPA), 119, 180

World War One, 54, 67, 69, 76, 90-91, 93; Central Bureau of Planning and Statistics, 67, 69; effects on use of social sciences, 67; War Industries Board, 67, 69

World War Two, 93, 96, 105, 107, 121-22, 130, 134, 155, 160, 167, 180, 182, 193, 214, 216, 245; effects on the Foundation, 120-124, 130

Yale University, 40, 117, 179, 231; School of Medicine, 202

Yellow fever, 102, 160, 210

YMCA, 180

Zipp, Samuel, 220

OTHER BOOKS IN
THE ROCKEFELLER FOUNDATION CENTENNIAL SERIES

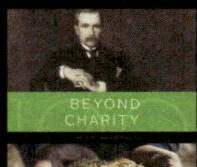

BEYOND CHARITY: A CENTURY OF PHILANTHROPIC INNOVATION

The creation of the Rockefeller Foundation in 1913 was in itself a marked innovation in the development of modern philanthropy. Foundation staff, trustees, and grantees had to learn by doing. The topical chapters in *Beyond Charity* explore the evolution of the Foundation's practice from the board room to the field office. For professionals or volunteers entering the field of philanthropy, each chapter offers an opening essay that highlights abiding issues in the field. The vivid stories and fascinating characters that illuminate these themes make the history come to life.

INNOVATIVE PARTNERS: THE ROCKEFELLER FOUNDATION AND THAILAND

For nearly a century, the Rockefeller Foundation and its Thai partners have been engaged in an innovative partnership to promote the well-being of the people of Thailand. From the battle against hookworm and other diseases to the development of rice biotechnology and agriculture, the lessons learned from this work offer powerful insights into the process of development. On the occasion of its centennial in 2013, the Rockefeller Foundation has commissioned a history of this innovative partnership.

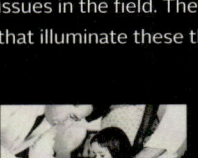

HEALTH & WELL-BEING: SCIENCE, MEDICAL EDUCATION AND PUBLIC HEALTH

Philanthropists who seek to improve health often find themselves torn between efforts to identify cures for disease and projects that strive to improve the social conditions that lead to better health. As this remarkable book shows, over a hundred years, the Rockefeller Foundation's efforts to balance these sometime competing objectives have fundamentally shaped the fields of public health and medicine.

FOOD & PROSPERITY: BALANCING TECHNOLOGY AND COMMUNITY IN AGRICULTURE

John D. Rockefeller recognized in his early philanthropy, even before the creation of the Foundation, that agricultural productivity is key to increasing overall wealth and health in the poorest of rural communities. Embracing the promise of science, the Rockefeller Foundation focused on the discovery of new technologies to enhance food production. But technology was never enough. New techniques and tools had to be adapted to local cultures and communities. This engaging book explores lessons learned from the Foundation's efforts to improve this most basic, but still so complicated, arena of human endeavor.

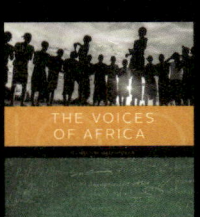

THE VOICES OF AFRICA: HUMAN CAPITAL AND DEVELOPMENT

In every society, development depends on investment in institutions and individuals. Wickliffe Rose, an early leader in the Rockefeller Foundation, called this "backing brains." But developing human capital is a risky proposition. This intriguing history explores the challenges and triumphs in the Rockefeller Foundation's efforts to invest in the people of Africa over the course of a century.

To find out more about how to receive a copy of any of these Centennial books, please visit www.centennial.rockefellerfoundation.org.